FITZWILLIAM MUSEUM

HANDBOOKS

ITALIAN MAIOLICA

Maiolica is a type of tin-glazed earthenware associated particularly with the Renaissance when its colourful decoration was at its peak, but it was made in Italy from the thirteenth century and is still in use today. This book provides an introduction to the history of maiolica, a glossary, a bibliography, and sixty-four colour illustrations and accompanying text, arranged chronologically to show some of the most characteristic styles of maiolica from about 1250 to 1920.

FITZWILLIAM MUSEUM HANDBOOKS

ITALIAN MAIOLICA

JULIA E. POOLE

SENIOR ASSISTANT KEEPER OF

APPLIED ART, FITZWILLIAM MUSEUM

PHOTOGRAPHY BY BRIDGET TAYLOR

ANDREW MORRIS AND

ANDREW NORMAN

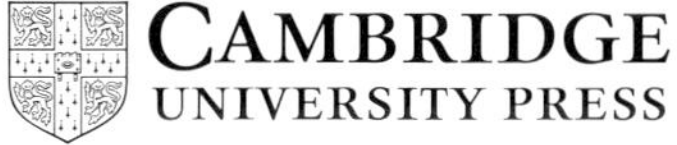

Published by the Press Syndicate of the University of Cambridge
The Pitt Building, Trumpington Street, Cambridge CB2 1RP
40 West 20th Street, New York, NY 10011–4211, USA
10 Stamford Road, Oakleigh, Melbourne 3166, Australia

First published 1997

Printed in Great Britain at the University Press, Cambridge

A catalogue record for this book is available from the British Library

Library of Congress cataloguing in publication data

Poole, Julia.
Italian maiolica / Julia E. Poole; photography by
Bridget Taylor, Andrew Morris, and Andrew Norman.
p. cm.–(Fitzwilliam Museum handbooks)
Includes bibliographical references and index.
ISBN 0 521 56316 X (hardback). – ISBN 0 521 56531 6 (paperback)
1. Majolica, Italian. I. Title. II. Series.
NK 4315.P65 1997
738.3′09′45–dc20 96–25471 CIP

ISBN 0 521 56316 x hardback
ISBN 0 521 56531 6 paperback

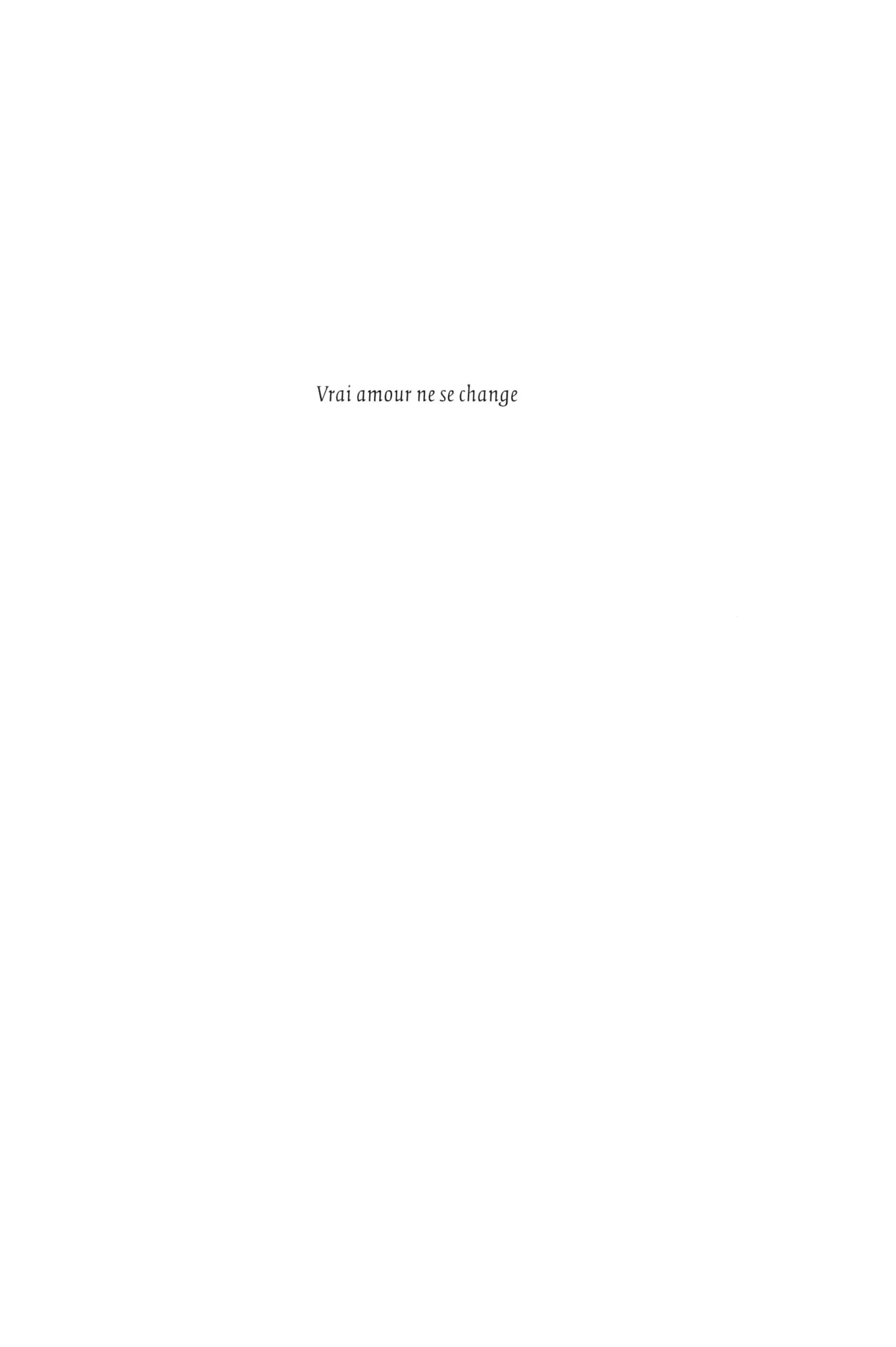

Vrai amour ne se change

CONTENTS

PREFACE

Italian maiolica has been collected in England since the eighteenth century. Among the best-known early collectors were the Norfolk gentleman, Sir Andrew Fountaine (1676–1753), the painter, Charles Jarvis (*c.* 1675–1739), and Horace Walpole (1717–97). A few examples were acquired by many English aristocrats and gentlemen who visited Italy, such as the ninth Earl of Exeter, who bought several old and new pieces at Naples in 1763 to add to the furnishings of Burghley House, near Stamford. For the next hundred years or so the most highly prized pieces were decorated in *istoriato* style with classical or biblical subjects. Many of these were derived from engravings after Raphael and other High Renaissance artists, and consequently maiolica was often described as Raphael- or Roman-ware in sale catalogues and inventories.

Between about 1840 and the end of the century – the heyday of maiolica collecting – taste gradually widened to include the maiolica first of the early sixteenth century, and then of the fifteenth. This period saw the formation of the great national collections in the British Museum and the Victoria and Albert Museum, and several outstanding private collections now in museums, including Sir Richard Wallace's at Hertford House, London, and Thomas Gambier-Parry's in Gloucestershire, now in the Courtauld Institute Galleries.

In this century appreciation of maiolica has become even more catholic. Enthusiasm for late medieval maiolica was triggered by discoveries in Orvieto in Umbria around 1900, and since then the development of archaeology in Italy has aroused intense and widespread interest in this field. It has also become clear that the dazzling Renaissance maiolica surviving in museums represents only the tip of an iceberg, and that simply decorated everyday pottery formed the bulk of production. In recent decades the soaring prices of Renaissance pieces have turned the attention of collectors and museums towards high quality maiolica of the seventeenth to early twentieth centuries. There has also been increasing interest in 'popular' maiolica made largely for a rural market in the eighteenth and nineteenth centuries.

The Fitzwilliam Museum's collection was begun in a small way in 1904, with the donation of a box of sherds excavated at Orvieto. It now stands at 522 pieces. The majority were bequeathed by five collectors: Charles Brinsley Marlay (1831–1912); Frederick Leverton Harris (1864–1926); Dr J. W. L. Glaisher (1848–1928); Louis C. G. Clarke (1881–1960); and Henry Scipio Reitlinger (1885–1950). Each of these collectors had different preferences in maiolica, and as a result the collection grew into one of the most representative in Britain. As with most collections outside Italy, the wares of the eighteenth to twentieth centuries are less well represented than those of the Renaissance. The collection also includes small groups of Italian medieval lead-glazed pottery and later slipware.

The sixty-four entries in this Handbook include maiolica from many of the major manufacturing centres, arranged in a roughly chronological sequence to illustrate the main developments in maiolica decoration. Their attributions should not always be regarded as definitive, because current research is tending to modify or change earlier opinions on the origins and dating of some groups of maiolica.

Further reading is provided for each entry. Works mentioned once are cited in full. Those mentioned more than once are cited by the author–date system.

INTRODUCTION

Maiolica is an Italian earthenware with an opaque white glaze containing tin-oxide. Its most outstanding feature is its splendidly colourful decoration which, unlike paintings or tapestries, remains unfaded, just as it was when it left the potter's workshop. Maiolica is usually associated with the Renaissance when its aesthetic quality was at its peak, but it had been made in Italy since the thirteenth century and is still in use today.

Its introduction long preceded the use of the word 'maiolica' which was probably derived from Maiolica, the medieval name for the Balearic island of Majorca, where ships carrying lustreware from Valencia stopped on their way to Italy. Alternatively it may have been a corruption of the Spanish name for lustreware, *obra de málequa* (Málaga ware). In fifteenth-century Italian inventories, lustreware was described as '*lavori di maiolicha*', and this usage continued during the first half of the sixteenth century and beyond. However, from at least the 1520s, the word was occasionally used to indicate tin-glazed ware without lustre, and as the century progressed this usage became increasingly common. In 1589 the potter, Leonardo Bettisi of Faenza, who so far as is known did not make lustreware, was referred to as '*maestro della maiorcha*', when he supplied tableware to the Grand Duke Ferdinando I of Florence. By the end of the century, 'maiolica' had become a general term for tin-glazed earthenware, but even then it was not always used. Tin-glazed ware was sometimes identified simply as '*vasi di terra*' (vessels or pots made of clay).

The tin-glaze technique originated in Mesopotamia (modern Iraq) during the ninth century, almost certainly in an effort to emulate white stonewares and early porcelains imported from China. It was soon found to provide an excellent surface for coloured decoration, and this was largely responsible for its popularity in later periods. The use of tin glaze spread through the Islamic Middle East and was taken to the Maghreb (west north Africa) and southern Spain when the Arabs conquered those areas. Reduced-pigment lustre decoration was also developed in the ninth century in Mesopotamia, and by the mid thirteenth century lustreware was being made in Málaga in Moorish Andalucia. In the early fourteenth century, the technique was taken by migrant potters to Christian Valencia where Manises became the most important centre. The high status of this luxury pottery in Italy in the fourteenth and fifteenth centuries is shown by its representation in paintings, and by its mention in inventories of household goods. Demand stimulated efforts to make lustreware in Italy, with success by at least the 1490s (see below). By then, however, tin glaze had been established in Italy for almost two hundred years.

How it was introduced around 1200 is not entirely clear. Tin-glazed wares from the Middle East and the Maghreb had been imported into Italy in the eleventh and twelfth centuries, including basins (*bacini*) which were used to decorate the facades of churches in Pisa, Genoa and elsewhere. But these imports do not appear to have led to imitation, and it therefore seems likely that the technique was introduced through the immigration of Arab potters, probably from the Maghreb or Sicily. In the thirteenth century much of the maiolica made in Sicily and southern Italy had polychrome decoration and has been known as 'proto-maiolica' since 1934. In central and northern Italy it was decorated in two colours, manganese-brown and copper-green, and is often referred to as '*maiolica arcaica*'. However, excavations during the last twenty years have shown that this division was not clear cut. Some late medieval maiolica from Lazio in central Italy is decorated in three colours, and some from Sicily is decorated in only one colour. Proto-maiolica is not represented in the Fitzwilliam's collection, and the discussion below concerns developments in central Italy.

Tin was an expensive raw material, much of it imported from England, and it was probably for that reason that maiolica made in the thirteenth and fourteenth centuries was only partly tin-glazed. The interior and lower parts of jugs, and the exterior of cups and bowls usually had a translucent lead glaze which appears yellowish-brown (no. 2). This practice became less common in the fifteenth and sixteenth centuries, but lead glazing persisted on the backs of some large dishes, such as Deruta *piatti da pompa* (nos. 13, 34), and on the interiors of some jars and jugs. Unglazed pottery for cooking vessels and various types of lead-glazed earthenware continued to be made alongside maiolica (no. 1). Slipware with incised decoration under lead glaze (no. 52) was widespread in northern and central Italy from the beginning of the fourteenth century until the eighteenth century when its production declined.

Improvements in kilns and glazes, and the introduction of new colours which could withstand high firing temperatures made possible the development of Renaissance-style maiolica. The medieval two-colour palette persisted in central Italy until the fifteenth century, but from about 1350 decoration in cobalt-blue was introduced. It was used with manganese-brown (no. 3), or on its own, and from the late fourteenth century might be in the form of a glaze-like relief-blue. This remained in fashion until about 1460 (no. 5), alongside maiolica decorated in normal cobalt-blue, much of it made between c. 1440 and 1460 with designs inspired by Islamic or Hispano-Moresque jars and dishes (no. 6). Meanwhile antimony-yellow or cobalt-blue were added to the brown and green palette (no. 4), and by about 1460 polychrome decoration was well established.

During the next seventy years the pace of change was astonishingly rapid, particularly in Tuscany, Umbria, Emilia Romagna and the Marches. Less information is available about developments in other areas, such as Naples and Venice. New forms were introduced, such as two-handled vases and dishes of different kinds, but the most outstanding change was the increasing sophistication of the decoration. Maiolica painters developed an immense repertoire of decorative designs and borders (nos. 7, 8, 14, 16, 18–20), which were combined with figural motifs, such as busts (nos. 7, 12), figures and animals (no. 14). Reduced-pigment lustre decoration, introduced by the 1490s in Deruta and Gubbio, was produced briefly in Faenza and Pesaro, and after 1498 at Cafaggiolo (nos. 13, 26, 15). It remained fashionable until the 1540s, and continued to be made in Deruta until late in the seventeenth century. Classical influence, already discernible in late fifteenth-century decoration, became more prominent in the early sixteenth (nos. 17–21). By then, aided by prints and book illustrations, maiolica painters were beginning to imitate frescos and oil-paintings by decorating dishes and other vessels with scenes from classical history and mythology, the Bible, or, more rarely, contemporary events. This *istoriato* maiolica (nos. 17, 22–4, 27–33, 35) was to dominate high-quality production from the 1520s until the 1560s, when it was gradually ousted from fashion by Faenza white ware decorated in *compendiario* style (nos. 39–42), and by grotesque decoration on a white ground from the Urbino district (nos. 44–5). These were adopted in other centres, such as Castelli (no. 47), Deruta (no. 46), and Montelupo, and continued for much of the seventeenth century.

The great boom in maiolica production during the Renaissance did not result simply from the existence of plentiful raw materials allied to technical progress and artistic skill. It was also influenced by the political geography of Italy, the existence of substantial markets, the nature of patronage, and changes in social habits which created a demand for luxury pottery.

Throughout the late Middle Ages and Renaissance, production of simply decorated maiolica for local consumption was widespread. By the end of the fifteenth century however, some towns had become renowned for their high-quality maiolica, and had developed distinctive styles or techniques of decoration. Some were large cities, such as Siena, but there was a tendency for them to be small towns whose foremost market was a large nearby city to which they were politically affiliated. Two prominent examples were Deruta, near Perugia, and Montelupo, near Florence. Other important centres developed in small or medium-sized towns which were the seat of a court, such as Faenza and Pesaro, ruled in the late fifteenth century by the Manfredi and the Sforza d'Aragona, and Urbino, which became one of the most important sixteenth-century centres under its Della Rovere Dukes. The remoteness of a centre was not necessarily a problem, provided that there was sufficient demand for its goods, such as the lustreware made in Maestro Giorgio's workshop in Gubbio. In the sixteenth century some of these maiolica towns developed a substantial export trade to more distant parts of the peninsula and Sicily, and to northern Europe (no. 41).

The great wealth in the hands of individuals and institutions in Italian cities meant that there was a steady demand for different types of high-quality maiolica. The production of painted pavement tiles was boosted by the vast amount of religious and secular building that took place during the fifteenth and sixteenth centuries. Tile pavements were laid in many family chapels in churches, such as that of the Basso della Rovere in Santa Maria del Popolo in Rome (*c.* 1484–98), and in domestic buildings, such as the Castello San Giorgio in Mantua (no. 9) and the Palazzo Petrucci in Siena (*c.* 1509–13). Large orders, like one for 5,000 tiles made in 1523 by an agent for the Duke of Urbino, might be divided between several workshops, three in that instance.

Most sizeable towns had one or more commercial pharmacies which required storage jars, and a high proportion of the output of maiolica workshops catered for that demand. Globular and cylindrical jars of different sizes were used for preserves, powders, ointments, and pills, and spouted vases, ewers, and bottles for syrups, oils, and waters (nos. 6–8, 20, 37–8). Similar jars were used for storage purposes in the home.

The patronage of hundreds of religious houses up and down Italy played an important part in encouraging maiolica production. Monasteries and convents commissioned large quantities of jugs, bowls, and cups for their refectories, and storage jars for the pharmacies of their hospitals, some of which treated the laity. These charitable institutions could be of substantial size, such as the hospital of Santa Maria Nuova in Florence, which could house 250 patients in 1427. Much of this maiolica was plain or simply decorated with the emblem of the order or a religious symbol, but wealthy institutions equipped their pharmacies with extensive sets of finely painted jars and ewers, often bearing the badge of the order or hospital (no. 5).

Popular devotional practices, such as praying in the home or street, the giving of votive offerings, and undertaking of pilgrimages, all created a demand for maiolica which has continued up to the present. Devotional maiolica included small-scale sculpture, reliefs (no. 51), painted panels, figures and busts, holy water stoups, and decorative dishes with religious subjects which could be bought as souvenirs to hang on the wall like a picture. Deruta, which is not far from the pilgrimage church of San Francesco at Assisi and on the route to Rome from the north, was making maiolica for this market by the early sixteenth century.

More significant in promoting the decoration of maiolica to a high aesthetic standard was the growth of demand for tableware from the wealthy and educated upper class, including ruling families, high-ranking ecclesiastics, and great merchant dynasties. At the beginning of the fifteenth century, the furnishing of even the grandest houses in Italian cities was still remarkably sparse by modern standards, and the amount of pottery used at table was confined to jugs and various types of bowls; dishes were beginning to appear, and ewers and basins were used for hand-washing. The very rich used silver dishes, and it was not until after the decoration of maiolica reached a high standard that the use of pottery became fashionable at that social level. It therefore seems probable that much of the initial demand for tableware came from people of middling wealth, who could not afford silver or did not wish to spend their money on it. By the early sixteenth century, maiolica were being ordered by people in the highest ranks of society, such as the Este of Ferrara. This implies that its status had risen and that it was now considered fashionable and desirable. Its splendid appearance and the intellectual content of *istoriato* decoration was undoubtedly a factor, but there were other possible reasons for its growing popularity. More varied and intricately prepared food was being presented at meals, which could account for the proliferation of dish forms, and fashionable diners now had their own plate to eat from and used forks instead of their hands to help themselves from serving dishes.

The development of services of tableware of increasing size and complexity was one of the great innovations of the late fifteenth and sixteenth centuries. Early services seem to have been quite small, up to about fifty pieces, but by the second half of the century they might comprise over 300 pieces, including sets of dishes of different shapes and sizes, flasks, cruets for oil and vinegar, salts, ewers and basins, and coolers for wine bottles. A *credenza* of 307 pieces was supplied by Leonardo Bettisi of Faenza to the Grand Duke Francesco de' Medici in Florence in 1568. Surviving dishes from numerous armorial services document the social range of the purchasers (nos. 23–4, 28, 41, 44). The extent to which the most exquisitely painted *istoriato* services were actually used is uncertain. The excellent condition of many of the dishes, suggests that they were little used, if at all, and that they may have been displayed on a *credenza* or buffet at meals in the same way as vessels of precious metals on formal occasions. Unfortunately no illustration of Italian maiolica displayed in this way is known. By contrast, the large numbers of dishes for different purposes listed in inventories of late sixteenth-century services, seems to imply that they were for use.

In addition to tableware, there was a demand for decorative objects, such as very large dishes, vases, elaborate inkstands, and small-scale figures. The growth of demand for these in the sixteenth century can be seen as part of a general wave of acquisitiveness, which gradually filled great *palazzi* and lesser houses in Italian cities with works of art and furnishings.

By 1600, the great period of maiolica was over. The seventeenth century was a transitional period in which some older centres including Urbino and Pesaro declined, while others came to the fore: Albisola, Savona, and Bassano in the north; Castelli, Naples, and Laterza in the south; and Palermo and Caltagirone in Sicily. Renaissance decorative styles were gradually displaced by ones which harmonised with baroque interiors. Among the innovations were imitations of Isnik pottery (no. 49), and late Ming blue and white porcelain (no. 50), which led to the use of this colour scheme for several varieties of European decoration. *Istoriato* decoration continued at Castelli, but in baroque style, and there was a revival at Urbania (formerly Castel Durante) in the 1660s and 1670s (no. 53).

By the early eighteenth century, the initiative in ceramic technology and design had passed to north-west Europe. Increasingly maiolica potters faced competition from French and German faïence, and Oriental and European porcelains (including Italian). Towards the end of the century, importation of English creamware and its adoption by Italian factories almost killed off the maiolica industry. Even so, the eighteenth century was not a period of unmitigated decline. In centres remote from large cities, especially in the south, such as Ariano Irpino in Campania or Caltagirone in Sicily, maiolica in a lively 'popular' style was made for a largely rural and unsophisticated market, and this genre continued in the nineteenth century (nos. 62–3). Between about 1715 and 1750 there was a revival of *istoriato* decoration at San Quirico d'Orcia, Siena and Bassano Romano (no. 56). In the second half of the century, attractive rococo-style tableware was produced on a large scale at the Ferniani factory in Faenza (no. 60), at Pesaro, in Naples, and at Milan, Lodi, and Nove. Some of this maiolica was decorated onglaze in enamels (no. 61), a technique introduced from France.

During the early nineteenth century, there was a more dramatic decline in production, but this was arrested in the 1840s and 1850s by the renewal of interest in Renaissance art. During the second half of the century, maiolica in Renaissance and later styles was revived in Pesaro, Rome, Florence, Deruta, and Faenza, to name but a few places, and the art of lustre decoration was rediscovered and practised at Pesaro, Gubbio, and Gualdo Taddino, and, after 1900, at Deruta. Inevitably, much of this maiolica lacks the vitality and originality of earlier periods, but at its best is extremely competent and decorative. One of the finest exponents of *istoriato* painting in this century was Ferruccio Mengaroni of Pesaro (1875–1925), whose work has frequently been mistaken for Renaissance maiolica (no. 64). Today Deruta, Faenza, and other towns continue to make maiolica, much of it intended for the tourist trade. The traditional techniques are also practised by studio potters working in a modern idiom.

THE MANUFACTURE OF MAIOLICA

Renaissance methods of maiolica manufacture are well known thanks to the description and illustrations by Cipriano Piccolpasso (1524–79), in *I tre libri dell'Arte del Vasaio* (The three books of the Potter's Art) which he wrote about 1557 for Cardinal de Tournon of Lyons (died 1562).

The basic raw material, red clay or chalky clay, was dug from river beds or pits. Impurities were removed and the clay was well kneaded before being thrown on a potter's wheel or pressed over or into plaster moulds to form vessels. Complex forms, such as ewers and vases, were made in more than one section and were assembled using slip to make the parts adhere. The first firing took place at about 1,000 degrees centigrade in a rectangular brick updraught kiln with the wood-fuelled fire under its floor. After removal, the pots, now either pale reddish-brown or cream in colour were ready for glazing.

The making of the tin glaze or '*bianco*' (white) was a complex process. First, white sand and potash in the form of calcined wine lees (from the inside of barrels) were heated in a pot in the kiln until they fused into a glassy lump. This was finely ground and suspended in water with oxides of lead and tin, the last rendering the glaze white and opaque. This sloppy liquid was applied to the pots, and after a short period drying they were ready for painting. If the body of the ware was dark, a preliminary coating of creamy-white slip was applied.

Piccolpasso shows the painters sitting down to their work with pots of pigment on a little table beside them. They used soft animal-hair brushes and had to be extremely deft because the pigment sank into the glaze and mistakes could not be rectified. Their pigments were based on metallic oxides: cobalt for blue; copper for green; antimony for yellow; manganese for purplish-brown; tin for white. Red was obtained by fluxing Armenian bole with lead, but it was difficult to fire successfully and occurs infrequently on Renaissance maiolica, mainly on pieces from Montelupo and Cafaggiolo. The painters relied heavily for ideas on a stock of drawings, prints, or book illustrations, particularly for *istoriato* designs. When the decoration was complete, a mark or inscription might be added (the exception rather than the rule), and high-quality wares were given a thin coat of translucent lead glaze called *coperta* (blanket). The pots were stacked in the kiln supported on pointed spurs, with the high-quality pieces protected by saggars, and were fired at about 950 degrees centigrade.

Lustre decoration was added after the second firing, so when the pots were painted spaces were left in the design where the lustre would later be applied, but this was not always done. The lustre used on maiolica is known as reduced-pigment lustre. The pigments were made of clay, cinnabar, vinegar, and compounds of silver for gold lustre, or copper for red lustre. After application, the ware was fired for the third time in a small kiln at a lower temperature than the second firing. Towards the end of firing the oxygen in the kiln was reduced by stoking the fire with brushwood so that the chamber became smoky. This resulted in the pigments being reduced almost to pure metal which adhered to the softened glaze, while the clay medium burned away. After removal from the kiln, the maiolica was cleaned and polished to reveal its full splendour. However, the potters were often disappointed with their labour, for Piccolpasso noted that 'oft times of 100 pieces of ware tried in the fire, scarce six are good'.

Further reading Alan Caiger-Smith, *Tin-Glaze Pottery in Europe and the Islamic World*, London, 1973. Cipriano Piccolpasso, *I tre libri dell'Arte del Vasaio, The Three Books of the Potter's Art*, translated and introduced by Ronald Lightbown and Alan Caiger-Smith, 2 vols., London, 1980. Alan Caiger-Smith, *Lustre Pottery*, London, 1985. Richard A.

Goldthwaite, 'The economic and social world of Italian renaissance maiolica', *Renaissance Quarterly*, 42 (1989), 1–32. Patricia Collins, 'Prints and the development of *istoriato* painting on Italian Renaissance maiolica', *Print Quarterly*, 4 (September 1987), pp. 223–35. Andrew Ladis, *Italian Renaissance Maiolica from Southern Collections*, Georgia Museum of Art, 1989, pp. 8–27. Chateau d'Ecouen, Musée national de la Renaissance, *Le dressoir du Prince, Services d'apparat à la Renaissance*, exhibition catalogue, 1995.

GLOSSARY AND ABBREVIATIONS

albarello A cylindrical storage jar of Islamic origin.

***berettino* glaze** Pale blue or greyish-blue tin glaze.

bianco sopra bianco Decoration in white on a greyish-white tin glaze.

catasto Cadastre. A property register for tax purposes.

compendiario A term derived from the verb *compendiare* to summarise, outline, or abridge. *Compendiario* decoration on maiolica is painted in a sketchy or summary style in a palette of blue, yellow, and orange, and sometimes also yellowish-green.

credenza A service of tableware taking its name from a piece of furniture on which vessels of precious metals were displayed at meals.

gadrooning A series of convex lobes.

grotesques Fanciful symmetrical decoration derived from Roman interior wall-paintings, usually incorporating mythical creatures, scrolls, medallions, and strapwork.

gules The heraldic term for red, usually shown in orange or purple on maiolica.

iconography The images or symbols in a particular work of art or associated with a particular subject in art, and their meaning. It may also mean the study of images and symbols in art.

impresa A personal device, usually accompanied by a motto, which together expressed something significant to the owner, such as a reference to an event in their life, or to beliefs or virtues they cherished.

istoriato Decorated with biblical, historical, mythological, or other scenes.

maiolica arcaica Ancient maiolica. A term for late medieval tin-glazed earthenware decorated in manganese-brown and copper-green.

MICF Museo Internazionale delle Ceramiche, Faenza.

neutron activation analysis A means of identifying the elements present in an object. A sample is exposed to thermal energy neutrons in a nuclear reactor, which make each element emit radiation in a unique pattern of gamma rays. These are passed through a detector to become a light pulse which is analysed to identify the amount of each element present.

Ovid Publius Ovidius Naso (43 BC – AD 18). Roman poet. His most celebrated work, *Metamorphoses*, is an important source of stories from classical mythology.

piatto da pompa A large dish for display.

peducci Pedestals. On maiolica *a peducci* describes a narrow, usually blue, running border of small pedestal-like motifs, scrolls, and pendants.

ricamo Embroidery. On *bianchi di Faenza*, decoration *a ricamo* describes patterns of radiating or crossing bands resembling embroidered ribbons.

Sacred monogram IHS, a transcription of the first three letters of the name of Jesus in Greek.

studiolo A study, but also a private chamber in which the owner kept paintings and other works of art.

thermoluminescence analysis A means of establishing an approximate date range for objects by heating a small sample of the fabric and measuring the amount of thermoluminescence (light) emitted from it.

1

JUG

UMBRIA, PROBABLY ORVIETO, OR NORTHERN LAZIO, THIRTEENTH CENTURY.

Height 16 cm. Dr J. W. L. Glaisher Bequest. C.2161–1928

Earthenware decorated in manganese and copper-green under lead glaze was widespread in the Arab world in the Middle Ages and was probably introduced from North Africa to Sicily and southern Italy by the migration of potters. By the beginning of the thirteenth century it was in use in the west of central Italy, in Rome and elsewhere in Lazio, and in Umbria.

Jugs formed a high proportion of the output of potters at this time, along with drinking cups, bowls and jars. The shapes of jugs differed from place to place, but they shared similar decorative motifs. These included wide green stripes with manganese edges, intersecting arcading, and scrolling foliage reserved in a green ground, all of which can be seen on the jug illustrated. Most of this pottery has been found in a fragmentary state in rubbish pits, and disused wells under buildings, or during road works, in towns such as Viterbo and Tuscania.

This jug was in a private collection at Orvieto before 1914, and is therefore likely to have been found in Orvieto or its vicinity. Its attribution is supported by more recent discoveries of jugs of similar type in the area, including one recovered in 1983 from a cistern under the Palazzo Faina in Orvieto. Underglaze-painted ware persisted in Umbria and Lazio after the introduction of tin-glazed earthenware in the first half of the thirteenth century, and probably went out of production in the early fourteenth. Other types of lead-glazed pottery, such as slipware, have continued to be made in Italy up to the present.

Further reading David Whitehouse, 'Ceramica Laziale', *Papers of the British School at Rome*, 44, NS 30 (1976), pp. 157–70. Guido Mazza, *La ceramica medioevale di Viterbo e dell'alto Lazio*, Viterbo, 1983. Barcelona, Museo de Cerámica, *Mediterraneum, Cerámica Medieval en España e Italia*, exhibition catalogue, Viterbo, 1992.

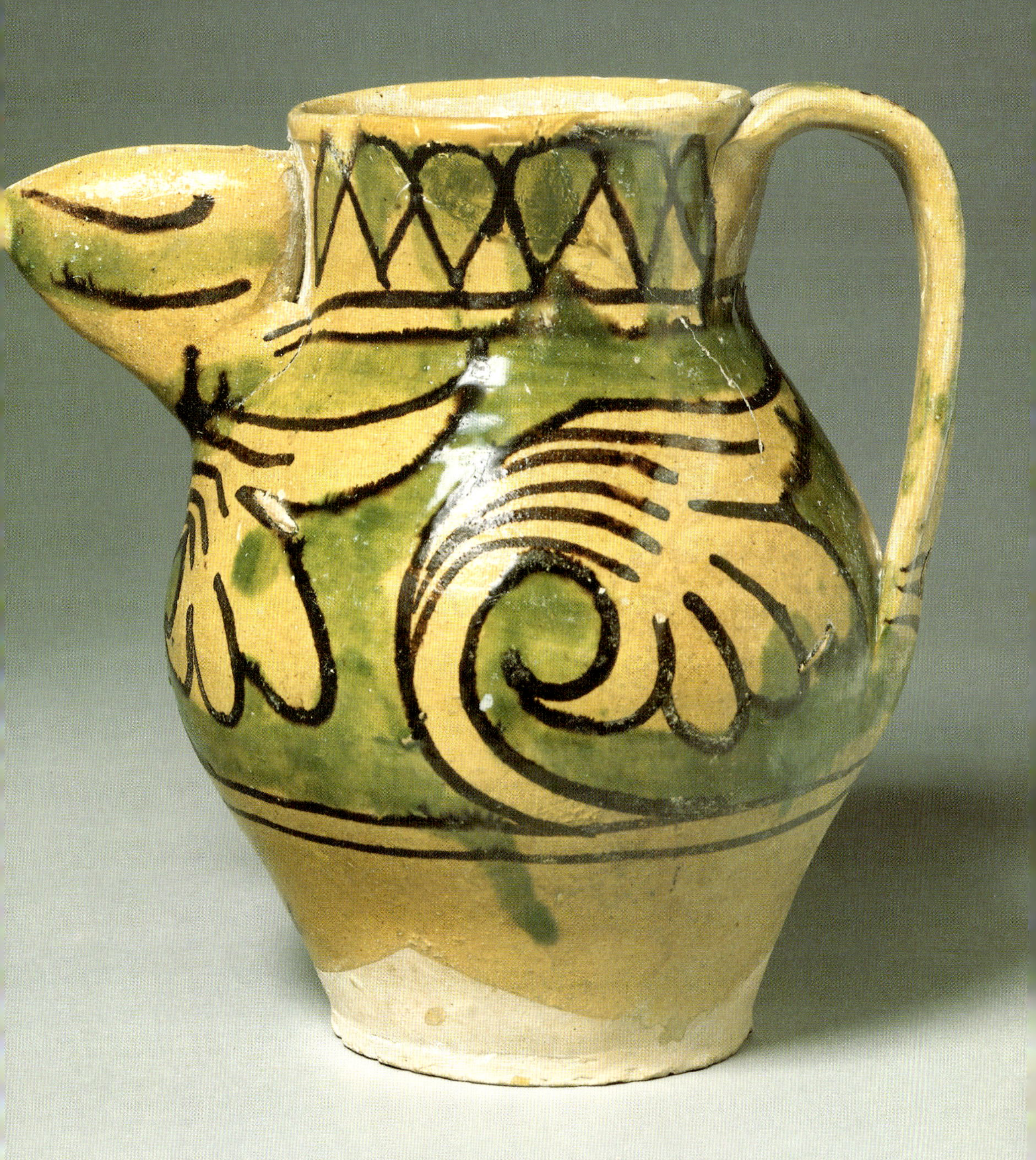

2

JUG AND PEDESTAL EWER

UMBRIA, PROBABLY ORVIETO,

c. 1275–1375

Heights 17.5 and 28.6 cm.
F. Leverton Harris Bequest, 1926. C.2162–1928 *and* C.89–1927.

This jug and ewer both have a pale buff body, tin-glazed and painted in manganese-brown and copper-green on the upper part, and lead glazed yellowish-brown inside and on the lower part. This combination of glazes was typical of late medieval tin-glazed ware which is sometimes described as *maiolica arcaica*. Its manufacture was introduced into central and some parts of northern Italy during the first half of the thirteenth century and it continued in production until the fifteenth century when it was gradually superseded by polychrome maiolica. During this period potters made many different forms of jugs, jars, flasks, bowls and two-handled cups. Despite the restricted palette, their decoration was surprisingly varied including plant, geometric, zoomorphic, heraldic and religious motifs. Mythical creatures, human figures and heads occur less frequently.

Pottery of this kind was first found in Orvieto around 1900 and since then vast amounts of it have been unearthed from the rubbish pits, wells and cisterns under domestic and other buildings, such as the Palazzo del Popolo. Of the two jugs shown here, the squat example with a restriction round its body, and a pelican beak spout, came from the same collection in Orvieto as no. 1, and the pedestal ewer with a trilobate mouth can be seen with others in a photograph taken there about 1909. So it seems very likely that they were found there or in the vicinity and were probably made locally.

It is still not possible to date late-medieval Orvieto maiolica very precisely, despite the study of finds from a controlled excavation conducted in 1983 and 1984 on the rubbish pits and cisterns under the Palazzo Faina. The ewer shown here was probably made in the late thirteenth or first half of the fourteenth century, and the jug, during the fourteenth century.

Further reading Spoleto, *Ceramiche medioevali dell'Umbria: Assisi Orvieto Todi*, exhibition catalogue ed. Grazietta Guaitini, Florence, 1981. Milan, Castello Sforzesco, *La ceramica orvietana del medioevo*, exhibition catalogue, Florence, 1983. Orvieto, Palazzo Papale, *La ceramica orvietana del medioevo 2*, exhibition catalogue, Florence, 1985.

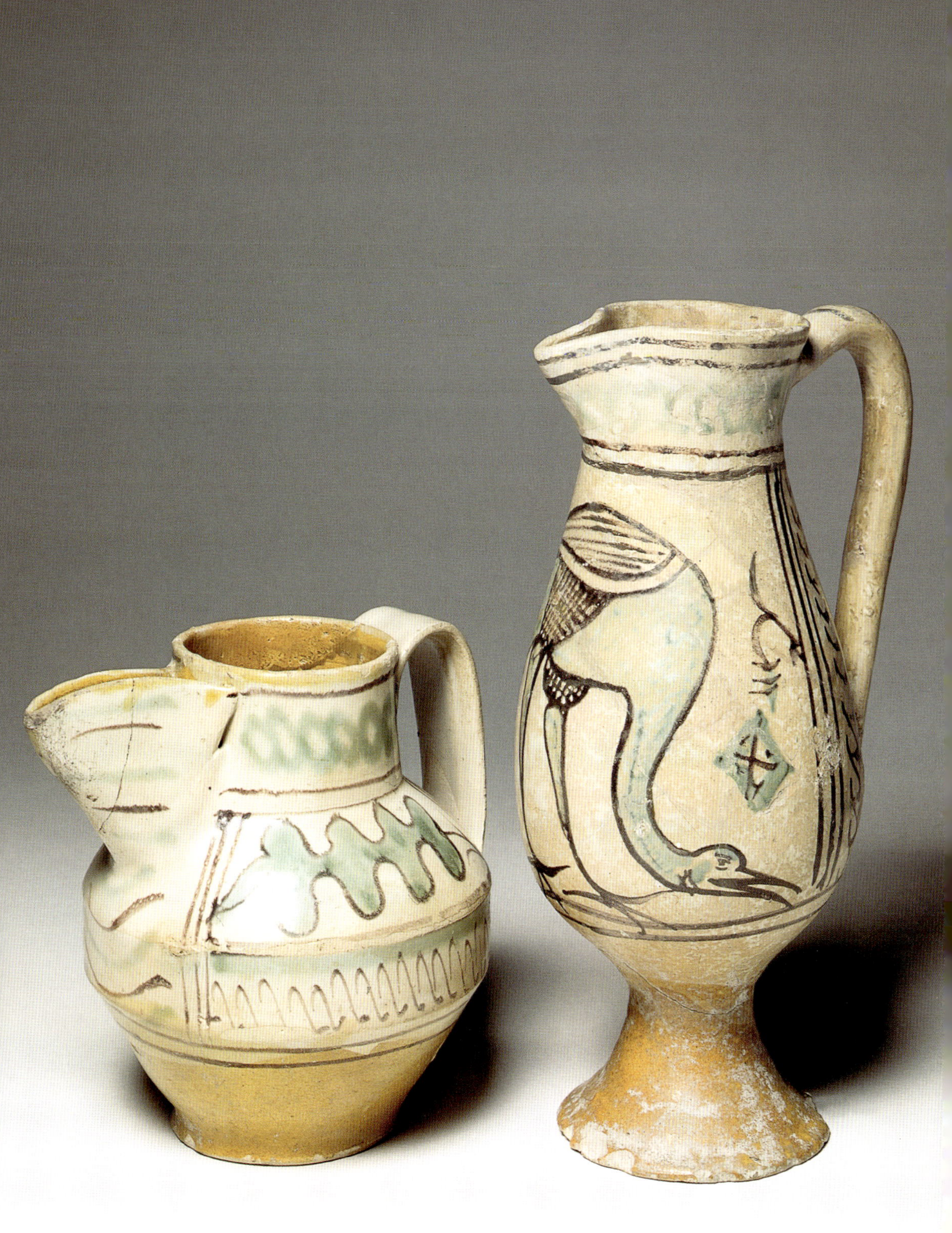

3

TWO-HANDLED BOWL

PROBABLY TUSCANY OR UMBRIA,

c. 1350–1425

Height 9.7 cm; width 34 cm.

H. S. Reitlinger Bequest, 1950. C.137–1991.

Decoration in manganese and cobalt-blue instead of copper-green (*maiolica arcaica blu*) came into use in central Italy around the middle of the fourteenth century. Its adoption was influenced by the use of this palette on *bacini* (basins) imported from the Maghreb. One of the earliest Tuscan examples is a jug said to have been found in the vault of the loggia of the Town Hall at Montalcino, which was probably built during the second quarter of the century. Jugs found during an excavation at the Palazzo Pretorio in Pistoia have been dated to the mid and late fourteenth century.

Maiolica arcaica blu is much less common than maiolica with manganese and copper-green decoration. This suggests that it was a luxury product made briefly in small quantities. Evidence from Pistoia indicates that it had probably gone out of use in the region of Florence by the end of the century, and was superseded by maiolica with decoration in relief-blue (see no. 5). Further south, in Lazio it persisted well into the fifteenth century.

This bowl formerly belonged to William Ridout (d. 1933), whose ceramic collection included 100 pieces of late-medieval maiolica, but its find site is not known. Its decoration resembles manganese and copper green bowls from Umbria, but a Tuscan origin cannot be excluded because double-armed cross motifs were also used there.

Further reading Guido Vannini, 'Firenze, Prato, Pistoia. Aspetti di produzione e consumo della ceramica nel mediovaldarno medievale' in ed. Gian Carlo Bojani, *Ceramica Toscana dal medioevo al XVIII secolo*, Monte San Savino, 1990, pp. 34–5, 62–3, pls. XXXVII, XXXVIII, where further bibliography is cited. Guido Mazza, *La ceramica medioevale di Viterbo e dell'Alto Lazio*, Viterbo, 1983, pp. 120–7.

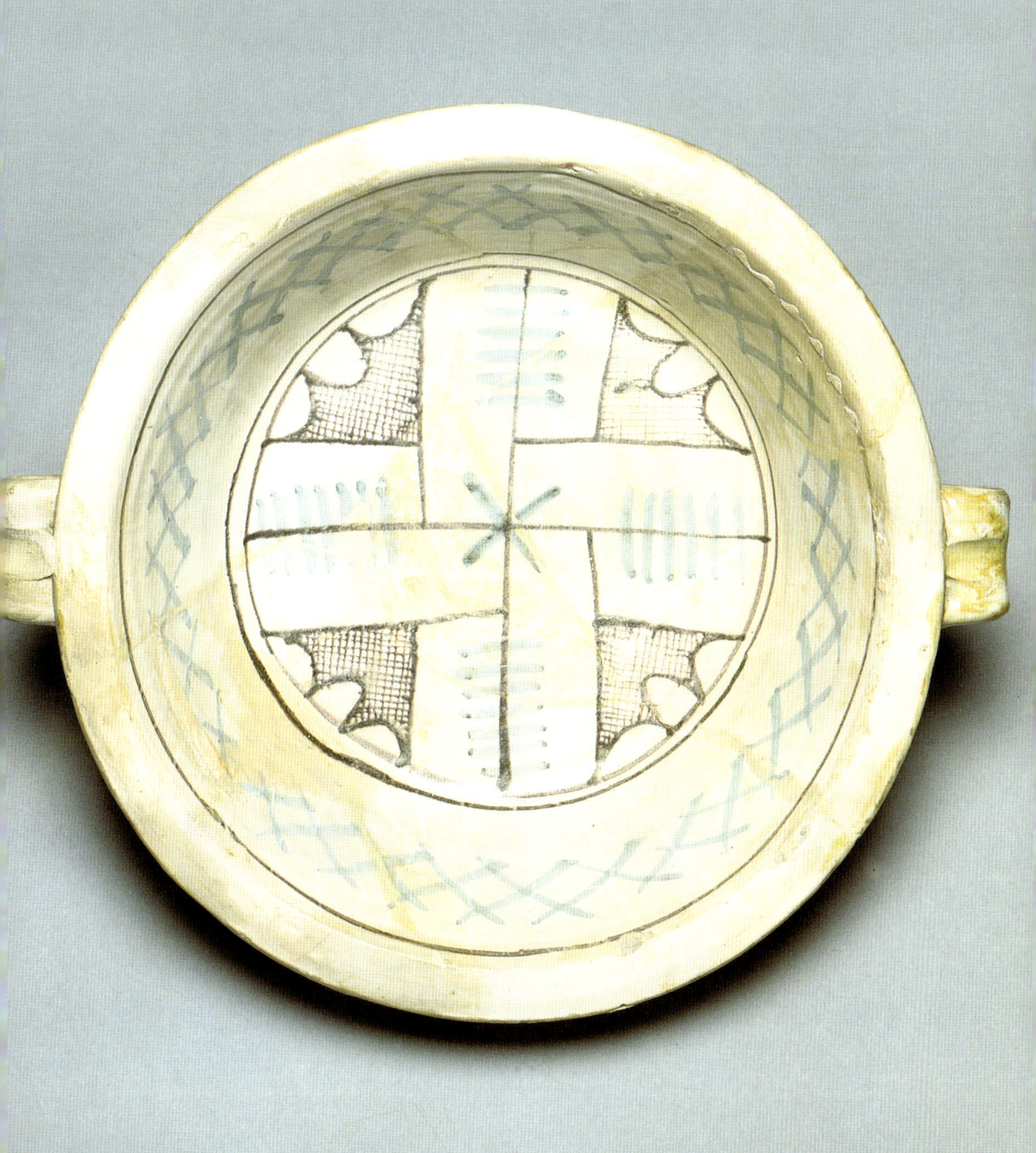

4

DEEP DISH OR BASIN

TUSCANY, PROBABLY FLORENCE OR ITS DISTRICT, *c.* 1420–50

The back is unglazed.
Height 7 cm; diameter 43 cm.
Purchased with the Glaisher Fund. C.25–1932.

Wide deep dishes or basins were used with ewers for hand-washing at meals and at other times. The finest were made of silver, and many later maiolica basins were moulded with inverted gadrooning and other ornament in imitation of embossing (see no. 21). A basin like this one might also have served as a cooler (*rinfrescatoio*). An example filled with glasses can be seen standing next to a group of jugs in a late fifteenth-century fresco in the Oratory of San Martino al Vescovo in Florence.

This basin illustrates one of the types of decoration which the great maiolica scholar, Gaetano Ballardini, named '*famiglia verde*', because of their predominantly green palette. Such terms can be misleading because they suggest that certain wares were related when they may not be. But *famiglia verde* is a convenient term for the transitional styles of decoration which evolved from *maiolica arcaica* in central Italy during the fifteenth century. One Tuscan type, of which this dish is representative, has touches of yellow, and retains medieval features, such as the use of manganese cross-hatching and non-figurative motifs. Another is a predominantly green version of relief-blue decoration with figural motifs surrounded by foliage (see no. 5), and a third includes naturalistic busts, animals, and curling leaves, and has a more even balance of the three colours.

The central design on this basin is still medieval in character, but the bound laurel wreath border, and use of yellow, are indications of progress towards the Renaissance style. A smaller dish with analogous decoration is in the Getty Museum, Malibu. Fragments of dishes with comparable decoration have been excavated in Florence and further south in Tuscany.

Further reading Cora, 1973, I, pp. 71–3, II, pls. 45–54. Hess, 1988, pp. 20–2, no. 4.

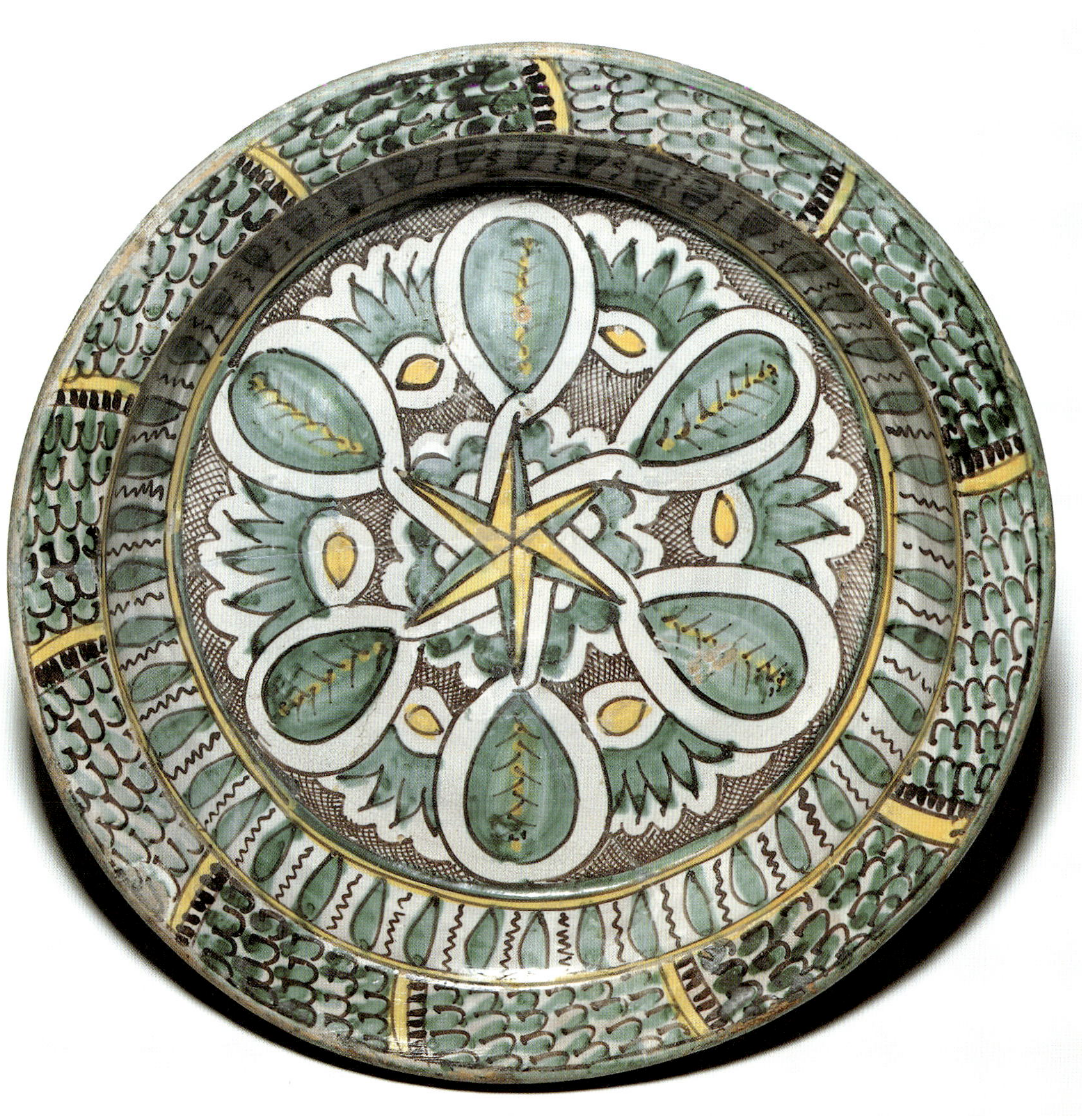

5

TWO-HANDLED PHARMACY JAR

FLORENCE OR ITS DISTRICT,

c. 1425–35

On each handle is a green crutch with two manganese asterisks below.
Height 20 cm; width 22.5 cm. L. C. G. Clarke Bequest, 1960. C.75–1961.

This jar is decorated in manganese and relief-blue (*zaffera a rilievo*), a glaze-like, upstanding pigment containing cobalt. It was probably introduced in Tuscany during the last quarter of the fourteenth century, as fragments found during excavations in Florence and nearby towns, such as Prato, Pistoia, and Montelupo, can be dated to the end of the century. Others have been found with fragments of Italo-Moresque type (see no. 6) which suggests that relief-blue decoration continued until the 1460s. It was also adopted in the Romagna, Lazio, and Umbria during the same period.

Relief-blue occurs on jugs, ewers, albarelli, and dishes, but the best-known examples outside Italy are Tuscan two-handled jars. Typically these have borders creating a panel on each side which is occupied by a central motif surrounded by stylized oak foliage. The main motifs include heraldic and other animals, fleurs-de-lis, and mythical or human figures. Some jars, however, are decorated overall with foliage, scales, or undulating lines. These motifs appear to have been derived from local and Islamic art, including heraldry, woven textiles, and ceramics.

This is one of at least twenty-one 'oak leaf jars' whose handles bear the crutch emblem of the hospital of Santa Maria Nuova in Florence. The hospital's archives record the purchase of large numbers of jars for its pharmacy in 1427 from Maso and Miniato di Domenico and, in 1431, from Giunta di Tugio, and the surviving jars may well come from one or the other of these consignments. The meaning of the two asterisks is uncertain. They may be the mark of a decorator, because one, two, or three asterisks occur on other jars of this kind.

Further reading Cora, 1973, I, pp. 73–82, II, pls. 55–115. Anna Moore Valeri, 'Florentine "zaffera a rilievo" maiolica: a new look at the Oriental influence', *Archeologia Medievale*, 11 (1984), pp. 477–500. Giovanni Conti, Allesandro Alìnari, Fausto Berti, *et al.*, *Zaffera et similia nella maiolica italiana*, Viterbo, 1991, pp. 15–94.

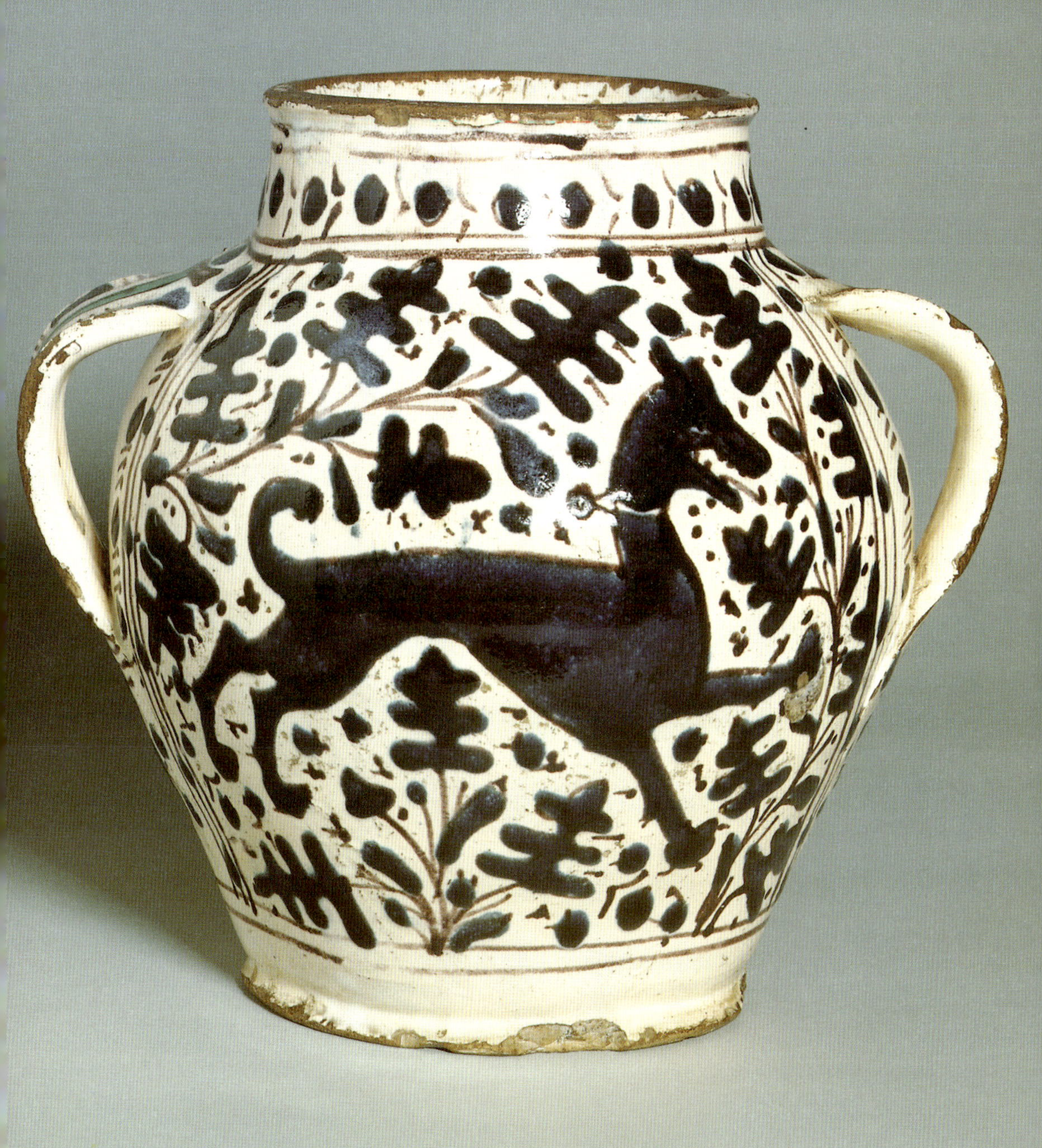

6

PHARMACY JAR (ALBARELLO)

FLORENCE OR ITS DISTRICT, *c.* 1440–60

Height 23.8 cm; diameter 14.1 cm.
Purchased with the Glaisher Fund. C.39–1931.

Large quantities of Hispano-Moresque blue and gold lustreware were imported into Tuscany and other parts of Italy from Valencia during the fourteenth and fifteenth centuries. The vessels imported included cylindrical storage jars, known as albarelli, which were of Islamic origin, and were also imported from the Middle East, mainly from Syria. '*Albaregli damaschini*' are mentioned in fifteenth-century inventories, and this term, originally denoting their origin, was sometimes used to indicate jars with blue decoration. Albarelli were used in pharmacies for the storage of powders, ointments and lozenges, cosmetics, herbs, and spices, and were covered with a parchment tied on below the flanged or slightly everted rim. In the home they were used for similar storage purposes or as flower vases.

Italian examples decorated in manganese and green in late medieval style date from the fourteenth or early fifteenth century. By the middle of the century they were being decorated with patterns derived from Valencian imports, mainly in blue with small amounts of manganese, or yellow to represent lustre. These Italo-Moresque designs included geometrical motifs and pseudo-Kufic script, small flowers and trefoil leaves, and stems of leaves with incised veins, like the ones on the jar illustrated here.

The front is decorated with a wreath enclosing the arms, *azure, a fess or between three fleurs-de-lis or (two in chief and one in base)* which correspond to those of the Pasini family. An almost identical jar is in the Fanfani collection at the Museo Internazionale delle Ceramiche, Faenza, and a smaller one without a lower border, was sold at Sotheby's in 1973.

Jars of this period are rarely inscribed with the name of the contents, and labelling only became common after about 1480.

Further reading Rudolf E. A. Drey, *Apothecary Jars*, London, 1978. Margaret Legge, *The Apothecary's Shelf; Drug Jars and Mortars 15th to 18th century*, Melbourne, 1986. Carmen Ravanelli Guidotti, *La donazione Angiolo Fanfani, ceramiche dal Medioevo al* XX *secolo, Museo Internazionale delle Ceramiche*, Faenza, 1990, pp. 26–7, no. 9, pp. 52–3, no. 17.

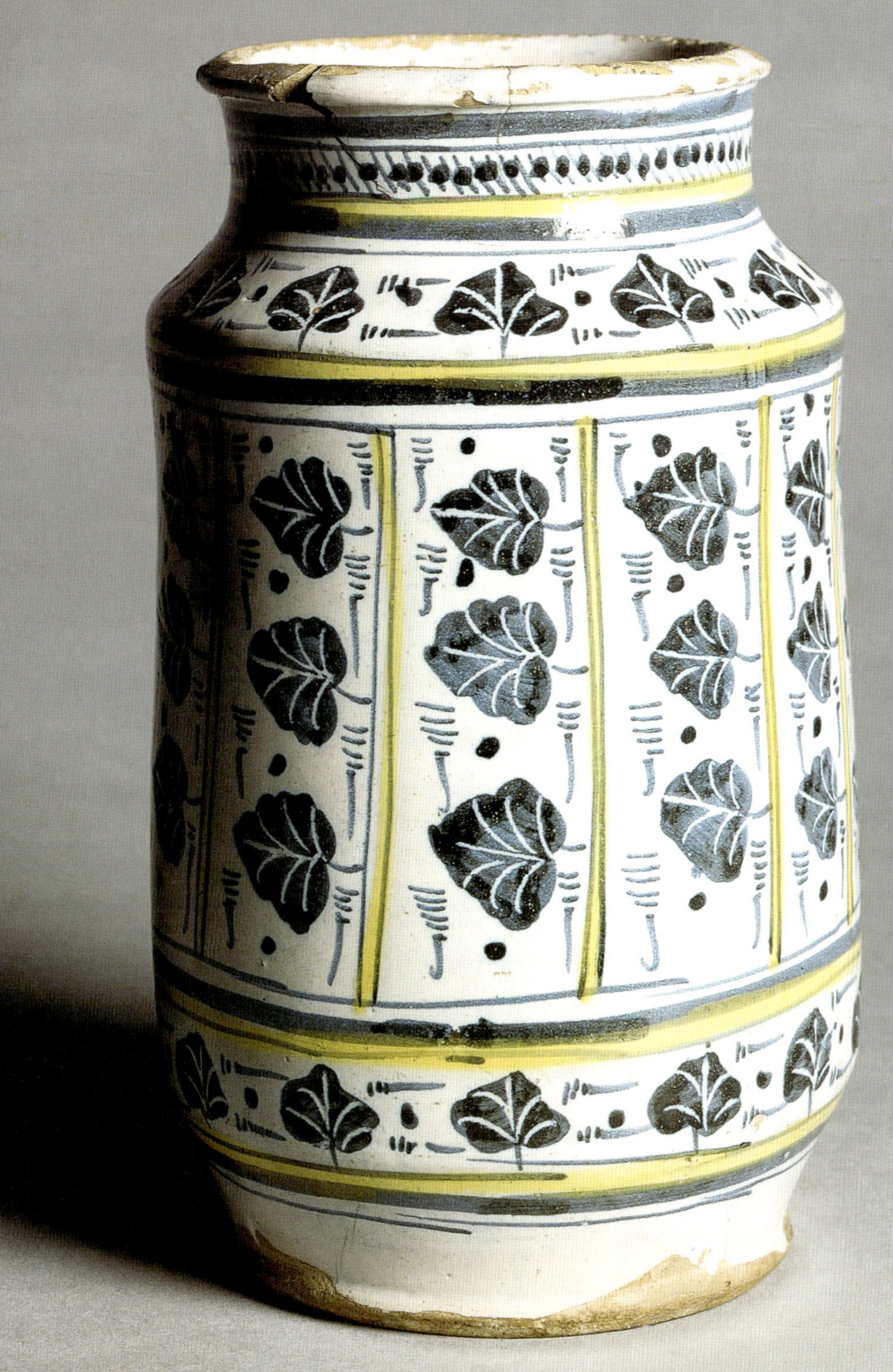

7

STORAGE JAR

PROBABLY PESARO, *c.* 1470–90

On the other side are three more profile busts of boys and parti-coloured fruits on coiling stems. Height 26.8 cm; diameter 20.3 cm.
F. Leverton Harris Bequest, 1926. C.60–1927.

This jar illustrates two of the most successful varieties of late fifteenth-century maiolica decoration: profile portraits (see also no. 12) and 'gothic foliage'. The latter was probably derived from the illuminated borders of manuscripts, and comprised elongated divided leaves, vigorously curving and scrolling back on themselves. The foliage is shaded in blue and manganese with small amounts of green and dark yellow, and is often combined with peacock's feather eye motifs or stylized buds. It occurs on pavement tiles, domestic, and pharmaceutical wares, and was widely disseminated throughout central Italy, including Rome and Naples. The style of the foliage varied from place to place, but it is not always possible to make secure attributions on that basis. In the early part of the century, this jar was attributed to Faenza, but the 'gothic foliage' more closely resembles fragments of such decoration found recently at Pesaro.

The jar is one of a small group which all have a rather broad form with a projecting rim, and upper borders of chevrons between yellow-ochre and blue bands. Three of them are decorated with profile busts: one, also in the Fitzwilliam (*c.*78–1961), is decorated with a man and woman separated by a vase of flowers, and two have young men. Most busts on maiolica are not portraits in the true sense, and in some instances can be shown to be stock images. However, on these jars the busts are so individual in character that they could have represented living boys. The painter appears to have been influenced by artists of the Ferrara school, such as Ercole Roberti.

Further reading Paride Berardi, *L'antica maiolica di Pesaro dal* XIV *al* XVII *secolo*, Florence, 1984, especially pp. 128–32. Alessandro Bettini, 'Le maioliche della discordia', *Ceramic Antica*, 1:2 (February 1991), pp. 12–18. Pierre-Alain Mariaux, *La majolique. La faïence et son décor dans les collections Suisses* XVe – XVIIIe *siècles*, exhibition catalogue, Musée Historique de Lausanne, Geneva, 1995, p. 71, p. 166, no. 17.

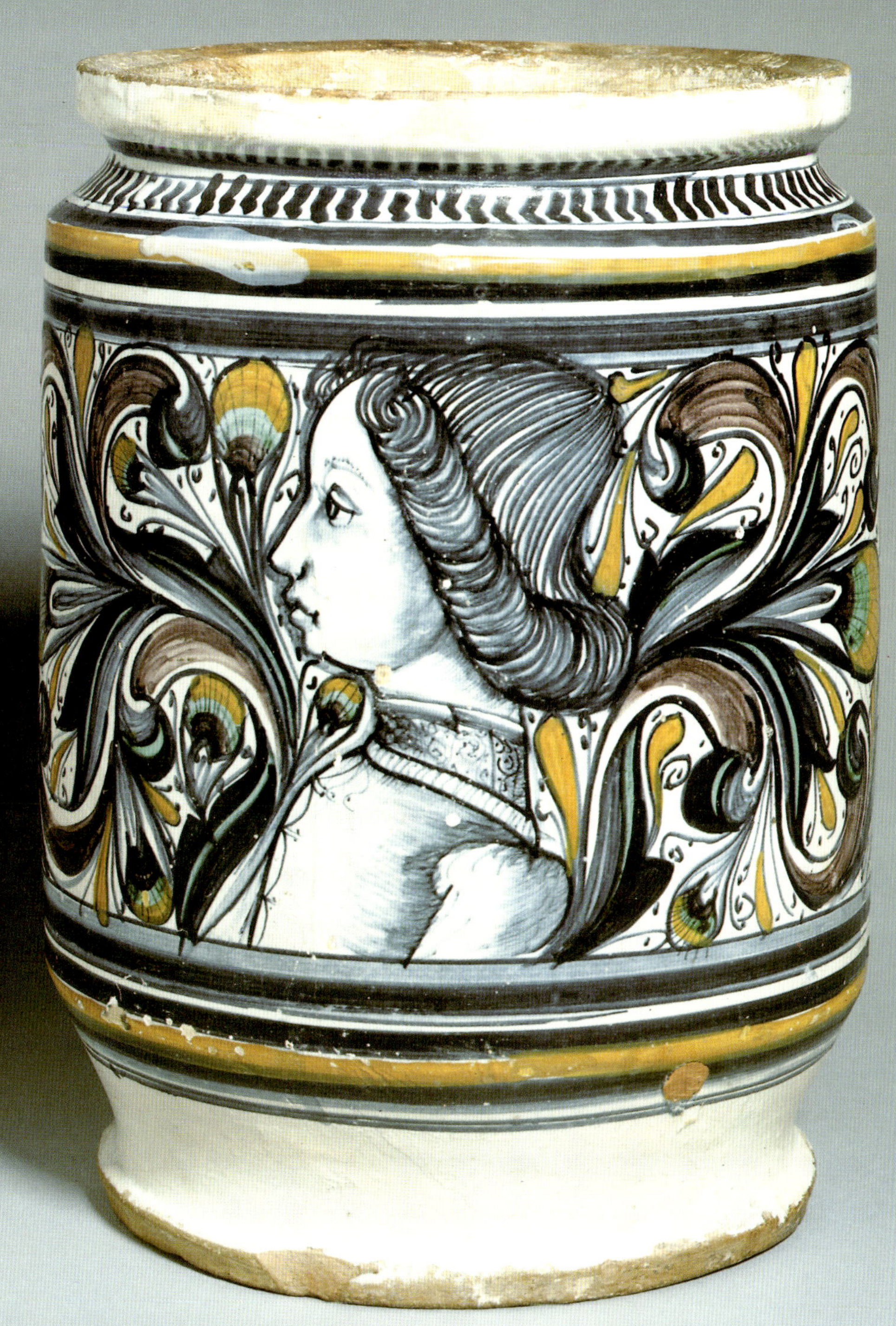

8

STORAGE JAR

PESARO, *c.* 1480–1500

Height 32.5 cm; diameter 14.3 cm.
Purchased with the Leverton Harris Fund. EC.27–1946.

Tall slender albarelli with waisted sides to facilitate lifting were made in many maiolica centres from the late fifteenth century onwards. Fifteenth- and early sixteenth-century examples were usually decorated with horizontal bands which emphasized the form of the jar – its neck, shoulder, waist, and the widest point above the base. Some jars had one wide field on the sides, others had two or more separated by bands which were generally placed with an unerring sense of proportion.

The zones of decoration might include 'gothic foliage' (see no. 7), 'persian palmettes', peacock's feather eyes, wavy rays, and a variety of repeating patterns of stylized flowers, tendrils, and leaves. Two jars with analogous zones of small flowers and trefoil leaves against a dotted background are in the Robert Lehman collection in the Metropolitan Museum in New York. Their size and colouring are also similar, and this suggests that they had a common origin, although maiolica painters were sometimes employed in more than one workshop on a contract or piece-work basis.

These jars are attributed to Pesaro because enough fragments with comparable decoration have been found there to infer that they were of local manufacture. The town was one of the most thriving maiolica centres between about 1450 and 1510, and numerous potters are mentioned in the records of local notaries. In 1486 Camilla and Giovanni Sforza d'Aragona, the rulers of Pesaro, forbade the importation of pottery other than jars for oil and water, in recognition of the excellence of local products.

Further reading Paride Berardi, *L'antica maiolica di Pesaro dal* XIV *al* XVII *secolo*, Florence, 1984, pp. 124–5, p. 254, figs. 31k and 31l. Albarelli, 1986. Rasmussen, 1989, pp. 32–3, nos. 18–19.

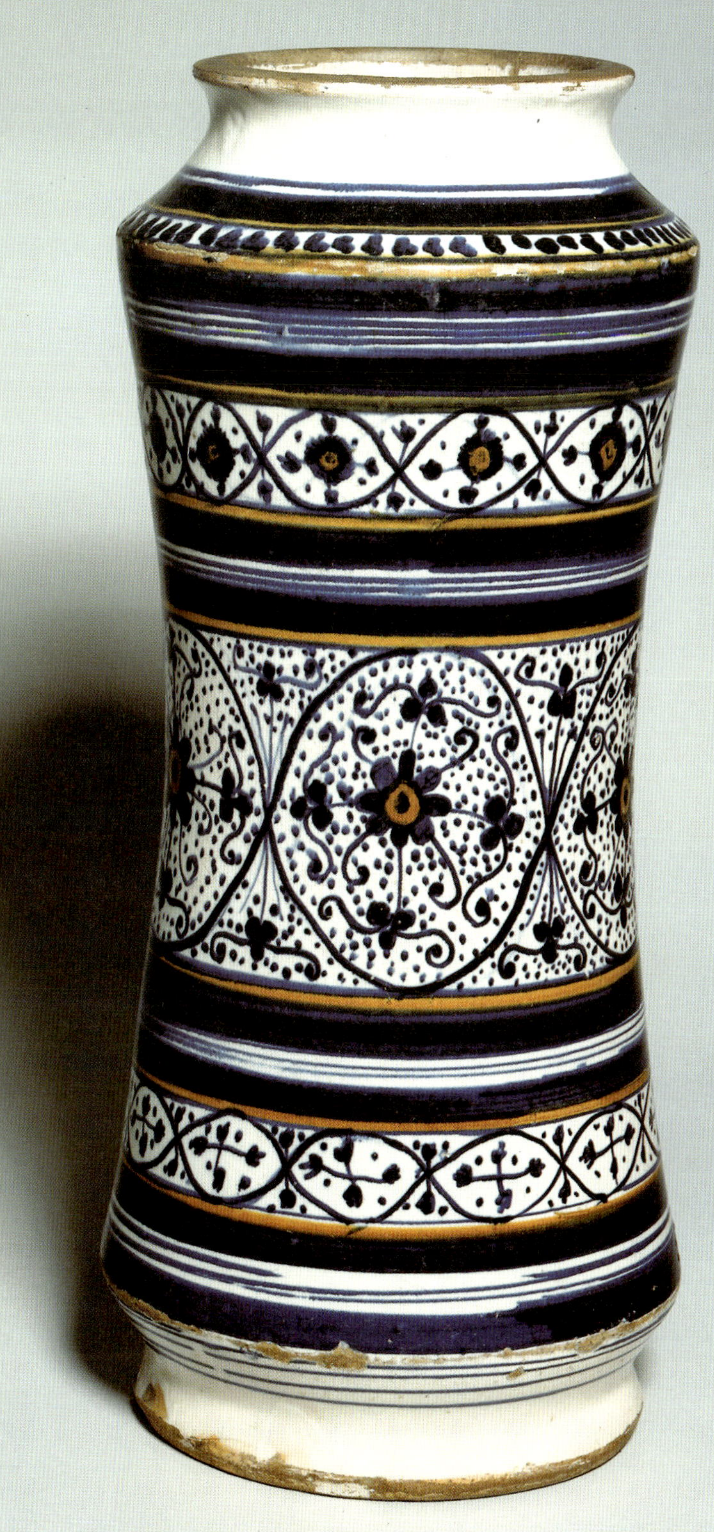

9

PAVEMENT TILE

PESARO, PROBABLY WORKSHOP
OF ANTONIO DEI FEDELI
(d. 1508), 1493–4

Height 23.9 cm; width 23.9 cm; depth 4.7 cm.
F. Leverton Harris Bequest, 1926. C.61–1927.

Tin-glazed pavement tiles were made in Italy in the thirteenth and fourteenth centuries, but it was not until the second half of the fifteenth century that the use of polychrome maiolica tiles became widespread in domestic and ecclesiastical buildings. Some pavements were patterned in tiles of two colours; others were made of tiles of different geometrical shapes painted with designs similar to those on domestic and pharmaceutical wares. The finest fifteenth-century pavement surviving *in situ* is in the Vaselli chapel in San Petronio, Bologna. It was painted by Pietro Andrea of Faenza and others about 1487.

This tile is decorated with a white hound muzzled and leashed, symbolizing fidelity, which was a device adopted by Gianfrancesco Gonzaga (1395–1444), first Marquis of Mantua. It was one of eight Gonzaga devices pictured on tiles commissioned from Pesaro in 1493 by Marquis Francesco II Gonzaga (1466–1519) for his villa at Marmirolo. However, on their arrival at the Castel San Giorgio in Mantua on 1 June 1494, some of them were laid in the *studiolo* of his wife, Isabella d'Este (1474–1539). The project seems to have been undertaken partly for aesthetic reasons and partly as a measure to rid the room of mice which had been nesting under the floorboards. Apart from this, maiolica pavements were not very practical in domestic situations because their colourful designs were gradually worn away by people's feet. The back of this tile, like that of the others from this pavement, was scooped out to produce three concentric circles. This may have been done to speed the drying of the tiles before firing or to prevent them warping in the kiln.

Further reading Mariarosa Palvarini Gobio Casali, 'Ceramic tiles for the Gonzaga', in Victoria and Albert Museum, *Splendours of the Gonzaga*, London, 1981, pp. 44–5. J. V. G. Mallet, 'Floor tiles with Gonzaga devices', *ibid.*, p. 173, no. 127.

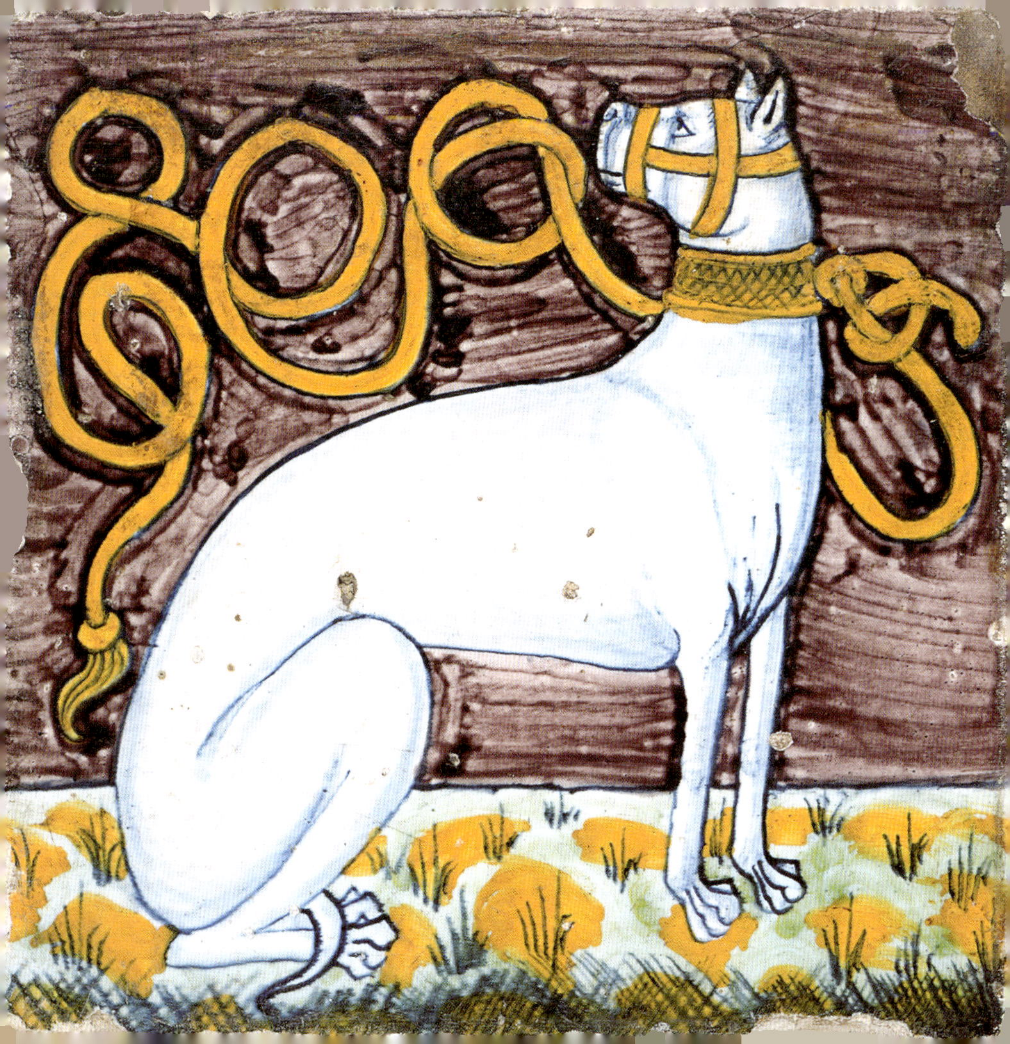

10

TWO-HANDLED VASE WITH FRUIT AND VEGETABLE COVER

FLORENCE, DELLA ROBBIA WORKSHOP, C.1490–1520

Height 39.5 cm; width 22.3 cm; cover width 24.2 cm.
L. C. G. Clarke Bequest, 1960. C.92A–1961.

This vase is one of a pair which may have been adjuncts of an altarpiece or have been used as ornaments in a domestic setting. They are made of tin-glazed terracotta, a medium developed by Luca Della Robbia (1399/1400–82) by 1441, and continued by his nephew Andrea (1435–1525) and his sons Giovanni (1469–1529/30), Luca the younger (1475–1548?), and Girolamo (1488–1566). Unlike most domestic and pharmaceutical maiolica which was tin-glazed and painted, sculpture and vases by the Della Robbia were decorated with coloured glazes and sometimes with gilding. Analysis of glaze from a roundel by Luca Della Robbia in the Victoria and Albert Museum, has shown that it contained a higher percentage of tin-oxide than ordinary maiolica glaze, which rendered it more opaque.

The workshop made moulded two-handled vases of two main types: one with a pronounced shoulder and incurved neck, the other, like this example, with an ovoid body and a short neck. Both types were decorated with combinations of gadroons, scales, interlace, Greek key, and, more rarely, plant ornament. The tops were made separately, and it is possible that the ones accompanying this pair are not those originally provided. A pair filled with flowers are shown standing on the ends of a bed head in a relief of the birth of John the Baptist on the font by Giovanni Della Robbia in San Leonardo, Cerreto Guidi. Vases like the Fitzwilliam's have usually been attributed to Giovanni Della Robbia, but an example with the scale pattern on the lower half has recently been attributed tentatively to Luca the younger.

Further reading Giovanni Cora, *Storia della maiolica di Firenze e del contado secoli* XIV *e* XV, 2 vols., Florence, 1973, pp. 173–9. Wilson, 1987, p. 76, no. 108. Giancarlo Gentilini, *I Della Robbia. La scultura invetriata nel Rinascimento*, 2 vols., Florence, n.d. (1992).

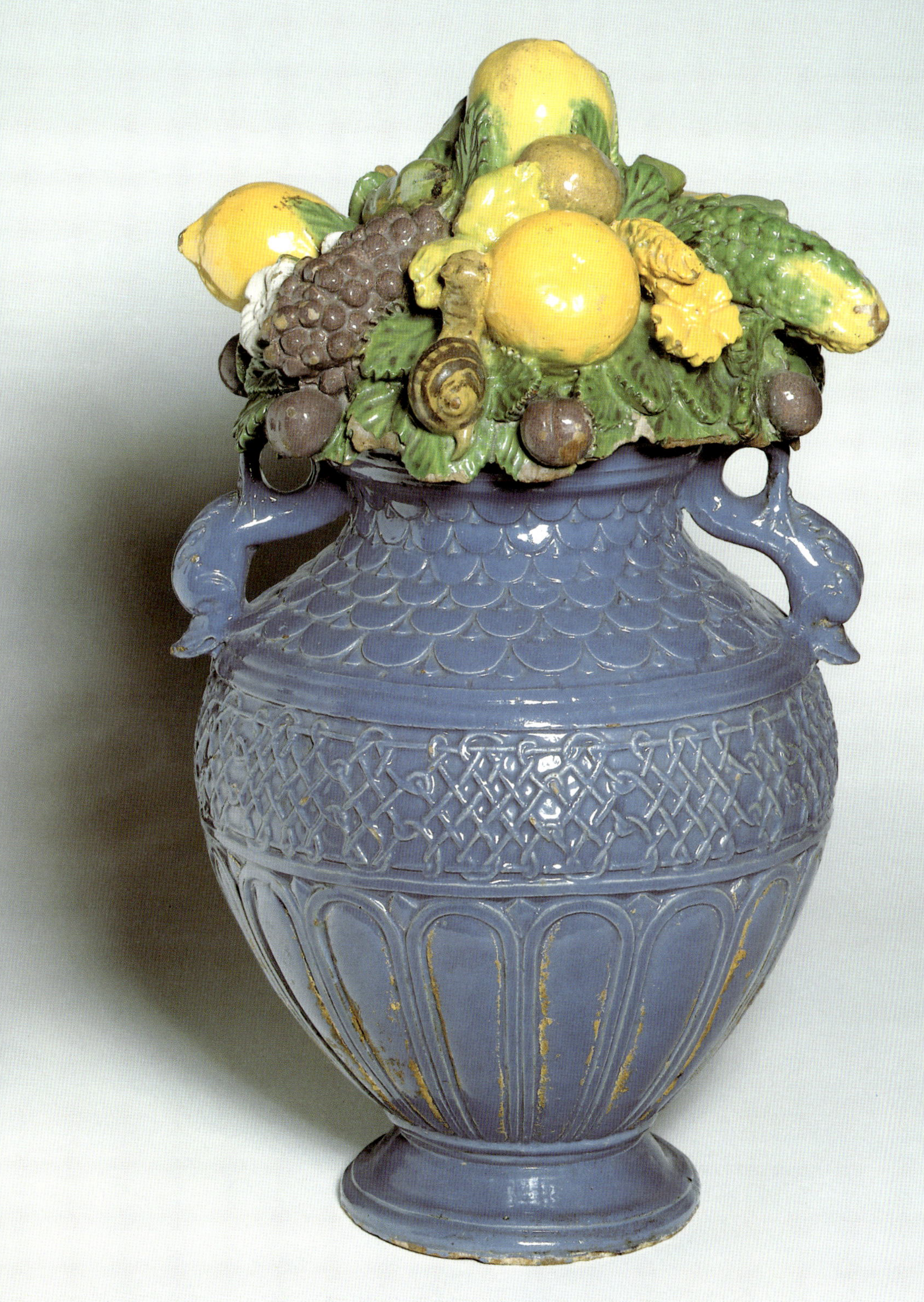

11

BUST OF AN OLD WOMAN

FAENZA, c. 1490–1510

Height 20.9 cm; width 24 cm.
Given by L. C. G. Clarke. C.1–1955.

The development of realistic bust portraiture inspired by Roman models was one of the great innovations in fifteenth-century art. Life then was often extinguished swiftly, and one reason for the popularity of busts and other forms of portraiture was that they satisfied the patron's urge to be commemorated as an individual with a distinct personality.

Maiolica is not a very satisfactory medium for three-dimensional modelling because the glaze tends to obscure details. Nevertheless, in the late fifteenth century small-scale religious and secular sculpture was produced in maiolica workshops. The rich dark blue on this bust resembles that on reliefs attributed to Faenza and, if not made there, it probably came from elsewhere in the Romagna or Marches, rather than from Tuscany or Umbria.

Maiolica busts of this date are rare. Two *belle donne* are in museums in Cleveland and Boston in the United States, and a third was last recorded there. The Fitzwilliam's bust is smaller, and stands apart in being a candid portrayal of gap-toothed middle age. Who, one wonders, would have wanted such a poignant reminder that youth and beauty fade? A possible answer, suggested by the rather squat proportions of the bust when viewed from the back, is that it portrays a court dwarf. Dwarves were valued for their ability to amuse, and one tiny woman is shown beside her mistress, the Marchesa Barbara, in Mantegna's *al seco* wall painting of Lodovico Gonzaga and his family in the Camera Picta (painted chamber) at Mantua.

The male busts in maiolica of this period are larger and more sculptural in character. They include a Christ in the J. Paul Getty Museum, Malibu and a St John the Baptist in the Ashmolean Museum, Oxford.

Further reading *Bulletin of the Museum of Fine Arts Boston*, 55:301–2 (1957), p. 109, pl. 75. John Pope-Hennessy, *The Portrait in the Renaissance*, London and New York, 1966. Edmund P. Pillsbury, *Florentine Art in Cleveland Collections. Florence and the Arts, Five Centuries of Patronage*, exhibition catalogue, Cleveland, 1971, no. 31.

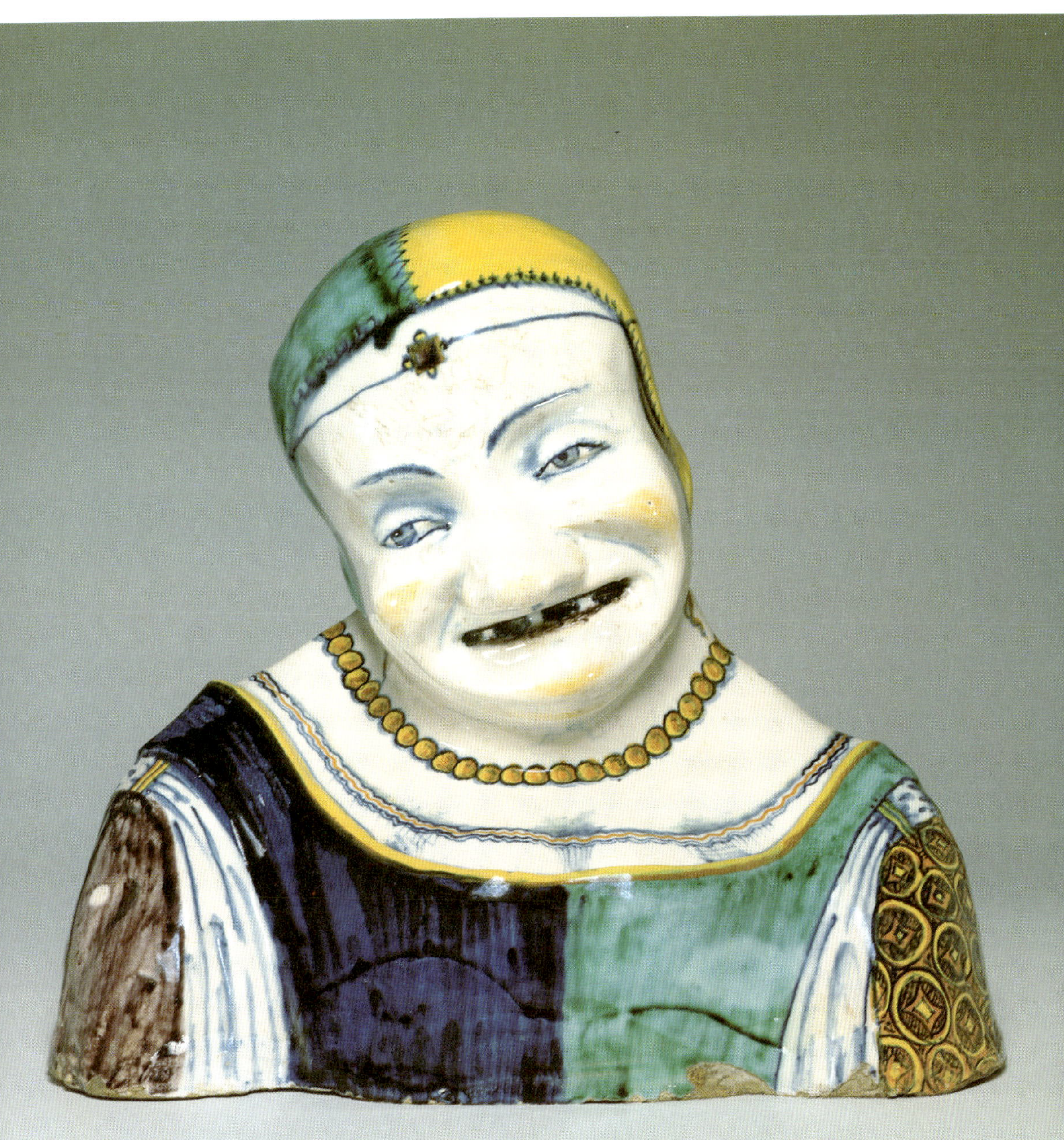

12

TWO-HANDLED VASE

DERUTA, *c.* 1490–1520

Height 23.5 cm; width 21 cm.
Purchased with the Glaisher Fund. EC.21–1939.

Deruta is a small Umbrian town about twenty kilometers south of Perugia. Documents show that pottery was being made there in the thirteenth century, and by the second half of the fifteenth century it had become one of the most important and prolific maiolica centres. Its potters supplied Perugia, and developed an extensive export trade in lustred and polychrome maiolica.

Two-handled vases similar in shape to this one were being made by at least 1491 when one labelled 'DERVTA' was depicted in an illuminated letter at the beginning of the Deruta *catasto*. They are said to have been made for use at banquets and weddings, a tradition which is supported by the decoration of many examples with love symbols, such as flaming hearts and clasped hands, or busts of young girls and men. Possibly they were the '*vasi da confectione*' sometimes provided with covers, which are mentioned in late fifteenth- and early sixteenth-century Perugian inventories, and were presumably filled with sweets such as sugared almonds.

This example is decorated on one side with a bust of a young man and on the other with a girl, both within garlands of laurel leaves and berries inspired by Roman sculptural ornament. The fashion for profile busts (as opposed to full-length profiles which had occurred in earlier paintings) was related to the growth of interest in Roman coins, and to contemporary medallic portraits inspired by them.

Further reading Spoleto, *Antiche maioliche di Deruta per un Museo Regionale della Ceramica Umbra*, exhibition catalogue ed. Grazietta Guaitini, Florence, 1980. Carola Fiocco and Gabriella Gherardi, *La Ceramica di Deruta dal* XIII *al* XVIII *secolo*, Perugia, 1994 (with English translation).

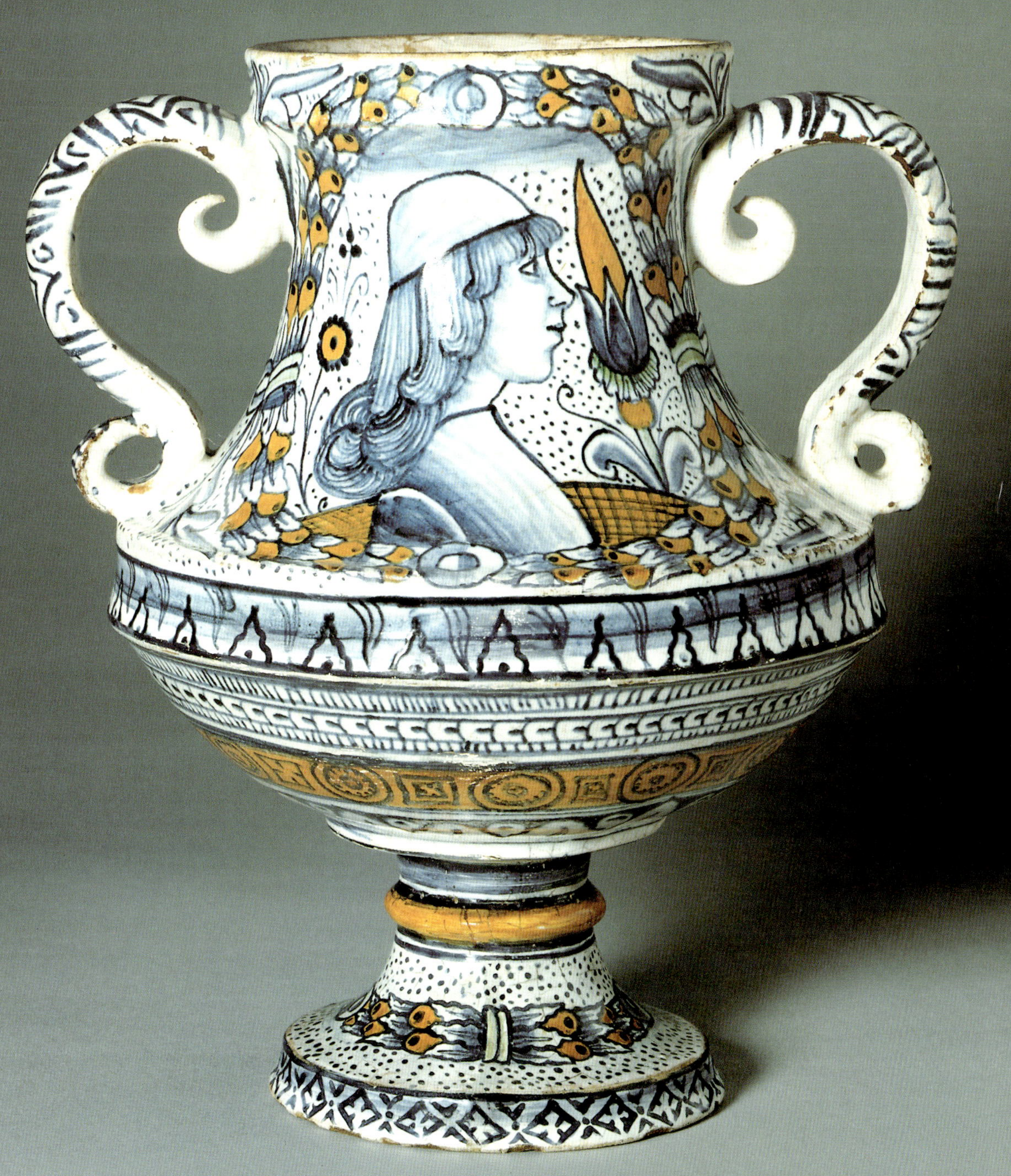

13

DISH

DERUTA, *c.* 1500–30

Height 7.5 cm; diameter 39.5 cm.
Purchased with the Glaisher Fund. C.24–1932.

Large decorative dishes, known as *piatti da pompa*, were a speciality of sixteenth-century Deruta potters. They are about 40 cm wide and have a distinctive profile with a slightly raised edge, broad rim, and curved well with a footring, which is usually pierced by two holes to take a cord for suspension. Curiously these are often incorrectly placed for suspension the right way up. The backs are almost always lead-glazed, and the fronts are tin-glazed and painted in polychrome or in blue embellished with gold lustre and, on some early examples, also red lustre. The gold pigment, actually derived from a compound of silver, varies in colour after firing from a very pale silvery-yellow to brassy- or brownish-gold.

The decoration of *piatti da pompa* includes armorials, religious and mythical subjects, horsemen, and hunting scenes. Busts and three-quarter-length figures of women are very common. They were not portraits, but belong to several physical types which, in the early part of the century, closely resembled women in paintings by Pinturicchio (1454–1515) and Perugino (1472–1523). They are usually accompanied by a scroll with a name followed by '*bella*', or a saying or quotation.

This dish is a very beautiful example. Its central design and border have a strong sense of movement and fill the surface perfectly without any sense of overcrowding. The same demure girl occurs on many other dishes, but usually facing to the left. The scroll is inscribed with a line from Petrarch's Sonnet XXIII, 31, '*LA VITA.EL.FINE. ELDI.LO DA. LASE RA.X.*', 'Life by its end, day by the evening, is praised' or, more idiomatically, 'The end crowns the life, the evening the day'. The 'X' seems to be a space filler or an indication that the verse continues.

Further reading Spoleto, *Maioliche umbre decorate a lustro, il rinascimento e la ripresa ottocentesca: Deruta, Gualdo Tadino, Gubbio*, exhibition catalogue ed. Grazietta Guaitini, Florence, 1982. Alan Caiger-Smith, *Lustre Pottery*, London, 1985. Fiocco and Gherardi, 1988–9, I, pp. 82–100.

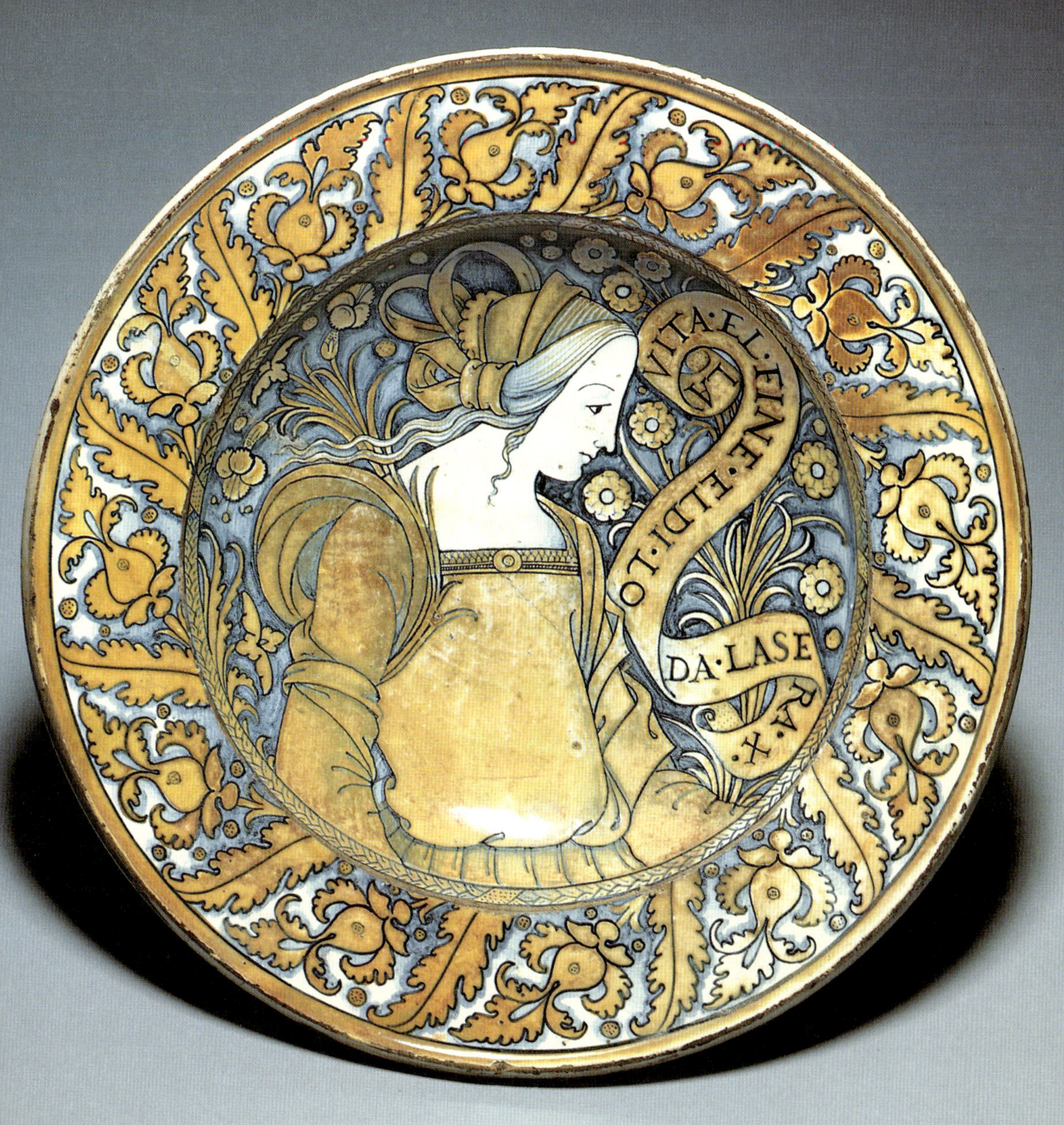
LA
VITA·EL·FINE·EL·DI·LO
DA·LASE
RA·X

14

DISH

MONTELUPO, c. 1500–25

Height 6.9 cm; diameter 34.7 cm.
H. S. Reitlinger Bequest, 1950. C.183–1991.

Montelupo is situated about 25 km from Florence at the confluence of the Pesa and Arno. During the fourteenth and fifteenth centuries it became an important maiolica manufacturing town, aided by ample local supplies of clay and timber, and easy transport by river to Florence or the port of Pisa. During the late fifteenth and early sixteenth centuries, trade with Florence boomed as the number of potteries there declined and Montelupo became its major supplier. In 1490 twenty-three potters signed a three-year contract to supply pottery to a Florentine merchant, Francesco Antinori. Possibly this fostered the existing custom of marking with initials which is very prevalent on pharmacy jars and jugs made in Montelupo.

Large decorative dishes with a flat base, curved sides, and slightly everted rim were made from around 1500 until the eighteenth century. Early examples usually have a central roundel surrounded by one of several border patterns. The ovals and lozenges on this example allow it to be dated to the early sixteenth century because a similar border occurs on a dish decorated with the arms of Pope Julius II and the date 1509. The border also occurs on fragmentary dishes excavated between 1973 and 1976 from a well in Montelupo which had been filled with potters' waste. Among the other finds was a dish dated 1514 and one with the arms of a Medici Pope, probably Leo X (ruled 1513–21).

Dishes of this kind appear to have been painted rather rapidly, with great verve but not much attention to detail. They are usually decorated in a bright palette, sometimes including touches of red, which in Tuscany is found mainly on pottery from Montelupo and Cafaggiolo. This combination of style and colouring produced bold vivacious designs which retain their effectiveness when viewed from a distance.

Further reading Guido Vannini, ed., *La maiolica di Montelupo. Scavo di uno scarico di fornace*, Montelupo, 1977. Fausto Berti, *La maiolica di Montelupo secoli* XIV–XVIII, Milan, 1986.

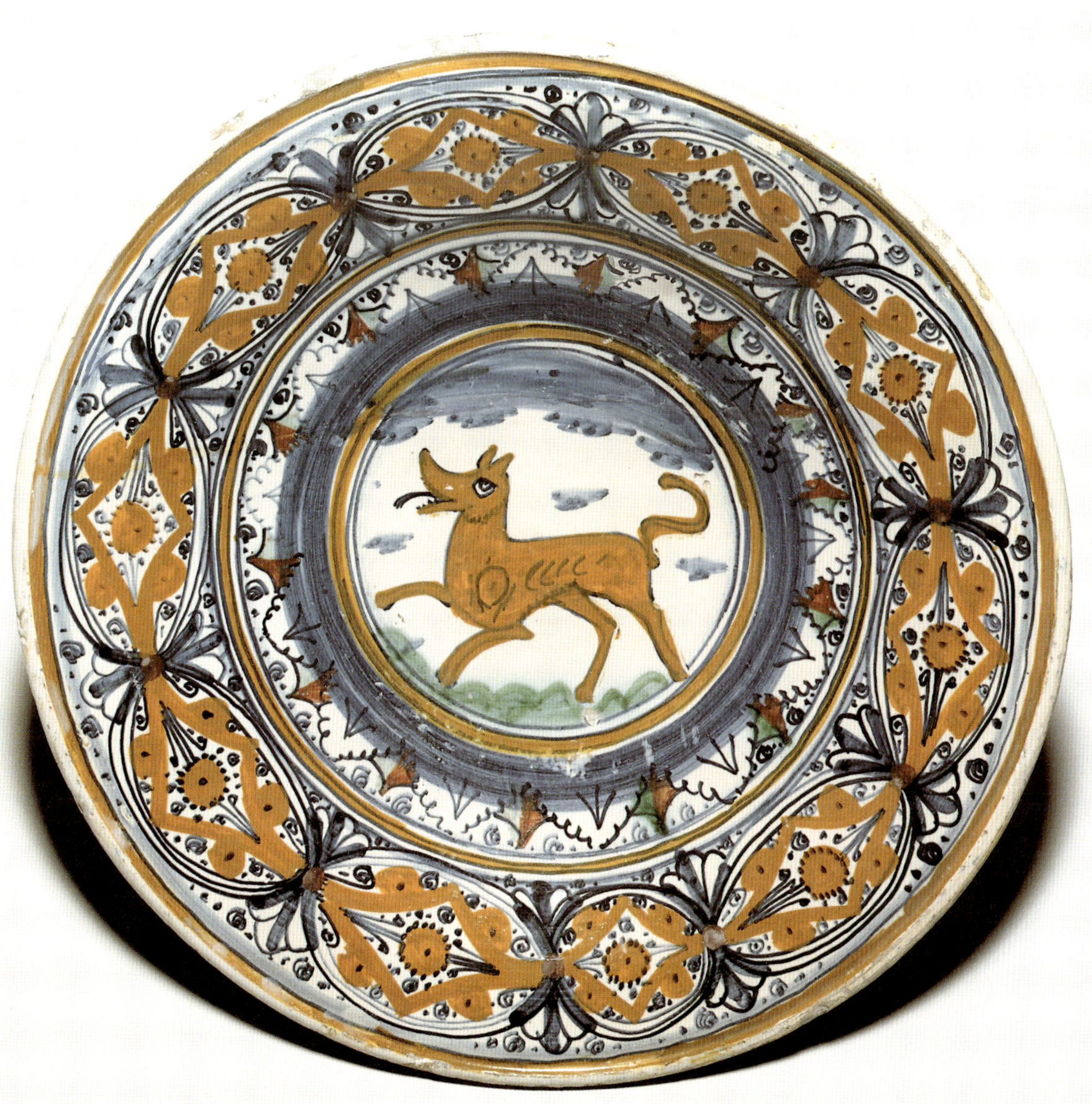

15

JUG

CAFAGGIOLO, *c.* 1500–20

Marked below the handle with SP in monogram with a stroke through the tail of the P. Height 18.3 cm; width 11 cm. Purchased with the Glaisher Fund. C.43–1931.

The mark on this jug probably stands for Stefano and Piero, sons of Filippo di Dimitri Schiavone of Montelupo. In 1490 they were among twenty-three potters there who signed a contract to supply pots to Francesco Antinori in Florence, and may have spent some time there before 1498 when they founded a pottery in buildings belonging to the castle at Cafaggiolo. This was owned by Lorenzo di Pierfrancesco de' Medici, known as Popolano, but the workshop seems to have been an independent concern. The mark occurs on several pieces bearing the place name, Cafaggiolo, and therefore demonstrates that lustreware was made there, as well as at Deruta and Gubbio. Unlike those centres, however, Cafaggiolo, does not appear to have made large quantities of lustreware nor to have made it over a long period, as far as we can tell without dated examples. The SP mark remained in use after Piero was succeeded by his son Filippo in 1507 and after the death of Stefano in 1532, when his seven sons continued the business and were probably responsible for setting up a pottery at Gagliano. Very little is known about Cafaggiolo maiolica after the middle of the century. Output probably declined gradually and eventually ceased in the 1570s or 1580s. Jacopo, one of Stefano di Filippo's sons, was still alive in 1576 and his son, Lorenzo, in 1583.

This jug was probably intended to be a cruet for use at table. The 'A' inside the top of the neck could stand for *acqua* (water) or *aceto* (vinegar), probably the latter, because a jug in the British Museum is inscribed with an 'O' for *olio*.

Further reading Cora and Fanfani, 1982. Alessandro Alinari, *Maioliche marcate di Cafaggiolo*, Museo Nazionale del Bargello, Florence, 1987.

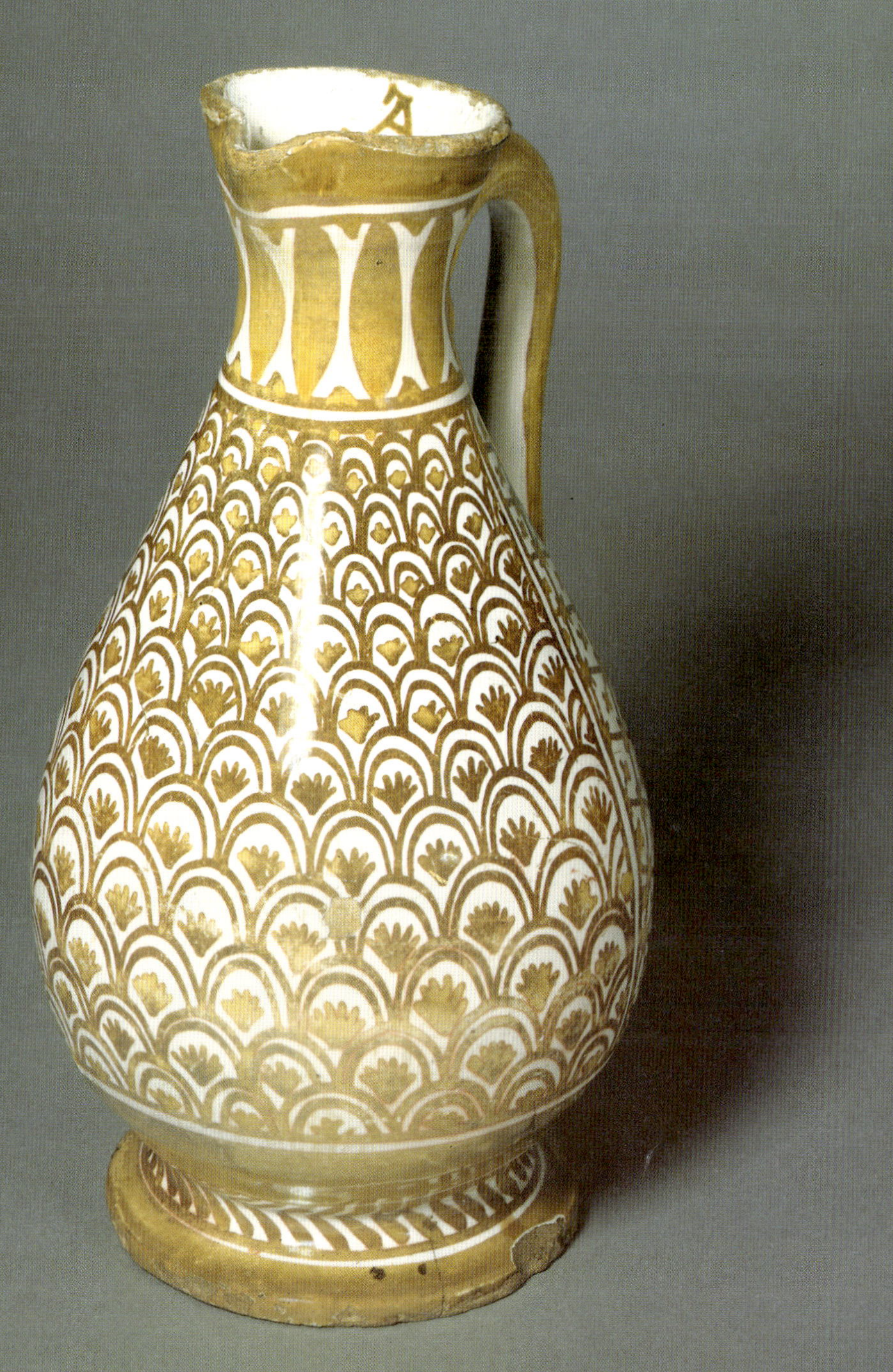
A

16

BROAD-RIMMED BOWL

CAFAGGIOLO, PROBABLY BY JACOPO, *c.* 1510–25

The back is inscribed in blue, 'J°: chafagguolo', and on the rim and sides there are four foliated spirals. Height 4.7 cm; diameter 24.2 cm. Purchased with the Leverton Harris Fund. C.4–1960.

Chinese porcelain was imported into Florence and other cities in Tuscany in small quantities during the fifteenth and early sixteenth centuries. The high esteem with which it was regarded can be gauged by its appearance in religious paintings, where its presence is an indication of the holy or favoured status of the characters portrayed. On his death in 1492, Lorenzo de' Medici owned fifty-one pieces, which was an exceptional collection. Porcelain was expensive and demand outstripped supply, so most people who could afford to indulge their taste had to be content with a few pieces, or with tin-glazed earthenware jugs and dishes decorated in blue *alla porcellana* by potters in Montelupo, Cafaggiolo, and elsewhere.

This is one of nine recorded broad-rimmed bowls (*tondini*) inscribed 'J° *chafagguolo*' on the back. Each has a different central motif, but with one exception all have borders of lozenges and foliated arabesques, and, on the back, three or four foliated stems surrounding the inscription. The blue on white decoration reflects the influence of Chinese porcelain, but the design itself is not Chinese. The first two letters of the inscription are probably an abbreviation for Jacopo as they resemble those in 'Jap° in chaffagguolo', on a dish decorated with an equestrian *Judith with the Head of Holofernes*, in the Victoria and Albert Museum. The painter was probably the Jacopo who was one of Stefano di Filippo's sons.

Further reading Marco Spallanzani, *Ceramiche orientali a Firenze nel Rinascimento*, Florence, 1978. Cora and Fanfani, 1982. Alessandro Alinari, *Maioliche marcate di Cafaggiolo*, Museo Nazionale del Bargello, Florence, 1987, pp. 27–32, nos. 1 and 2. Hess, 1988, pp. 66–8, no. 21.

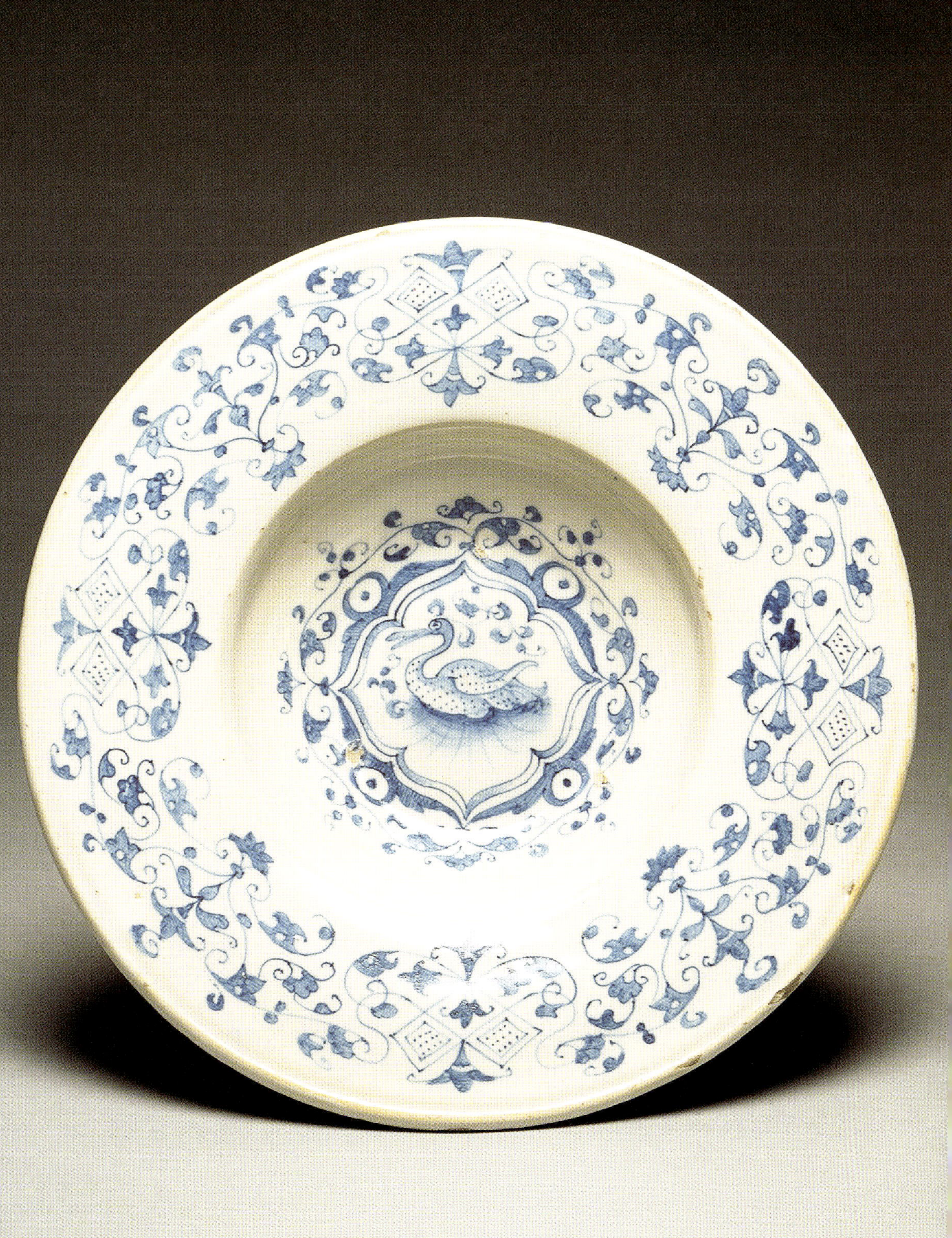

17

DISH: CAESAR'S HORSE

CAFAGGIOLO, PROBABLY BY
JACOPO, DATED 1514

On the reverse, below the date, is the alchemical symbol for tin.
Height 5.2 cm; diameter 40.4 cm. F. Leverton Harris Bequest, 1926. C.86–1927.

To judge by surviving pieces, maiolica made in the early years of the Cafaggiolo workshop was aimed mainly at the upper end of the market. A high proportion of it is decorated with the coats of arms of Tuscan families, or with classical subjects or motifs, which would have appealed to educated patrons.

The Roman military Triumph was one of the classical themes which captured the imagination of Renaissance rulers, not surprisingly, as they were frequently at war. The most celebrated portrayal of the military Triumph in art was the nine canvases painted by Andrea Mantegna for the ducal palace at Urbino between 1486 and about 1492, which are now at Hampton Court. These inspired many other Triumphs, including one by Benedetto Bordon, reproduced in a series of large woodcuts by Jacob Argentoratensis, published in Venice in 1504. One of the woodcuts showing Caesar's horse was the source for this dish. Each scene was labelled with an alphabet letter, hence the 'H' below the hound. The next in the sequence, labelled 'I', is reproduced on a dish in the Victoria and Albert Museum. Both dishes are dated 1514 (the latter in Roman numerals), and both were in the same collection in the 1850s, which suggests that they originally formed part of a set showing the whole *Triumph*.

The painter, probably Jacopo, one of Stefano di Filippo's sons, omitted a boy behind the horse, but otherwise followed the print closely, including the horse's curious feet which followed the Roman writer, Suetonius' description of Caesar's horse as having hooves which 'were cloven in such a way as to look like toes'.

Further reading Cora and Fanfani, 1982, see no. 10. Ronald Lightbown, *Mantegna*, 1986, pp. 140–53. Jean Michel Massing '*The Triumph of Caesar* by Benedetto Bordon and Jacobus Argentoratensis. Its iconography and influence', *Print Quarterly*, 7:1 (March 1990), 2–21.

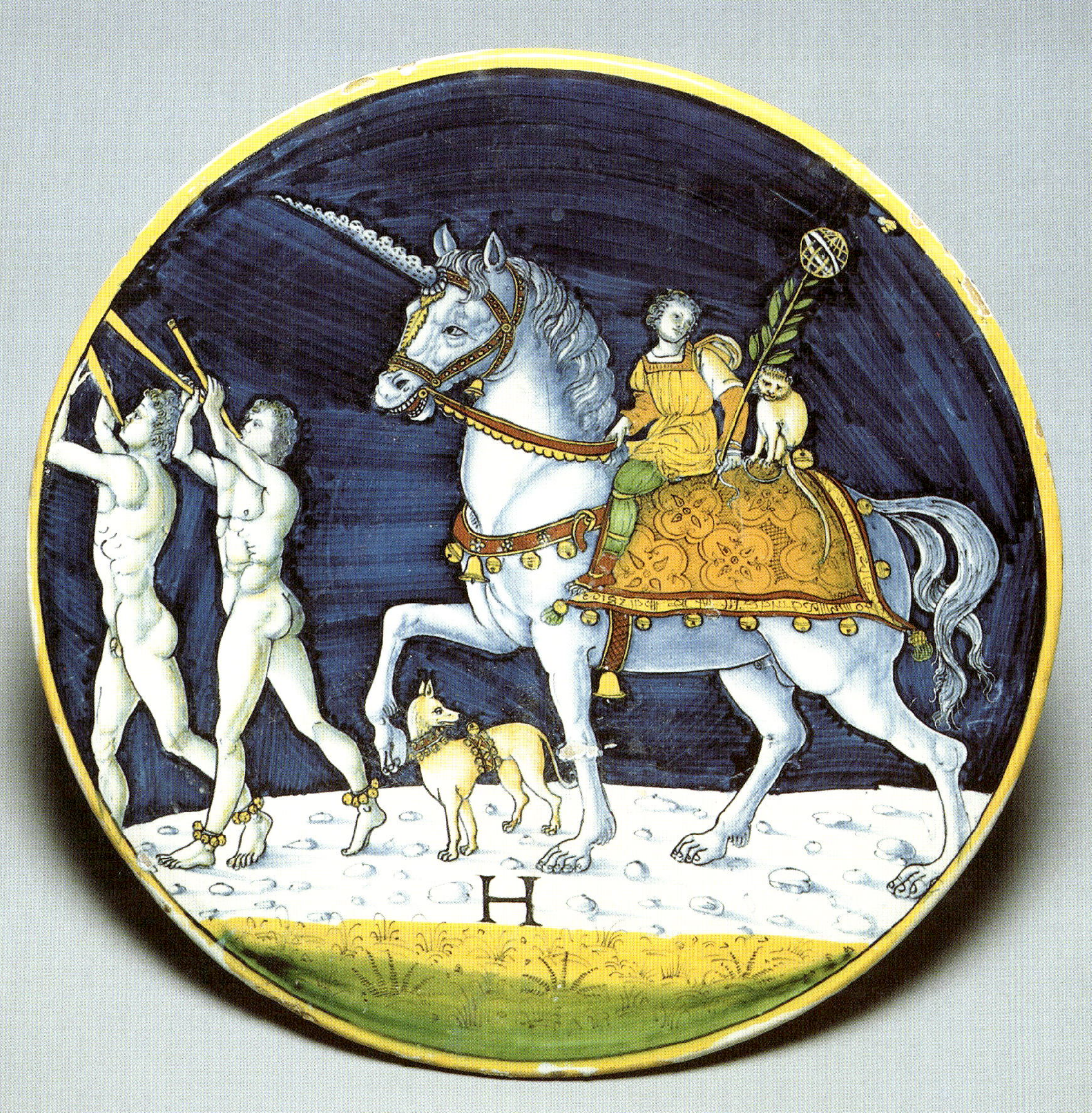
H

18

PLATE

PROBABLY MADE IN THE MARCHES,

c. 1510–30

On the back in blue, a circle round the rim enclosing three groups of stylized foliage separated by cusped lines. Height 1.9 cm; diameter 22.6 cm. Purchased with the Glaisher Fund. EC.19–1939.

In the early sixteenth century classical influence on maiolica decoration became more pronounced. This development was linked to the increasing availability of printed designs inspired by Roman sculpture and architectural decoration, including book illustrations, and ornamental engravings by artists such as Nicoletto da Modena, Giovanni Antonio da Brescia, and, later, Agostino Veneziano and Enea Vico. On maiolica the repertoire of classical motifs included *putti*, military trophies, Roman busts, and grotesques (see nos. 19 and 20), usually reserved in blue, orange, or lustred grounds. On dishes and plates this decoration may cover the whole surface, or be arranged symmetrically as a border surrounding the well. The seemingly endless permutations of these classical motifs make this one of the most fascinating and beautiful classes of maiolica.

A splendid bowl whose decoration includes *putti* and trophies was signed (but not necessarily painted) by the potter, Giovanni Maria, and is inscribed as made in Castel Durante in 1508. Consequently dishes of this kind have been associated with his workshop in Castel Durante, or in Urbino, assuming that he was the same Giovanni Maria who was recorded there in 1520, 1530, and 1538. He also spent time in Venice in 1523. However, disparities between the style and quality of dishes of this type, indicate that they were painted by several artists, probably in more than one workshop. Neither the front nor the back of the Fitzwilliam's plate closely resembles the decoration of the bowl of 1508, and, although it might have been made in Giovanni Maria's workshop, it could equally well have originated in another workshop in the Urbino district, or elsewhere in the Marches, such as Fabriano.

Further reading Bernard Rackham, 'Die Majolikamaler Giovanni Maria von Castel Durante I', *Pantheon*, 2 (1928) pp. 435–45; Part II, *Pantheon*, 3 (1929), pp. 288–92. Rasmussen, 1989, pp. 100–4, no. 62. Wilson, 1993, pp. 130–3.

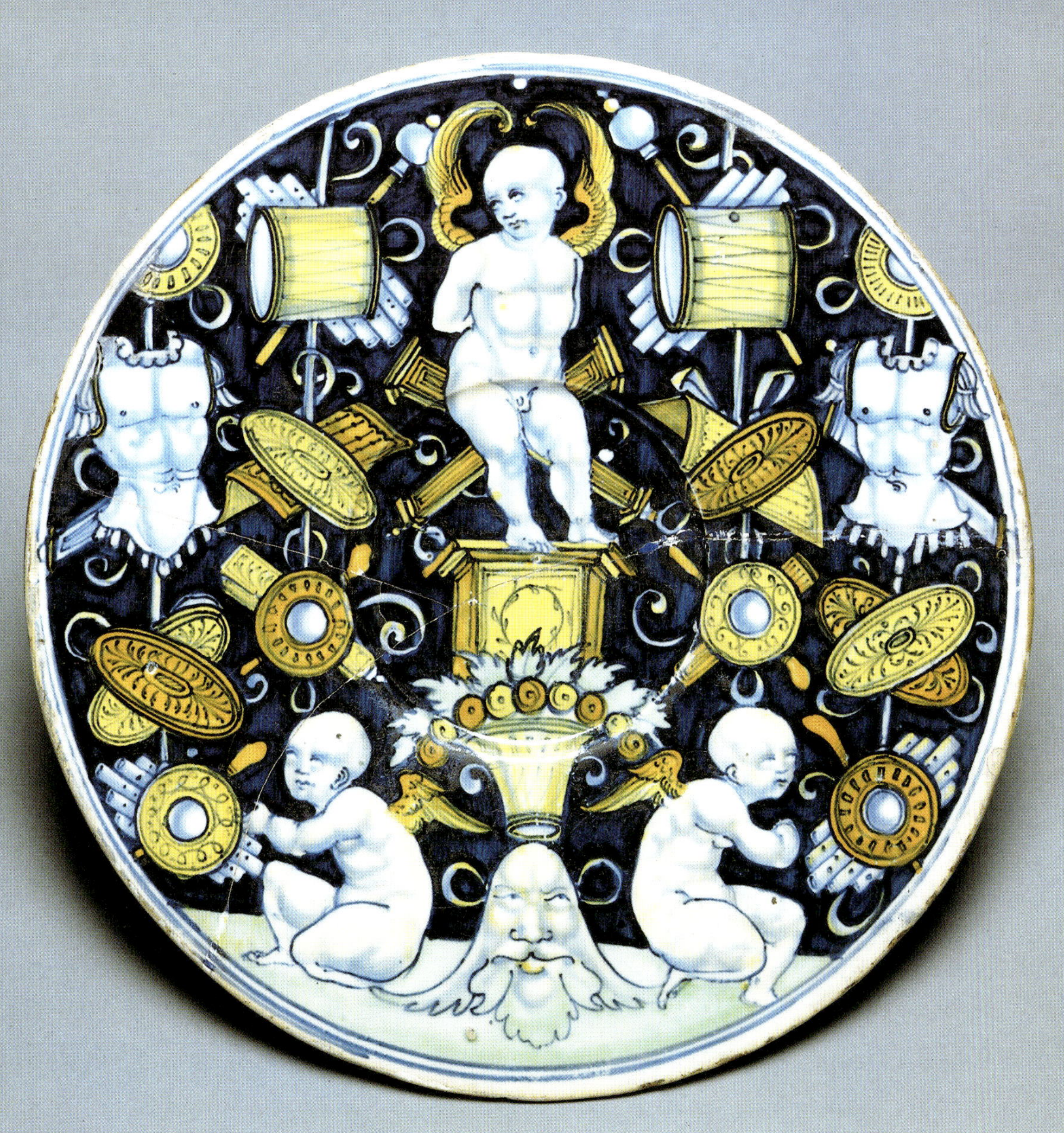

19

DISH WITH BROAD RIM

FAENZA, ATTRIBUTED TO THE 'ASSUMPTION PAINTER', DATED 1520

On the back is a crossed circle with a small circle in one quarter and arrows in the others, surrounded by two rows of transversely striped petals. Height 4 cm; diameter 28.6 cm. Purchased with the Leverton Harris Fund. EC.36–1942.

The discovery about 1480 of the painted rooms of Nero's Golden House in Rome is regarded as the catalyst which initiated the fashion for grotesque decoration in the early sixteenth century. According to Benventuo Cellini in his *Autobiography*, the term *grottesche* was derived from *grotte*, the word used to describe these by then subterranean chambers. The earliest grotesques on maiolica, dating from the first decade of the sixteenth century (one dish is dated 1507), did not resemble Roman decoration closely because they had coloured grounds, usually blue or orange, but occasionally yellow or black (for white ground grotesques see nos. 44–6). They occur on tiles, and domestic and pharmaceutical wares from most of the major centres.

The border of this dish illustrates Faenza polychrome grotesque decoration reserved in a dark blue ground. Another Faenza variety was painted in white and blue on a pale blue (*a berettino*) glaze. Dated maiolica of both types ranges from 1519 to 1538. The sides of the well are decorated in *bianco sopra bianco* technique, barely visible in a reproduction. The young man in the central medallion resembles St Sebastian, but is more likely to be a lover serving as a target for Cupid's arrows. The sensation of being bound and tortured by love, as inescapably as a prisoner at an executioner's stake, was a common theme in Renaissance art and occurs frequently on maiolica. The painter was named after a panel decorated with the *Assumption of the Virgin* in the Victoria and Albert Museum. The sign on the back occurs on numerous Faenza dishes up to about 1540, and is usually surrounded by striped petals or stylized flowerheads and foliage separated by squiggles. It probably represents an inflatable ball used in the game *pallone*, but its significance is not yet known.

Further reading Nicole Dacos, *La decouverte de la Domus Aurea et la formation des grotesques à la Renaissance*, London and Leiden, 1969. Rackham, 1940, I, pp. 84–6, nos. 267–9, II, pl. 43. Norman, 1976, pp. 103–8, C 44. Hess, 1988, pp. 88–90, no. 27. Wilson, 1989, pp. 54–5, no. 23.

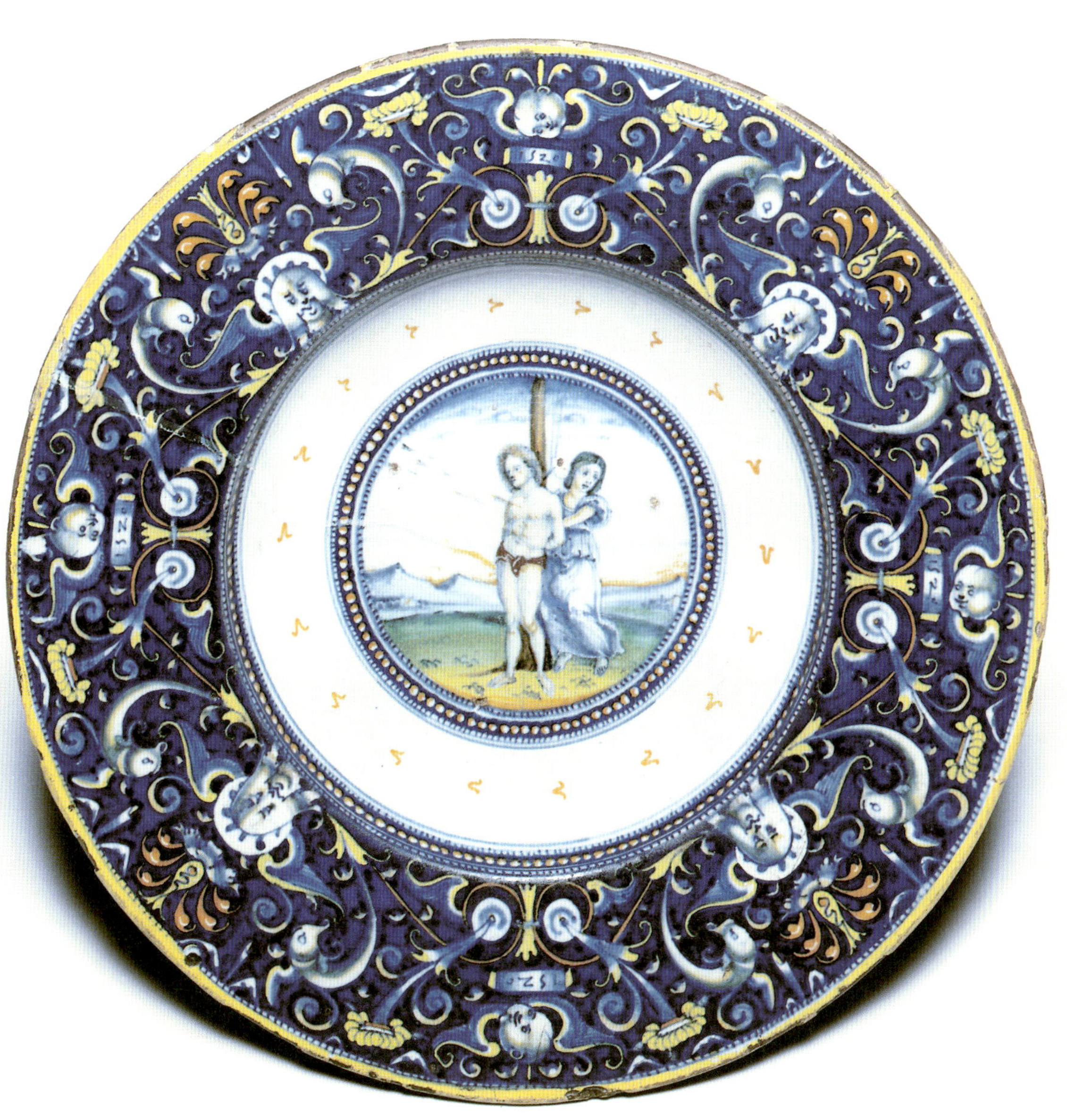

20

TWO-HANDLED PHARMACY JAR

PROBABLY MADE IN TUSCANY, c. 1510–30

Height 37 cm; width 30.1 cm.
H. S. Reitlinger Bequest, 1950. C.185–1991.

This pharmacy jar illustrates another type of grotesque decoration with larger, more three-dimensional motifs than those on no. 19. Eight more jars of similar form are known, including one labelled 'GENTZIANA' (Gentian) in the Victoria and Albert Museum, and one labelled 'COMINO PESTO', (crushed Cumin) in the British Museum. The first word on the Fitzwilliam's jar may be an abbreviation for SALI (salts) or SALVIA (sage) The 'P' at the end of the label probably stands for PRAEPARATIO (preparation). The similarities in the size, decoration, and lettering of all eight suggests that they were made in the same workshop and probably belonged to the same set. One of two jars in the Museo Civico at Massa Marittima bears the coat of arms *gules* (shown orange) *a lion rampant argent holding an axe*, and its identification may provide a clue to their original home.

The form and colouring of the jars suggests that they came from Tuscany, and Montelupo and Siena have both been proposed as their place of manufacture. The figure and landscape in the panel on the Fitzwilliam's jar seems to support an attribution to Siena, because they are similar in style to a series of late fifteenth-century panels representing famous men and women attributed to the Master of Griselda with Neroccio de' Landi (1447–1500) or Signorelli (active 1470–1523). The pavilion and trees in particular are reminiscent of those in the background of *Alexander the Great* in the Barber Institute, Birmingham. The grotesques seem close in form to those on two albarelli in the Museo di Capodimonte, and a pharmacy ewer in the MICF, which are presently attributed to Siena. However, neutron activation analysis of samples from the body of this jar and the example in the British Museum did not match the results from maiolica securely attributed to Siena or Montelupo.

Further reading Wilson, 1987, pp. 76–7, no. 109. Mario Bellini and Giovanni Conti, *Maioliche italiane del Rinascimento*, Milan, 1964, pl. 78 C. Ravanelli Guidotti, 1990, p. 133, no. 72.

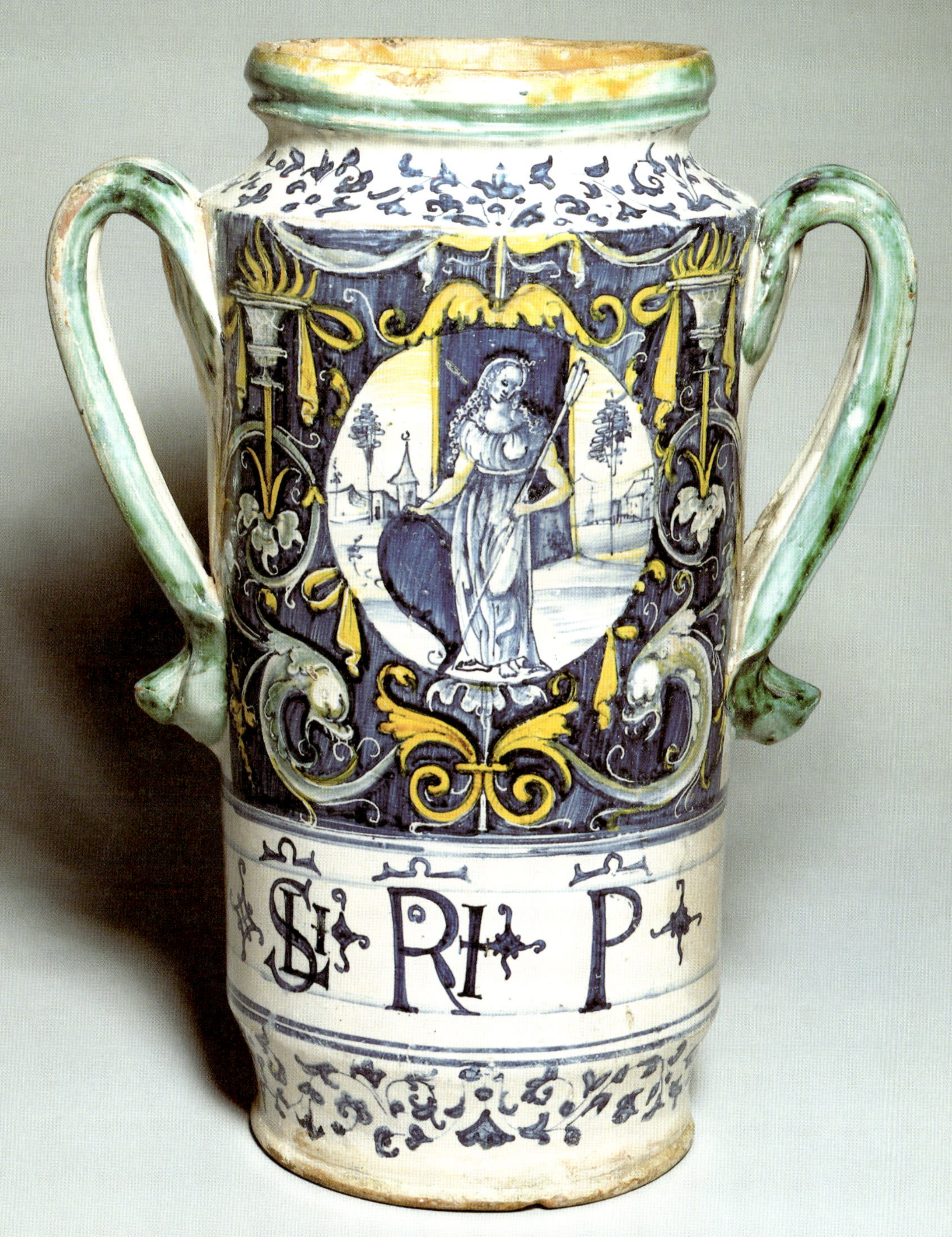

21

BASIN FOR A EWER

PROBABLY CAFAGGIOLO, ATTRIBUTED TO THE 'VULCAN PAINTER', C. 1520–30

Height 5.5 cm; diameter 46.3 cm. Purchased with the Leverton Harris Fund and with a contribution from the National Art Collections Fund. EC.19–1946.

This basin is one of the most brilliant and enigmatic pieces in the Fitzwilliam's collection and has fascinated maiolica scholars since it was exhibited by Baron Lionel de Rothschild at the *Special Exhibition of Works of Art* at South Kensington in 1862. Before its acquisition by the Fitzwilliam, it was attributed to Faenza or Siena, but since then it has usually been assigned to Cafaggiolo, although it does not bear the SP monogram mark which occurs on many dishes and jugs from the pottery. The painter was named after a dish in the Victoria and Albert Museum, decorated with Vulcan at his Forge, surrounded by a border of trophies and putti with the same intense blue background, pale green, and touches of red which appear on the Fitzwilliam's basin.

The meaning of the central medallion remains obscure because the arms, *per fess gules and argent, overall a tree eradicated* have not been identified securely. They are close to the arms of the Dini family of Florence, but lack the word LIBERTAS in chief (at the top). The animals could represent individuals or families engaged in a feud over territory, for the inscription 'E COSI VA CHE TROPO VOLLE' means 'This is what happens to him who wants too much.' The battle between satyrs, satyresses, and centaurs may represent the battle between the lapiths and centaurs after the wedding of Hippodamia. The rim is decorated with grotesques surrounding oval 'cameos' of heroes and heroines from the Bible and from Roman history: Marcus Curtius, Dido, David, Judith, Mucius Scaevola, Lucretia, Horatius, and an unidentified woman. These are another instance of classical influence associated with the collecting of small antiquities such as cameos, intaglios, and coins.

Further reading Rackham, 1940, I, pp. 109–11. Roberto Weiss, *The Renaissance Discovery of Classical Antiquity*, Oxford, 1969, pp. 180–202. Alessandro Alinari, 'The Vulcan painter and the Fall of Phaethon', in Wilson, ed., 1991, pp. 80–5.

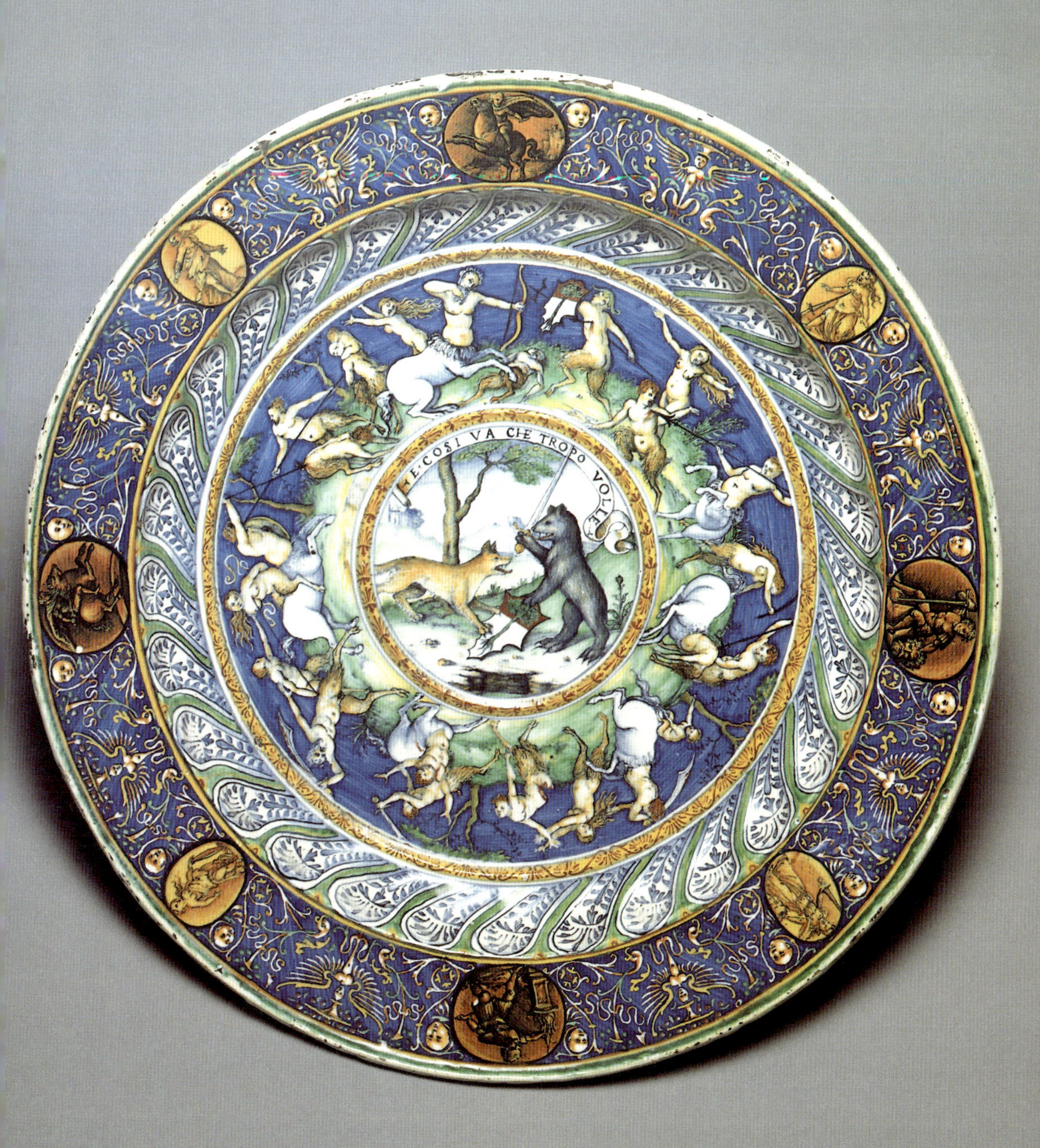
E·COSI VA CHE TROPO VOLLE

22

DISH: DOGE AGOSTINO BARBARIGO SUPERVISING THE LOADING OF MONEY FOR THE RELIEF OF NAPLES ON TO A SHIP

PROBABLY MADE IN FAENZA OR IN VENICE, *c.* 1500–20

On the reverse, a blue spiral, blue and orange circles and a yellow zig-zag border filled with transverse blue lines. Height 4 cm; diameter 28 cm. F. Leverton Harris Bequest, 1926. C.62–1927

This is a rare portrayal on maiolica of a recent historical event. The French had invaded Naples in February 1495 and the ousted Aragonese king, Ferdinand II, appealed to Venice for help. By the end of March, an anti-French treaty known as The Holy League had been concluded. The League was made public on Palm Sunday, 1495, and afterwards money was collected and despatched by sea to Ferdinand II. The sacks on the ship are labelled with their contents: Papal, Hungarian, Ancona, and Venetian ducats. The two carried by the sailor on the left are labelled '*March*', probably small silver *marchesane* or *marcelli*, and '*Troni*', silver *lire* introduced by Doge Niccolò Tron (1471–4). The notice on the ship's rigging, '*fate fate fatte / et non parole*' (action, action, action and not words), indicates that Venice was sending practical assistance and not just vain promises.

The attribution of the dish has caused much speculation. The subject is so specifically Venetian that it is only natural to consider that it was painted there soon after the event. However, no firm evidence for the manufacture of maiolica in Venice in 1495 has been published, and *istoriato* dishes from any centre before 1500 are uncommon. In view of the dish's shape, certain aspects of the figures, and the decoration of the reverse, it is more likely to have been made in Faenza between about 1500 and 1520. If made elsewhere, it was probably decorated by a painter trained in Faenza. The reason for its existence remains a mystery, as does its ownership before 1922.

Further reading Gaetano Ballardini, 'L'insigne "Piatto Leverton" con un episodio della spedizione di Carlo VIII in Italia', *Faenza*, 10:3–4 (1922), pp. 132–43. F. Leverton Harris, 'An Italian maiolica plate', *Burlington Magazine*, 40 (June 1922), pp. 278–83.

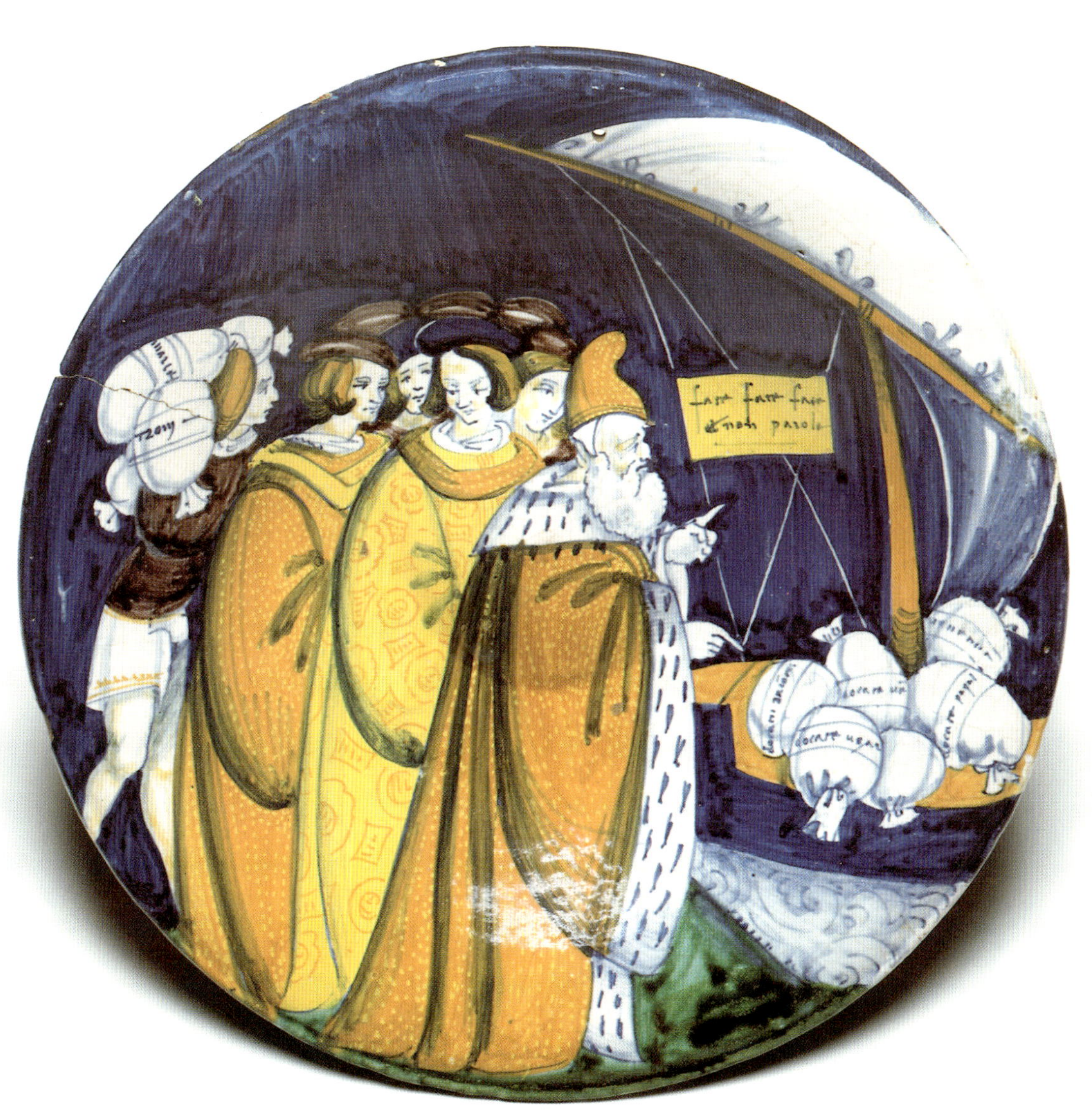
fatti fatti fatti
et non parole

23

PLATE: MERCURY, HERSE AND AGLAUROS

WORKSHOP OF MAESTRO GIORGIO, GUBBIO, DATED 1522

The back is marked in the middle in thick dark yellow lustre, '1522/ .M°.° G'. Height 2.7 cm; diameter 26 cm. L. C. G. Clarke Bequest, 1960. C.79–1961.

This *istoriato* plate is decorated with the story of Mercury and Aglauros, told by Ovid in *Metamorphoses*, Book II. Mercury had fallen in love with Herse the beautiful daughter of King Cecrops of Athens. Determined to see her, he went to the palace, but her sister Aglauros refused to admit him and demanded much gold, for her compliance. Mercury returned with the gold but Aglauros was so consumed by envy of Herse, that she refused to budge from outside her door. So Mercury waved his caduceus to open the door and turned Aglauros into stone, so that she could never move again.

The figures of Mercury and Aglauros were based on a woodcut illustration in *Ovidio metamorphoseos vulgare*, published in Venice in 1497, and repeated in several editions before 1522. The coat of arms, which occurs on two more plates now in St Petersburg and New York, has not been identified.

The mark on these plates indicates that they were lustred in the workshop of Maestro Giorgio. They were almost certainly made there too, because they appear to be by the painter of a dish decorated with the *Judgement of Paris*, which is marked '*M° giorgio/1520 a dj2 de otobre/B.D.S.R ingubio*' in blue, and must therefore have had its second firing in the workshop. Giorgio was the leading Gubbio potter in the 1520s and was renowned for his lustreware. He was probably living in Gubbio by 1492. He was granted citizenship in 1498 and had his own workshop from 1499 to 1546, when it passed to his two sons, Ubaldo and Vincenzo. He died in 1555.

Further reading Ballardini, 1933–8, I, fig. 114, no. 119. Alfred N. Kube, *Leningrad State Hermitage Collection, Italian Maiolica XV-XVIII Centuries*, ed. O. E. Mikhailova and E. A. Lapkovskava, Moscow, 1976, no. 90. Catherine Join-Dieterle, *Musée du Petit Palais, Catalogue de Céramiques I*, Paris, 1984, pp. 172–3, no. 54. Fiocco and Gherardi, 1995, pp. 25–43. Wilson, 1993, pp. 163–6.

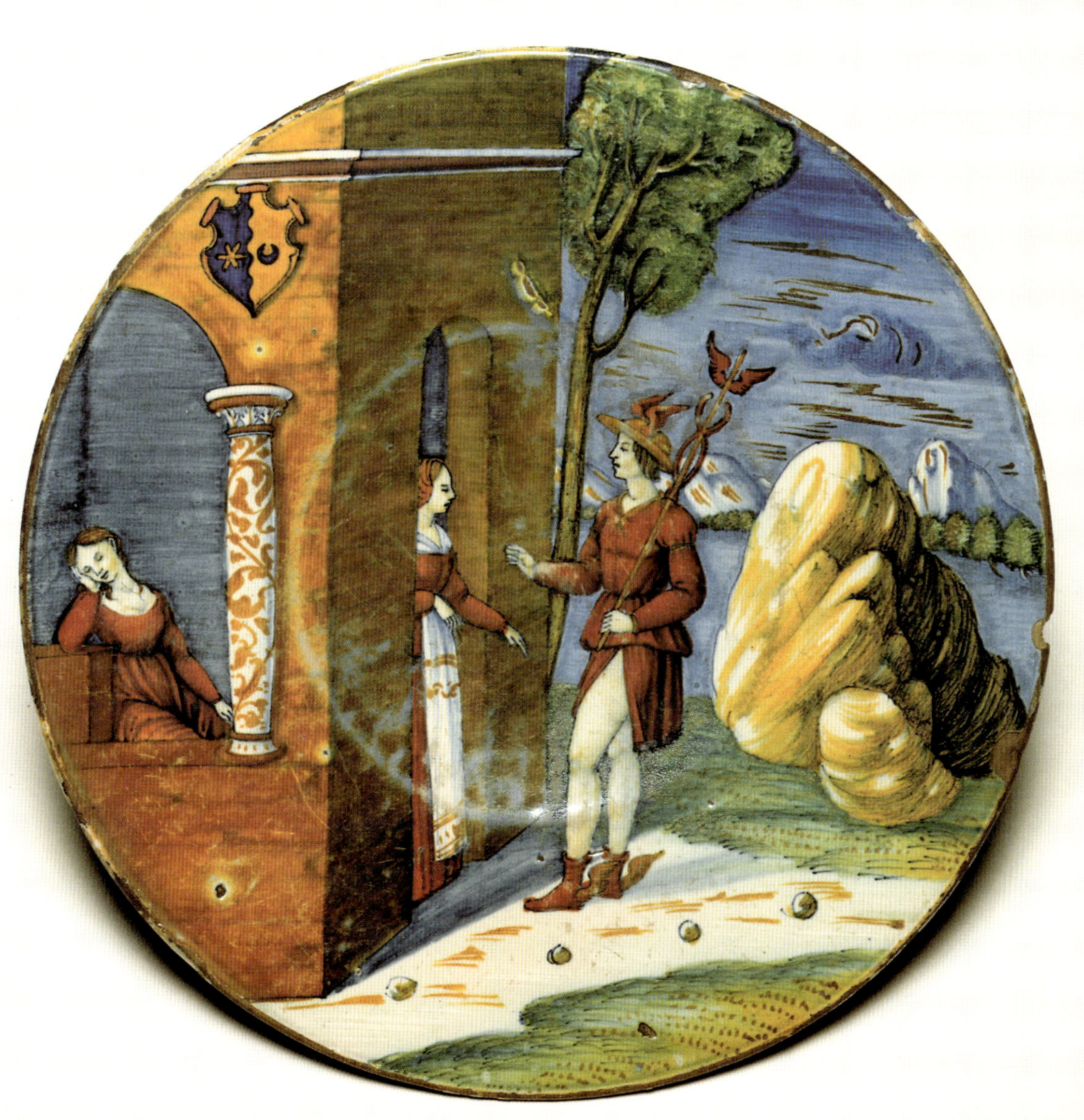

24

DISH FROM THE ISABELLA D'ESTE SERVICE: PELEUS AND THETIS

PAINTED BY NICOLA DI GABRIELE SBRAGHE, URBINO, C. 1524

Height 3.9 cm; diameter 30.2 cm. Purchased with the Glaisher Fund. EC.30–1938.

The potter, Nicola di Gabriele Sbraghe, known as Nicola da Urbino, was a workshop owner in Urbino from at least 1520 until his death at the end of 1537 or in January 1538. He was also a brilliant maiolica painter, whose work has been identified by comparison with five pieces of *istoriato* maiolica monogrammed or signed by him. Nicola painted in an exquisitely delicate manner, and was unusually imaginative in his adaptation of printed sources and in the creation of architectural and landscape backgrounds. His output of the 1520s, which includes several armorial services, is regarded as the acme of maiolica decoration.

This dish formed part of a service owned by Isabella d'Este (1474–1539), widow of Francesco Gonzaga, fourth Marchese of Mantua (1466–1519). It was probably given to her in the late autumn of 1524 by her daughter, Eleonora, Duchess of Urbino. Twenty-one dishes and one fragmentary dish are known, two decorated with biblical scenes and the rest with subjects from classical mythology or history. Each dish also bears the arms of Gonzaga impaling Este, and one or more of Isabella's *imprese* or her initials YS intertwined. On this dish the arms are surrounded by *bianco sopra bianco* decoration, and the rim is decorated with the story of Peleus and Thetis from Ovid's *Metamorphoses*, Book XI. Having found the sea goddess, Thetis, asleep on the shore, Peleus entreated her to make love, but she refused and escaped by transforming herself into different forms. After praying to the sea god Proteus for advice, Peleus successfully overcame the goddess' scruples and she conceived the ill-fated hero, Achilles. Nicola based the figures on a woodcut in *Ovidio metamorphoseos vulgare*, first published in Venice in 1497. Two *imprese* are shown: 'XXVII' sounding like *vinti sète*, (you are defeated), and gold bars in a crucible, which Isabella's husband adopted in 1495 to signify his integrity after successfully withstanding an accusation of treachery.

Further reading Victoria and Albert Museum, *Splendours of the Gonzaga*, London, 1981. Wilson, 1987, pp. 44–51, nos. 49–64. Carmen Ravanelli Guidotti, 'Un singolare ritrovamento: un piatto del servizio di Isabella d'Este-Gonzaga', in Wilson, 1991, pp. 13–23.

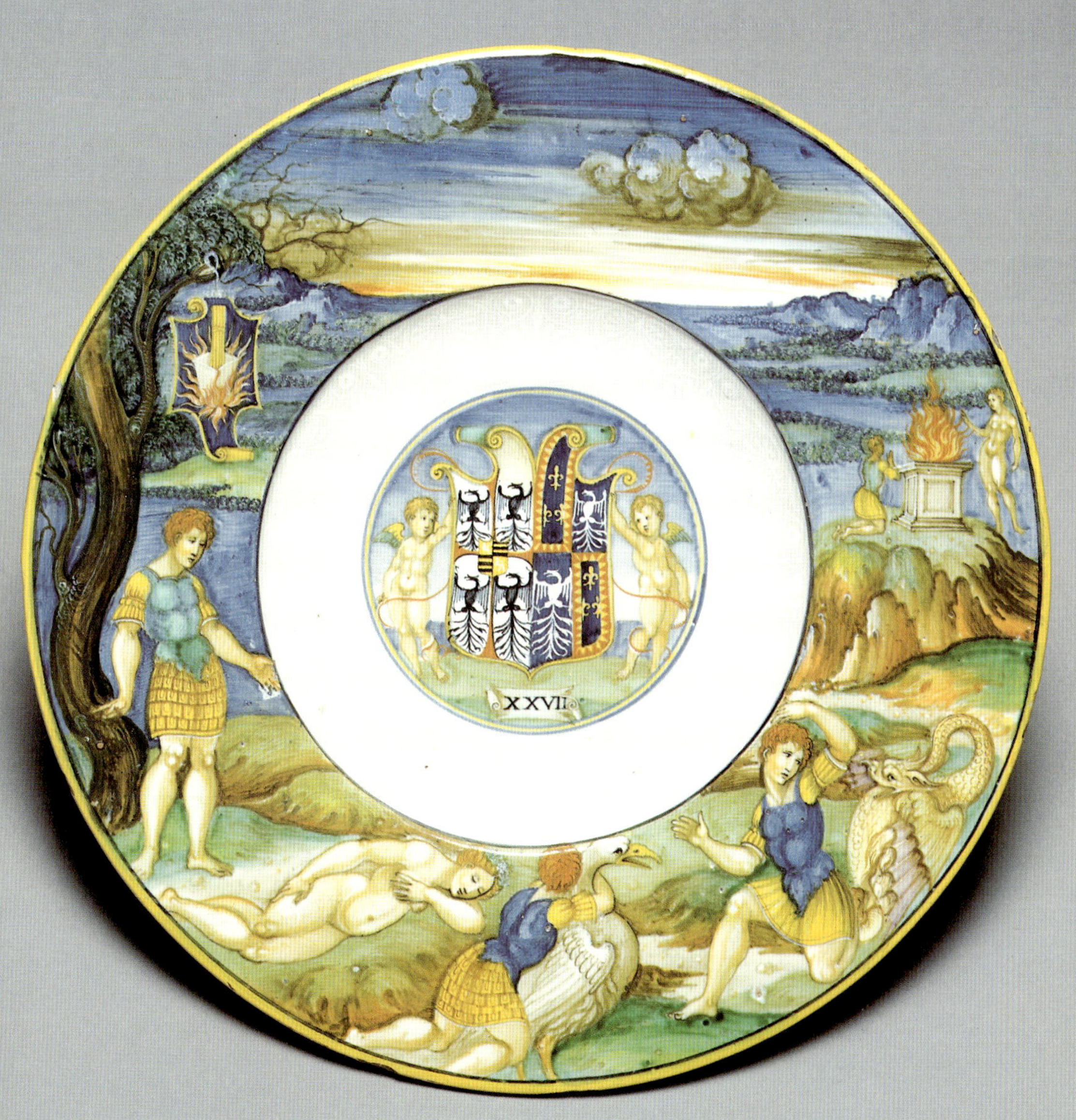
XXVII

25

TWO SHALLOW FOOTED BOWLS

URBINO OR CASTEL DURANTE, c.1520–30

Height 4.7 cm; diameter 22.7 cm.
C. B. Marlay Bequest. MAR.C.65–1912. C.63–1927

Between about 1520 and 1540 in the Urbino district and at Gubbio, the preferred form for *belle donne* dishes had shallow curved sides and a low foot, like those illustrated here. The image usually had a blue background, and the girl's name was written on a scrolling ribbon projecting on either side of her head, or on an arched scroll over it, usually followed by B or BELLA, or less frequently DIVA (divine), GRAZIOSA (charming), or UNICA (unique). This suggests that they were made for specific girls, but it is debatable whether real girls were known by the outlandish names which occur on some dishes. A few of the girls are so unusual in character that it is conceivable that they were true portraits, but the majority of these numerous dishes belong to several stock types which the painters adapted to suit their customers' requirements. The Fitzwilliam's LAVRA is an attractive but not outstanding example. Her complexion, fashionably straight nose and modest expression resemble those of Nicola di Gabriele's female figures of the mid 1520s, but its former attribution to him seems over-enthusiastic.

A rare sub-group of these *belle donne* is decorated with profile busts of girls wearing parade helmets. The earliest known, now at Pesaro, is named FAUSTINA and dated 1522. Others probably painted in the 1520s include the Fitzwilliam's MARTA, and DEIDAMIA and BRADAMANTE (a character in Ariosto's *Orlando Furioso*) respectively in the Kunstgewerbe Museum, Berlin, and the Musée National de Céramique, Sèvres.

The fashion for these dishes must have been influenced by contemporary interest in portraiture, and possibly also by lives of illustrious women, such as Foresti's *De claris mulieribus*, Ferrara, 1497. They are said to have been given by boys to their girlfriends, hence the term *coppe amatorie*, but firm evidence that this was true is lacking.

Further reading Hausmann, 1972, pp. 239–46, nos. 175–7. Giacomotti, 1974, pp. 243–9. Maria Mancini Della Chiara, *Maioliche del Museo Civico di Pesaro, Catalogo*, 1977, no. 105. Wilson, 1987, pp. 144–8. Rasmussen, 1989, pp. 104–6, no. 63 and pp. 244–5.

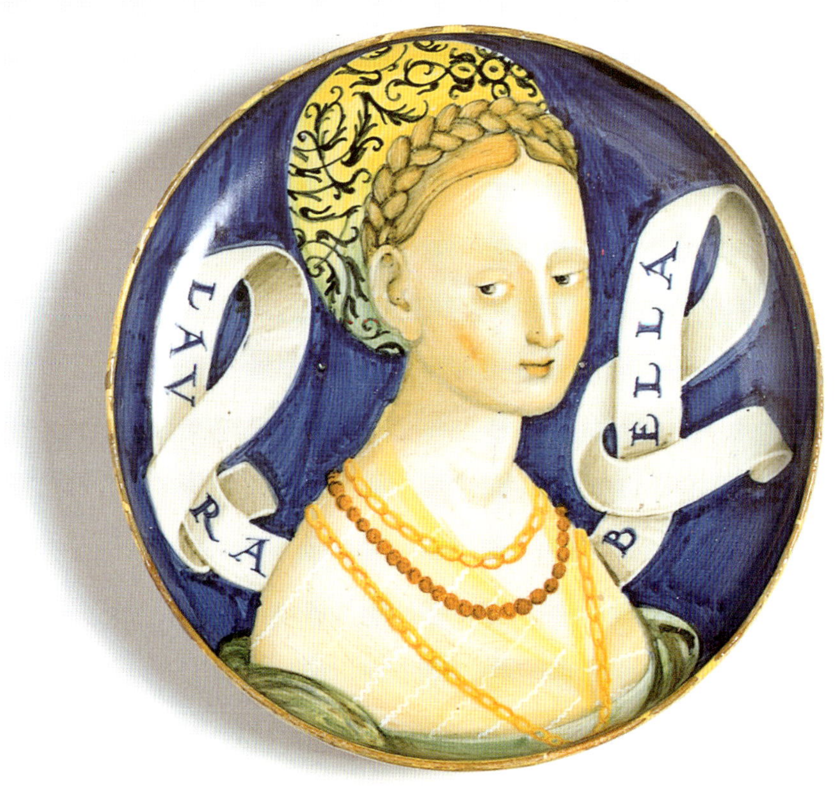
LAVRA
BELLA

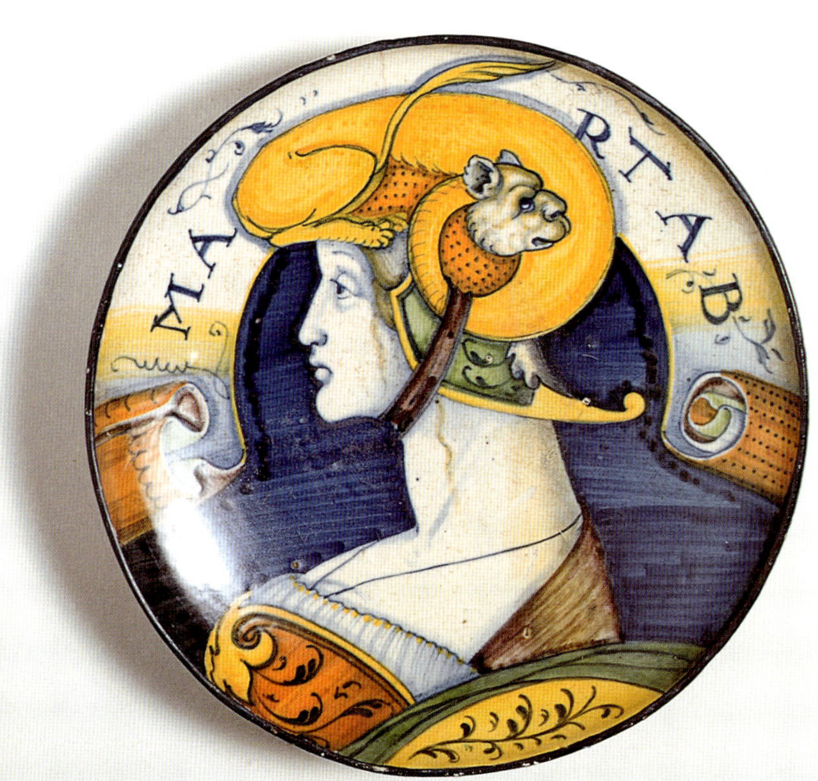
MA
RTAB

26

SHALLOW BOWL STANDING ON A LOW FOOT

GUBBIO, WORKSHOP OF MAESTRO
GIORGIO ANDREOLI, *c.* 1530–40

Height 5.8 cm; diameter 24.7 cm.
F. Leverton Harris Bequest, 1926. C.106–1927.

Shallow bowls like this one, often called *coppe*, were made in large numbers in Maestro Giorgio's workshop. They were formed by pressing clay over a mould so that the interior of the bowl was decorated in relief. The central medallion usually encloses one of a range of stock motifs: a figure or bust, a religious or secular symbol, or a coat of arms. The sides have radiating leaves, stylized buds, or rays. The designs are outlined in blue and filled in with dark gold and red lustre. On this example the central medallion encloses the *Agnus Dei* (Lamb of God) holding a banner with a cross, which symbolized victory over death, won by Christ's sacrifice on the Cross.

The earliest roughly datable bowl of this type, in the Victoria and Albert Museum, has a medallion with the arms of Pope Julius II (ruled 1503–13), and the latest, puzzlingly, has the same arms in relief but painted over with the arms of Paul III (ruled 1534–49). A few examples are dated between 1530 and 1532. A bowl with the Sacred Monogram, dated 1530 is in the British Museum; one with St Sebastian is in the Civic Museum in the Castello Visconteo at Pavia; and one with the *Agnus Dei*, dated 1532, formerly in the Liechtenstein collection, Vienna, was sold in New York in January, 1996.

The backs of these bowls are usually decorated with a few curved strokes or loose spirals, and some are signed with an 'N' in lustre. This initial also occurs on lustred *istoriati* and *belle donne* dishes up to 1540, and is presumably the mark of the lusterer. It has been associated, not very convincingly, with Vincenzo Andreoli, one of Maestro Giorgio's three sons.

Further reading Watson, 1986, pp. 98–9, no. 38; Wilson, 1987, p. 108, no. 172; Curnow, 1992, pp. 47–8, no. 42; Fiocco and Gherardi, 1995, pp. 40–1 and pp. 78–80, nos. 22–3.

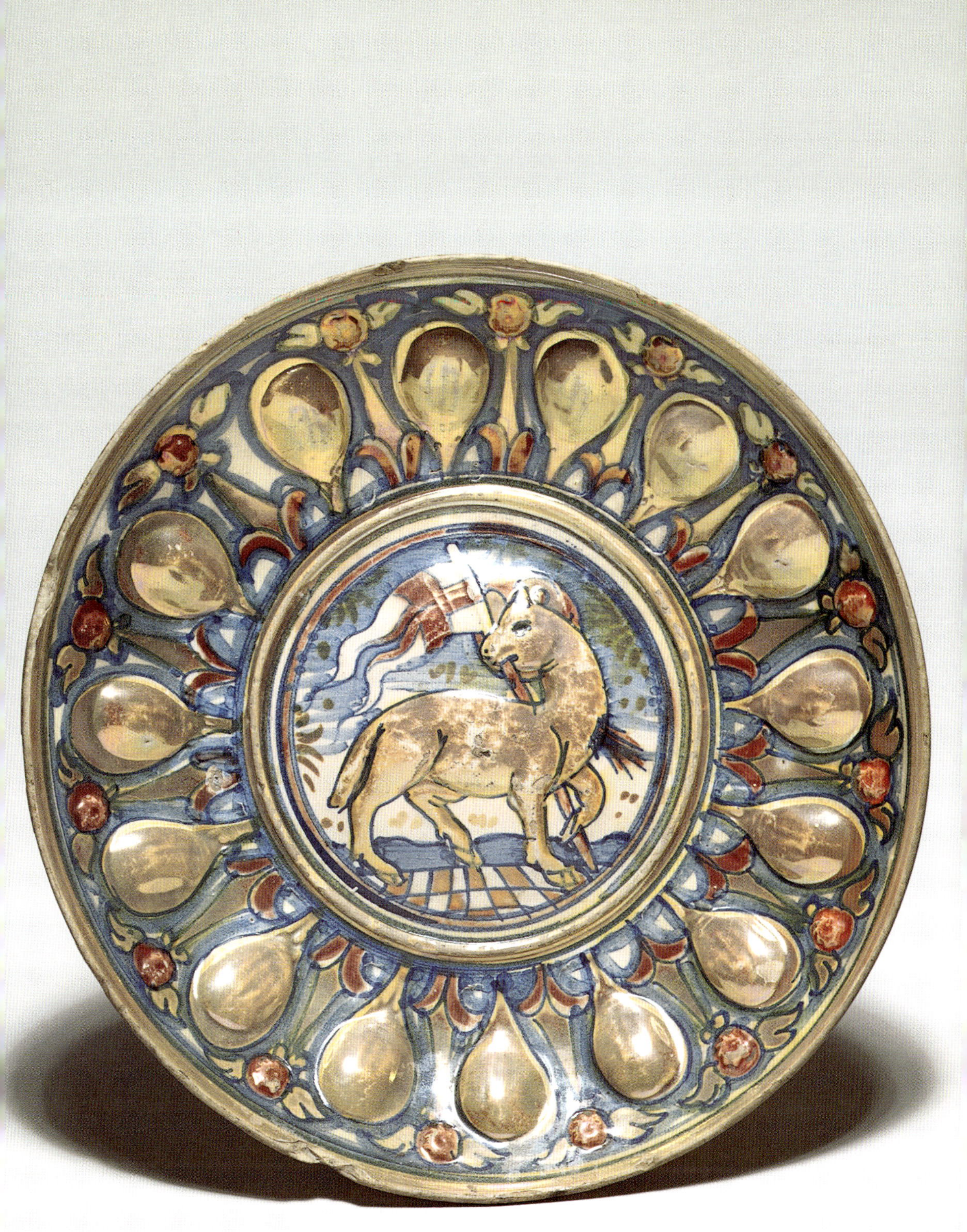

27

COVER FROM AN ACCOUCHEMENT SET BOWL

URBINO, PROBABLY PAINTED BY THE 'MILAN MARSYAS PAINTER', *c.* 1531

On the underside, two putti support an unidentified coat of arms flanked by the letters 'ELI' and 'PYA'. Height 1.9 cm; diameter 19.2 cm. C. B. Marlay Bequest. MAR.C.60–1912.

The safe delivery of a baby was an even greater occasion for rejoicing during the Renaissance than it is today, because the mortality of mothers and infants was high. From the fifteenth century it was customary to give the new mother a little maiolica service to use during her recovery. In Romagna and the Marches these became known as *un servizio da impagliata* because the word *impagliata* was used to describe a woman during her lying-in after childbirth. According to Cipriano Piccolpasso (*c.* 1523/4–79) in *I tre libri del Arte del Vasaio*, written about 1557, the services usually had five pieces arranged on top of each other: a standing bowl covered by a trencher, a drinking bowl on a foot, and a salt and its cover.

Accouchement sets are mentioned in many fifteenth- and sixteenth-century inventories, but, apart from a salt in the Victoria and Albert Museum, only bowls and covers appear to have survived. Most of them are decorated with scenes of childbirth, the washing of babies, or women with small children. Others have childbirth scenes from the Bible or classical mythology, or subjects connected with qualities, such as valour, which it was hoped the child would acquire. The *Holy Family* on the Fitzwilliam's cover was derived from the *Adoration of the Shepherds*, engraved by G. G. Caraglio after Parmigianino. The probable painter is named after the subject of an *istoriato* dish in the Castello Sforzesco, Milan. The letters on either side of the arms have not been explained conclusively. They might be abbreviations for Elisabetta *piacevole* (agreeable or pretty) or *pia* (pious), as the arms are not those of the Pia family. A dish painted by Francesco Xanto in 1531 with the *Judgement of Paris* bears the same arms (Fitzwilliam Museum, C.86–1961).

Further reading Carmen Ravanelli Guidotti, *Donazione Paolo Mereghi ceramiche europee ed orientali*, MICF, Faenza, 1987, pp. 205–7, no. 84. Claudia Silvia Däubler, 'La tazza da parto nella Collezione Pringsheim', *CeramicAntica*, 4:6 (June 1994), pp. 26–39.

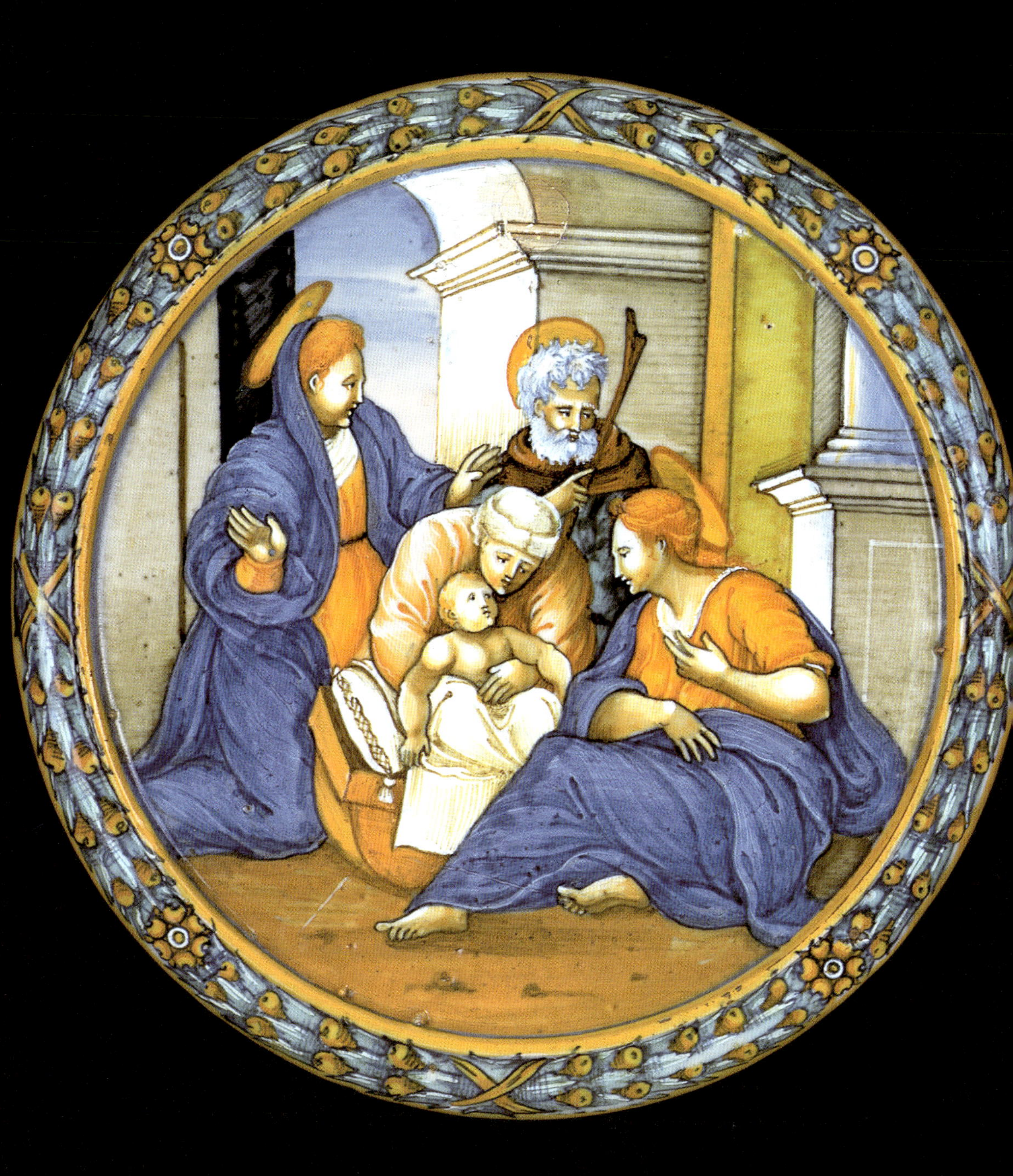

28

DISH FROM THE PUCCI SERVICE

URBINO, PAINTED BY FRANCESCO XANTO AVELLI DA ROVIGO, DATED 1532

The reverse is inscribed '.1532./Nel agitato Legno truova/ Orlando di Ruggier' l'armi/Nel.XXXVII. cãto del furioso d/.M.L. Ariosto./ frã: Xãto .A./da Rouigo ĩ/Urbino.' Height 2.7 cm; diameter 26.5 cm. M. L. Horn Bequest, 1953. C.10–1953.

This is one of thirty-six dishes recorded from a service bearing the arms of a member of the Pucci family of Florence. Most of the dishes are decorated with scenes from classical mythology or history, but this dish and another in the British Museum differ in having scenes from one of the greatest romantic epic poems, *Orlando Furioso* by Ludovico Ariosto (1474–1533). The action shown on the Fitzwilliam's dish takes place after the hero, Ruggiero, had abandoned his ship in a storm off the coast of Egypt, leaving on board his horse, Frontino, his armour, and his magic sword, Belisarda. These were found by a Christian warrior, Orlando, who took the sword for himself, and distributed the armour and horse to his companions, Oliviero, and Brandimarte, in preparation for a battle with a Saracen, Gradasso.

The painter, Francesco Xanto Avelli, was a native of Rovigo, near Padua, and was recorded in Urbino between 1530 and 1542. During that period he marked or signed numerous dishes and panels, many of which are also inscribed with their subject and its literary source. His reference to canto 37 of *Orlando Furioso* on this dish, shows that he used the first edition of 1516, because in the second edition of 1532 the action takes place in canto 41. Xanto constructed his scenes by copying or adapting figures from a wide range of prints, in one instance as many as twelve for one dish. On this one however, all the figures and the horse were taken from the *Abduction of Helen*, engraved by Marcantonio Raimondi after Raphael.

Further reading Julia Triolo, 'Francesco Xanto Avelli's Pucci Service (1532–1533): Part One', *Faenza*, 74:1–3 (1988), pp. 32–43; 'Part Two', *Faenza*, 74:4–6 (1988), pp. 228–82. Timothy Wilson, 'Xanto and Ariosto', *Burlington Magazine*, 132 (May 1990), pp. 321–7. Wilson, 1993, pp. 199–201, pp. 205–9.

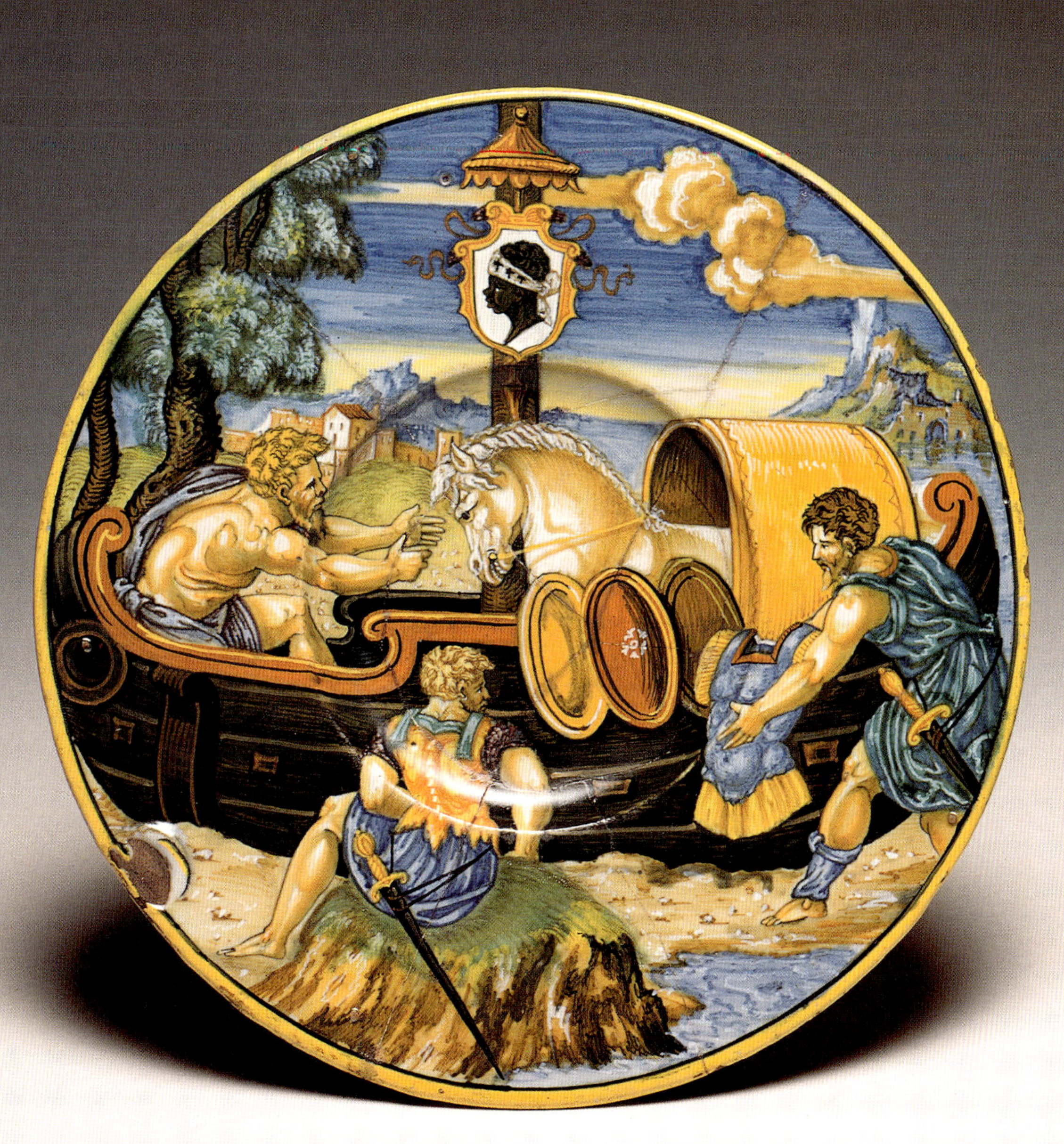

29

DISH: THE QUEEN OF SHEBA LISTENING TO THE WISDOM OF SOLOMON

URBINO, WORKSHOP OF GUIDO DURANTINO, C. 1535

The back is inscribed 'La Reina Sabba / Ande adudire la sa / pientia đ Salomone ❦/nella botega đ M⁰ Guido / durâtino jn Vrbino'. Height 4 cm; diameter 28.2 cm. M. L. Horn Bequest, 1953. C.17–1953.

Guido Durantino was the son of Nicolò Schippe, also known as 'pelliparius', a skinner in Castel Durante. He was living in Urbino by 1516 and was recorded as a potter there from 1519 until his death, probably not long after he made his second will in October, 1576. In the 1520s he had business dealings with the potter and maiolica painter, Nicola di Gabriele Sbraghe, and the earliest known dish inscribed as made in his workshop was painted in 1528 by Nicola. The latest was dated 1542, but much of the finest *istoriato* maiolica made in Urbino between then and the 1560s has been attributed to the workshop. It is not known whether Guido himself was a painter, because no maiolica is known which he inscribed as painted by himself.

This dish was probably made about 1535 because the style of painting and the writing on the back resemble those on dishes in two armorial services which Guido's workshop made in that year for Cardinal Antoine Duprat, Chancellor of France, and Anne de Montmorency, Constable of France. Religious subjects remained popular with lay and clerical patrons of maiolica workshops, despite the dominance of classical influence on art and architecture during the Renaissance. The *Judgement of Solomon* and the *Queen of Sheba listening to the wisdom of Solomon* both occur frequently on maiolica.

Most of the maiolica attributed to Guido's workshop is in *istoriato* style, but when, in 1565, his son, Orazio, asked for a division of their assets and set up his own workshop, Guido was left with the white wares, Venetian-style wares, and everyday crockery. Presumably the workshop had been making these previously and continued to make them until his death.

Further reading J. V. G. Mallet, 'In Botega di Maestro Guido Durantino in Urbino', *Burlington Magazine*, 129 (May 1987), pp. 284–98. Wilson, 1993, pp. 218–22.

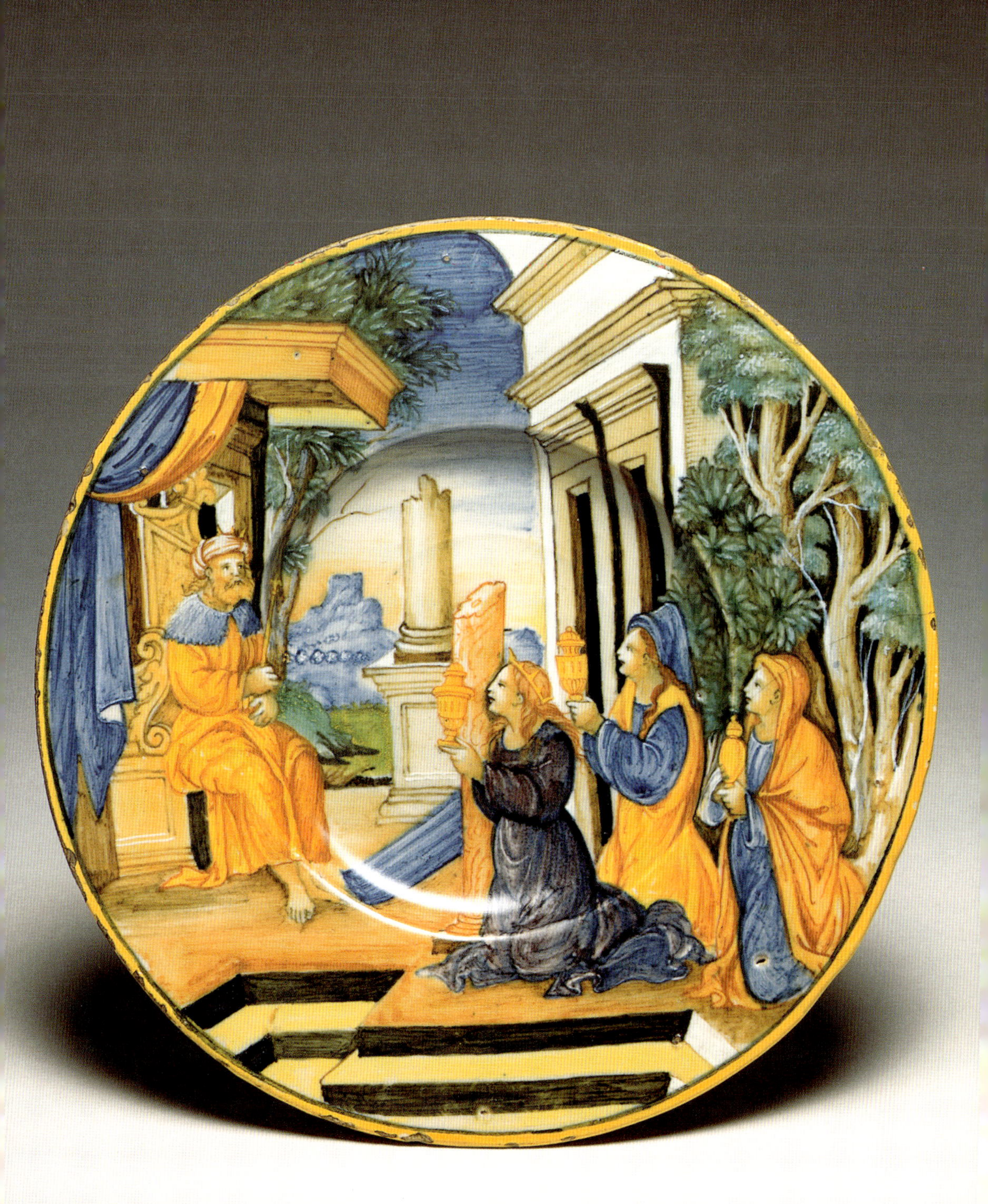

30

PLATE: ATALANTA'S RACE AGAINST HIPPOMENES

FAENZA, PAINTED BY BALDASSARE MANARA, 1534

The back is decorated with orange and yellow scale pattern surrounding the date and initials 'MD/XXX/IIII/>B<M' in dark blue. Height 2.7 cm; diameter 22.8 cm. Purchased with the Glaisher Fund. EC.23–1939.

Hippomenes won the hand of the fleet-footed and heartless Atalanta by defeating her in a race. He succeeded, when other young men had failed and forfeited their lives, by throwing down three golden apples one after the other. Atalanta could not resist stooping to pick them up, and after picking up the third was hampered by their weight. On this plate Hippomenes is shown twice, once behind Atalanta and again dashing ahead to claim her hand from her father King Schoenius.

The initials '>B<M' on the back stand for Baldassare Manara, a member of a long established family of potters in Faenza. He is first recorded in 1529 and probably died between 1546 and 15 June 1547 when he was described as dead in a document. The earliest dishes attributed to him are dated 1532, and he signed or initialled others in 1534 and 1535, and a circular plaque in 1536. Manara's style is distinctive but uneven in quality. Some dishes painted within a short space of time appear childish or naive, and others more mature and accomplished. One of his best signed dishes is the *Triumph of Time*, in the Ashmolean Museum, Oxford.

This plate illustrates several typical features of his scenes, such as pebbly paths, grass with small flowering plants, and slightly topsy-turvy buildings in the distance. He probably adapted the iconography from a woodcut in an Italian translation of Ovid's *Metamorphoses* published in Venice in 1522. The arms have not been identified.

Further reading Rackham, 1940, pp. 263–4, nos. 800–3. Wilson, 1987, pp. 70–1, no. 102, p. 144, no. 221. Hess, 1988, pp. 61–3, no. 19. Wilson, 1989, pp. 56–7, no. 24. Carmen Ravanelli Guidotti, 'Da un'idea di Giuseppe Liverani, la proposta per una monografia su "Baldassarre Manara figulo faentino del XVI secolo"', *Faenza*, 77:3–4 (1991), pp. 147–57.

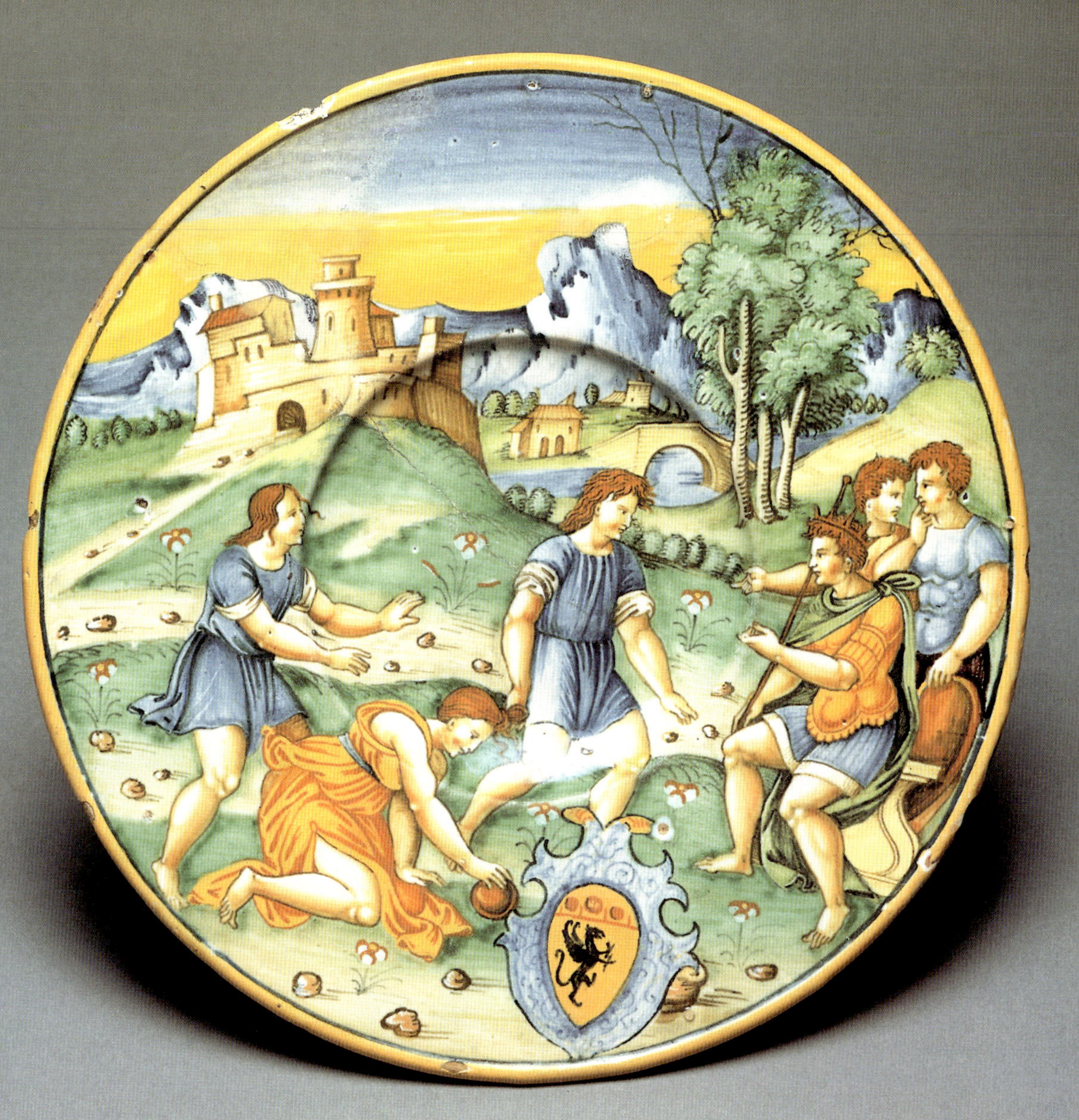

31

DISH: THE JUDGEMENT OF PARIS

URBINO, PERHAPS WORKSHOP OF GUIDO DURANTINO, *c.* 1545–50

The back bears the arms of Cardinal Tiberio Crispi and the inscription 'SORDENT. PRAE FORM/INGENIVM VIRTVS/REGNA.AVRV̂' (Genius, valour, domination and wealth are despised in comparison to beauty). Height 5 cm; diameter 45.4 cm. F. Leverton Harris Bequest, 1926. C.59–1927.

The *Judgement of Paris*, engraved by Marcantonio Raimondi after drawings by Raphael, was one of the prints most frequently used as a source by maiolica painters, but was rarely copied in its entirety as it is here. Paris is shown with the goddesses Hera, Athena, and Aphrodite who had been brought to him by Hermes with a message from Zeus that he was to award a golden apple to the fairest. Rejecting the bribes of power and wisdom offered by Hera and Athene, Paris awarded the apple to Aphrodite, who offered to assist him in gaining the love of Helen, wife of Menelaus, King of Sparta, whose beauty was equal to her own. The inscription on the back of the dish referring to Paris' choice was also copied from the print.

The dish's owner, Cardinal Tiberio Crispi (1497–1566), was promoted to the cardinalate in December 1544 by the Farnese pope, Paul III (ruled 1534–49). Like many cardinals, Crispi marked his promotion by impaling his arms with those of the pope, so their presence on the dish indicates a date after December, 1544. Another feature which links the dish to Crispi is the nude woman with a unicorn which the painter inserted into the *Judgement* in the upper left background. This is believed to be an *impresa* adopted by Crispi, but might also refer to his links with the Farnese family who had four unicorn *imprese*, including a unicorn placing its front hooves in a maiden's lap.

In the early eighteenth century the dish may have belonged to the painter, Charles Jarvis (?1675–1739), because it corresponds to the description of lot 555 in the posthumous sale of his effects. By 1850 it was in the possession of Richard Ford (1796–1858) at Heavitree, near Exeter, and remained in his family until 1919.

Further reading *Dizionario Biografico Italiano*, XXX, Rome, 1984, pp. 801–3. Maria Cristina Villa, 'Il giudizio di Paride in un rinfrescatoio urbinate di gusto cortese', *CeramicAntica*, 5:11 (December 1995), pp. 10–25.

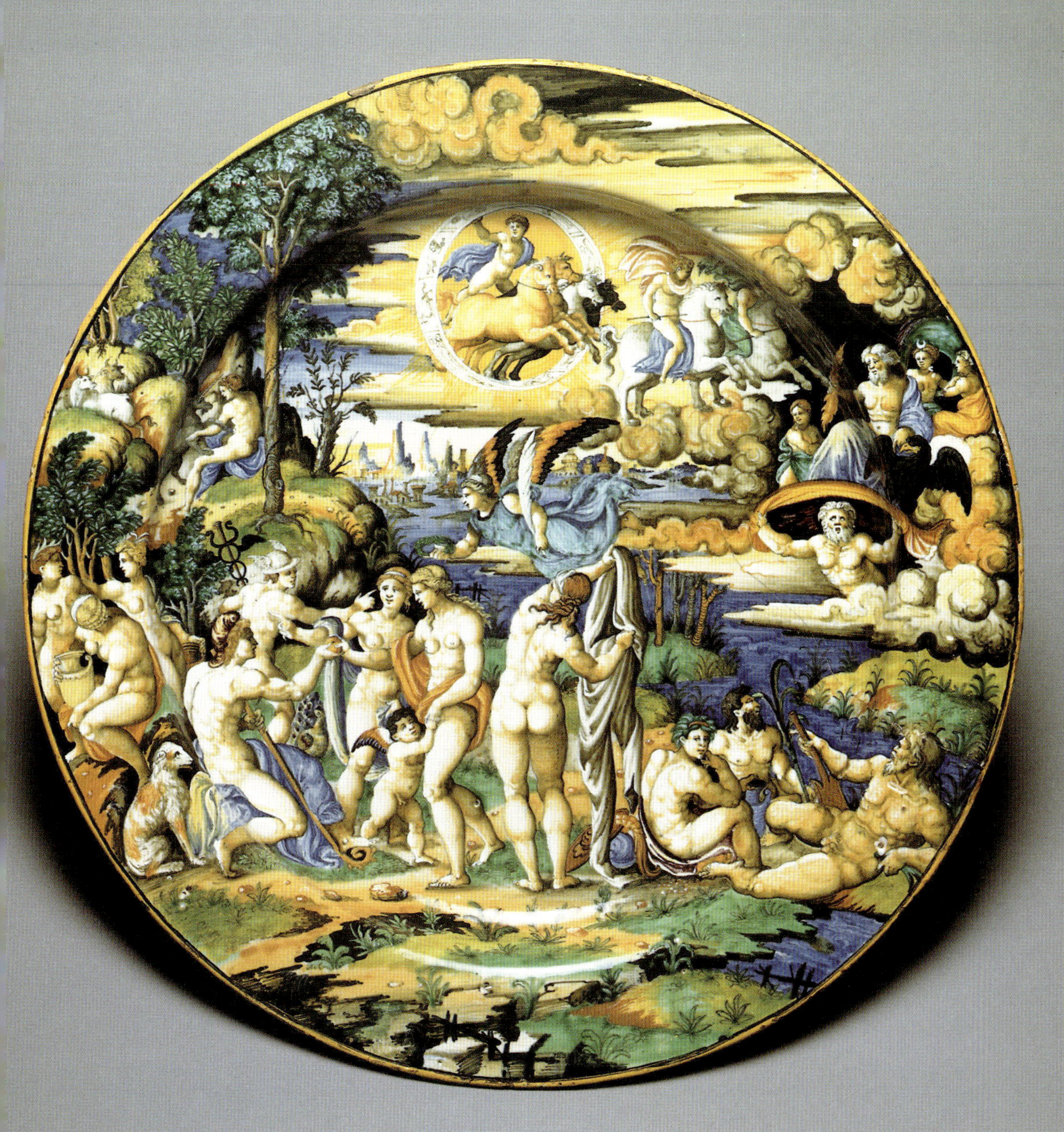

32

TRILOBATE CISTERN: THE TRIUMPH OF GALATEA OR AMPHITRITE

URBINO, PROBABLY WORKSHOP OF GUIDO DURANTINO, *c.* 1550–70

Height 23.3 cm; width 48.5 cm; depth 49.5 cm. Purchased with the Cecil C. Mason Fund and grant-in-aid from the Victoria and Albert Museum. C.1–1964.

Large oval or circular cisterns (*rinfrescatoii*), usually made of metal, can be seen in many Renaissance and later paintings of banquets or informal meals. They were filled with cold water or ice to cool wine flasks and were placed on the floor by the table from which drinks were served, or near the dining table. No illustrations of maiolica cisterns in use have been identified, but as a good number have survived, it seems likely that they were set on a table with other maiolica rather than on the floor.

Trilobate cisterns have a central foot formed by three lions' paws and three handles in the shape of grotesque masks with horns which curl on either side of the rim like scrolls. This complex and fanciful form is a good illustration of mannerism in maiolica. None of the *istoriato* examples is dated, but on stylistic grounds the earliest appear to have been made in the 1540s. The latest dated example, decorated with grotesques, was made in the workshop of Francesco Patanazzi in 1608.

Istoriato decoration inside trilobate cisterns includes scenes from Roman history, classical mythology and the Bible; the outsides usually have landscapes with buildings. This example and several others are decorated internally with marine triumphs, which were appropriate to their function as water holders. The inspiration for these scenes was Raphael's fresco of the *Triumph of Galatea* in the Villa Farnese in Rome, which was widely known through an engraving by Marcantonio Raimondi. Yet strangely, only one of the extant cisterns, in the Wallace Collection, is decorated with a close copy of it. However, the *putti* flying overhead on this and other cisterns, indicate that the painter was familiar with the print, or with Marcantonio's *Parnassus* which has *putti* flying over Apollo and the Muses.

Further reading Giacomotti, 1974, pp. 338–40, nos. 1034–5. Norman, 1976, pp. 228–9, C111, pp. 236–8, C116. Ravanelli Guidotti, 1985, pp. 168, 170–2, no. 126.

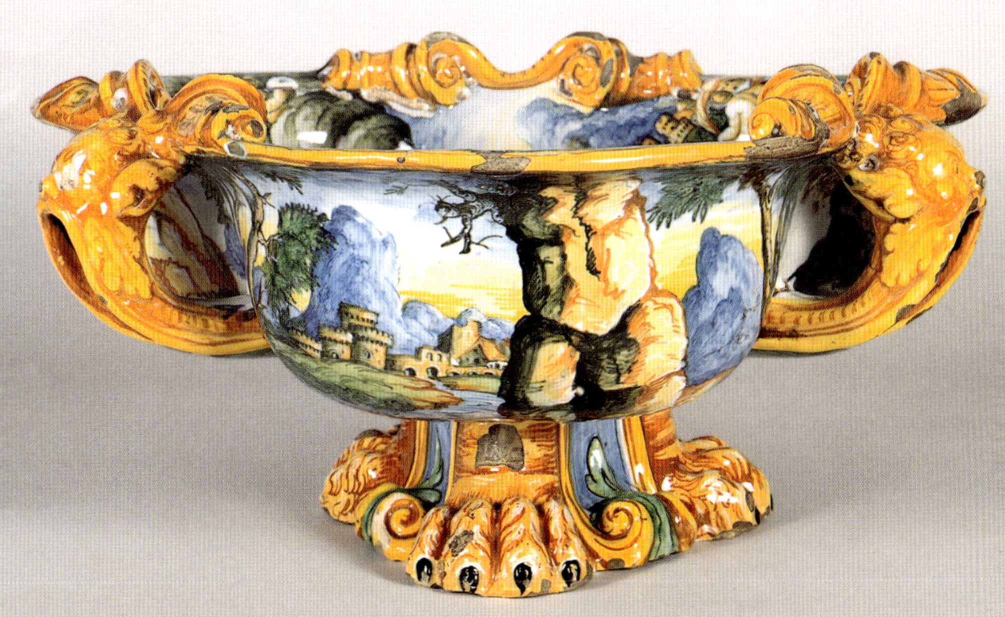

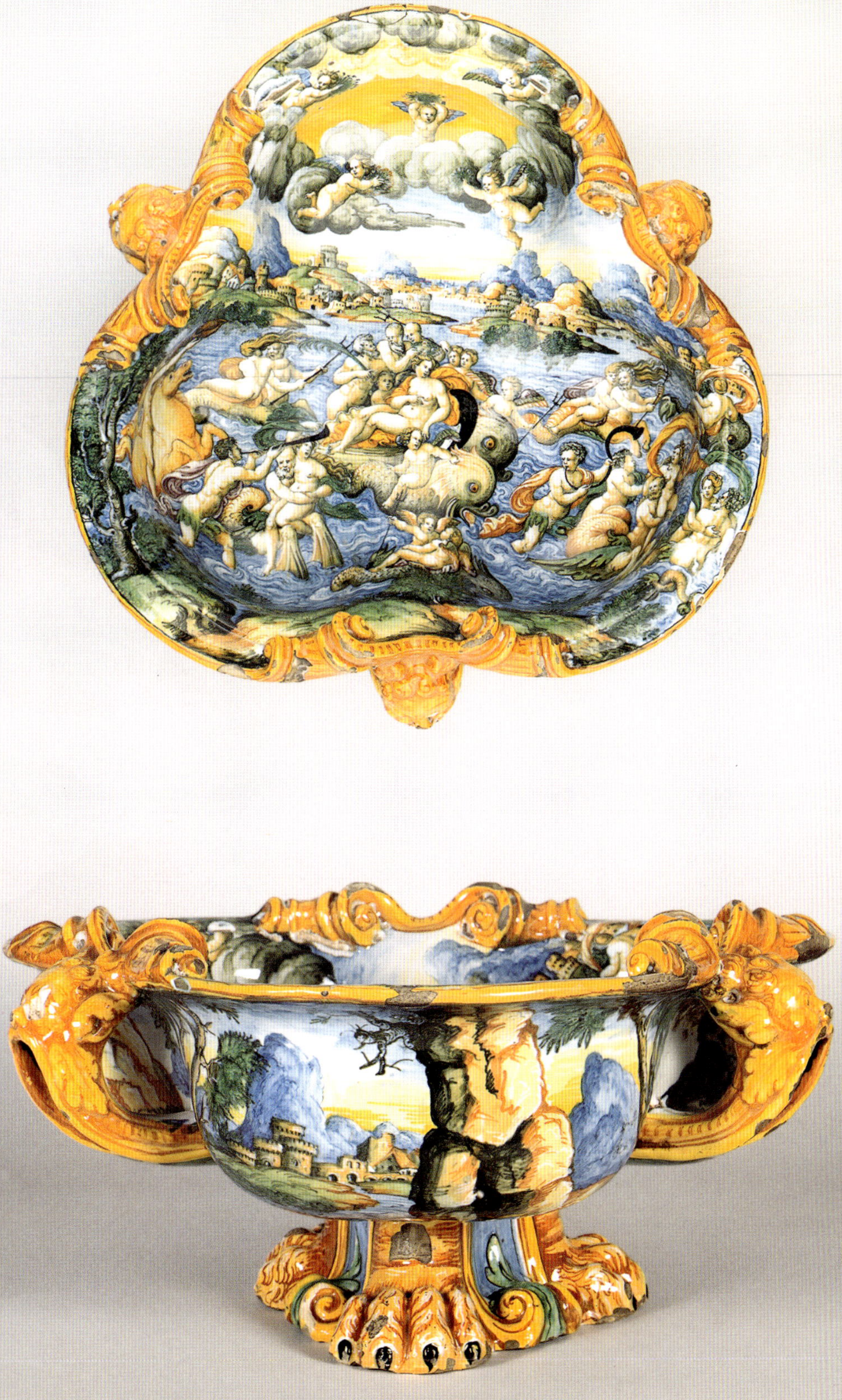

33

DISH: HERO AND LEANDER

PESARO, ATTRIBUTED TO SFORZA DI MARCANTONIO, DATED '.61.' (1561)

Inscribed on the reverse 'Leandro in Mare &./ Hero alla finestra/.61./.S.' Height 4.2 cm; diameter 30 cm. Purchased with the F. Leverton Harris and L. D. Cunliffe Funds. C.21–1995

During the second and third decades of the sixteenth century the maiolica industry in Pesaro was less flourishing than in the previous century. This situation improved after Guidobaldo II della Rovere succeeded to the dukedom of Urbino in 1538, because he preferred to live at Pesaro. The presence of the court stimulated local industries and from around 1540 Pesaro became a significant producer of *istoriato* maiolica.

Sforza di Marcantonio da Casteldurante was recorded as a potter, and sometimes also as a painter, in Pesaro between 1550–2, and 1563 and making his will in 1580. He signed himself 'SFORZA' on two panels dated 1567, respectively in the British Museum and the Museo Civico Medievale, Bologna. Dishes signed '.S.', in 1561 and in some years up to and including 1576, are attributed to him on the basis of similarities with these panels. Sforza's choice of subjects, iconography, and inscriptions, suggest that he had been in contact with Francesco Xanto in Urbino, probably in the late 1530s.

Xanto painted several dishes with versions of *Hero and Leander* between 1532 and 1538. He probably knew the story from a translation of Ovid's *Heroides*, but on the backs of the dishes he quoted from Petrarch's *Trionfi*, III, 21, 'Leandro in mare ed Hero a la fenestra'. The first dish decorated with this subject which is attributed to Sforza was painted in 1546; the latest, now at Braunschweig, is dated 1576, and initialled '.S.' Both, like this one, have an inscription from Petrarch, and the figure of Leander used by Xanto, which was taken from a Marcantonio Raimondi school print, the *Battle with the Cutlass*. The three dishes illustrate the persistence of popular themes over a long period, and the repetitive nature of much maiolica painting.

Further reading Grazia Biscontini Ugolini, 'Sforza di Marcantonio: figulo pesarese cinquecentesco', *Faenza*, 65 (1979), pp. 7–10; Lessmann, 1979, pp. 345–51. Albarelli, 1986. Wilson, 1987, pp. 67–8, no. 98. Wilson, 1993, pp. 210–14.

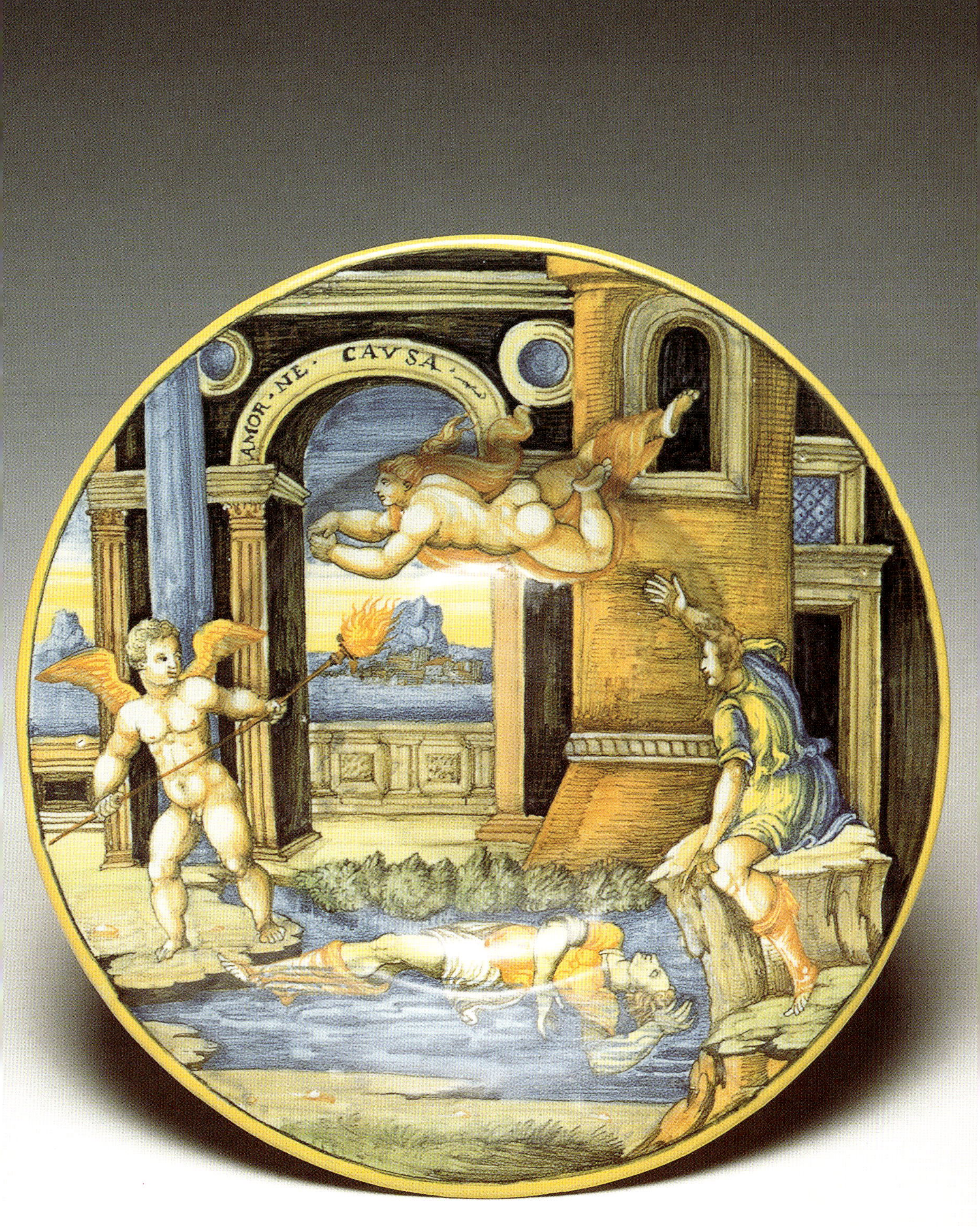
AMOR · NE · CAVSA

34

DISH: A TURK ON HORSEBACK

DERUTA, PROBABLY MANCINI WORKSHOP, *c.* 1535–55

On the reverse, two dark blue spirals and an M or W with an extra stroke crossed diagonally. Height 9.5 cm; diameter 40 cm. F. Leverton Harris Bequest, 1926. C.100–1927.

Deruta polychrome *piatti da pompa* (see no. 13) with borders of rays, panels of scales and formal plants were made over a long period and most of them cannot be dated precisely. A rough estimate can be obtained by comparing their borders with dishes decorated with the arms of popes and cardinals, or with arms of couples whose marriage date and death dates are known. The earliest recorded, in the British Museum, bears the arms of Hadrian VI (1522–3) and the latest, in the Musée Ariana, Geneva, those of Pius IV (1559–65). Foliated scrolls resembling those on this dish appear on a dish in the Chateau d'Ecouen, with the arms of Clement III, dated 1531, and on one in an Italian private collection, showing a man trying to shave an ass, dated 1556.

These dishes were probably made in the Mancini workshop which was operating by at least 1521. Equestrian Turks closely resembling this one appear on several dishes, including one in the British Museum which also has similar marks on the reverse. Their popularity as maiolica decoration may have been connected with the repulse of the Turks from Vienna in 1529 or the continuing threat of a Turkish invasion. The style of painting has aspects in common with that of the unknown 'Master of the Pavement of San Francesco' (dated 1524), and of Giacomo Mancini who signed dishes between 1541 and 1545 (see no. 35).

Further reading Giacomotti, 1974, pp. 144–5, nos. 488–90, pp. 148–53, nos. 498–509. Wilson, 1987, pp. 1, 102, no. 158. Fiocco and Gherardi, 1988–9, I, pp. 110–36.

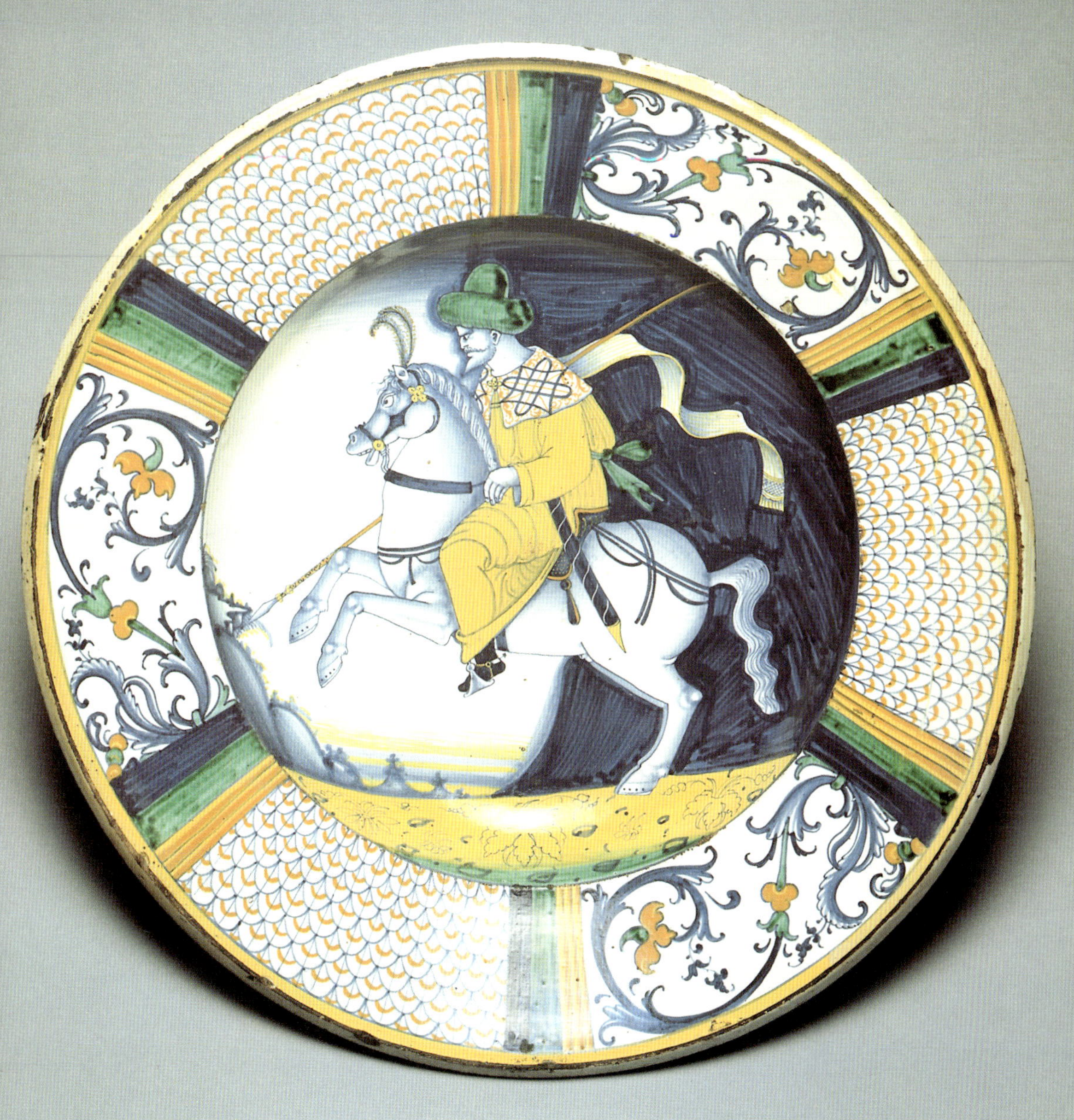

35

PANEL: THE CRUCIFIXION

DERUTA, WORKSHOP OF GIACOMO MANCINI, KNOWN AS EL FRATE, PROBABLY 1556

On the reverse, in black 'DIRVTI/ISSVI'. Height 40 cm; width 41.3 cm. C. B. Marlay Bequest. MAR.C.57–1912.

This panel is one of the most ambitious examples of *istoriato* maiolica from Deruta. It is attributed to Giacomo Mancini, known as 'El Frate' (the Friar), who was the most significant exponent of *istoriato* decoration there in the mid sixteenth century. Several lustred and polychrome dishes signed by him between 1541 and 1545 survive, and these have enabled others to be attributed to him. By the 1550s his style had matured, but several characteristics of his hand remained constant, providing links with his earlier work. One of the most noticeable was his treatment of horses' heads and ears, which can be seen clearly on this panel, as can the tousled hair which many of his figures have. Some of his finest work was done in the 1560s, such as a large dish decorated with *Parnassus*, dated 1564, in the Musée Alexis-Forel at Morges. He died in or shortly before 1581 when his sons divided the family goods between them.

This *Crucifixion* may have been influenced by two prints, both of which include horses: a *Calvary*, by a follower of Marcantonio Raimondi, and another dated 1541, probably after Francesco Salviati. The sun and moon are shown to express the mourning of the whole universe at Christ's death. The scorpions on the banner and on one shield conventionally indicate that the holders were sinners.

Further reading Carola Fiocco and Gabriella Gherardi, 'Una targa della collezione Cora attribuibile alla bottega del Frate da Deruta', *Faenza*, 70:5–6 (1984), pp. 403–14. Carola Fiocco and Gabriella Gherardi, 'Aspetti dell'istoriato derutese: l'opera tarda di Giacomo Mancini detto "Il frate" e della sua bottega', *Faenza*, 81: 1–2 (1995), pp. 5–9.

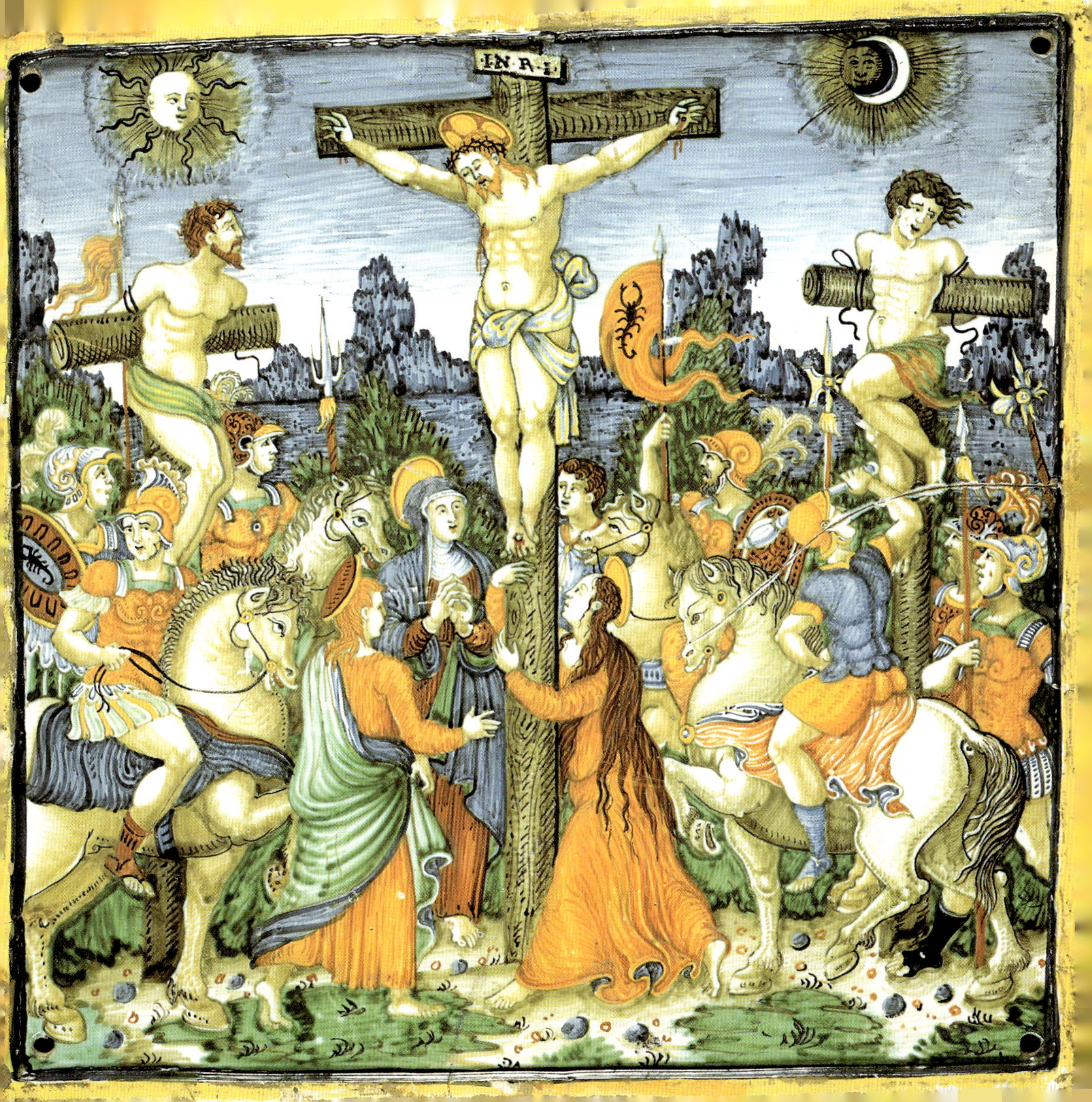
I.N.R.I.

36

PLATE

PROBABLY MADE IN VENICE OR PADUA.

c. 1545–1600

Height 3.2 cm; diameter 23 cm.

Dr J. W. L. Glaisher Bequest. C.2211–1928.

Maiolica with a pale blue (*a berettino*) glaze was a speciality of Venetian potters in the sixteenth century. In fact the colour of the glaze varies considerably from smooth, very pale greyish-blue to coarser lavender-blue. Much of it was decorated in darker blue and white with varieties of foliage, landscapes with buildings, townscapes, or busts of men and women. Foliage designs '*alla porcellana*' can be dated by German coats of arms to the second and third decades of the century. The other types are generally given a wide date range of between about 1540 to 1570 or 1600, but they persisted well into the seventeenth century. Some of the finest dishes with foliage decoration have been attributed tentatively to the workshop of Maestro Lodovico, who signed a dish now in the Victoria and Albert Museum, and was active around 1540.

This plate is representative of another group of *berettino* wares which are decorated with polychrome fruit, flowers, and foliage. These, like foliage and landscape designs, were illustrated by Cipriano Piccolpasso in *I tre libri dell'Arte del Vasaio* (The Three Books of the Potter's Art), which he completed about 1557 for Cardinal de Tournon of Lyon. He described them as 'truly Venetian, very pretty things', and noted that they cost 'five lire a hundred', two lire more than foliage designs and one less than landscapes with buildings. None of them are signed, so it is not possible to attribute them to a particular pottery, and some examples may have been made on the mainland at Padua.

The backs of Venetian *berettino* wares are usually decorated with wreaths of blue stylized foliage, or with outline petals or arches radiating from the base or footring. On many dishes these overlap and some writers described them as *a canestro* (basketwork).

Further reading Angelica Alverà Bortolotto, *Storia della ceramica a Venezia dagli albori alla fine della Repubblica*, Florence, 1981. Timothy Wilson, 'Maiolica in Renaissance Venice', *Apollo*, 125 (March 1987), pp. 184–9. Angelica Alverà Bortolotto, *Maiolica a Venezia nel Rinascimento*, Bergamo, 1988.

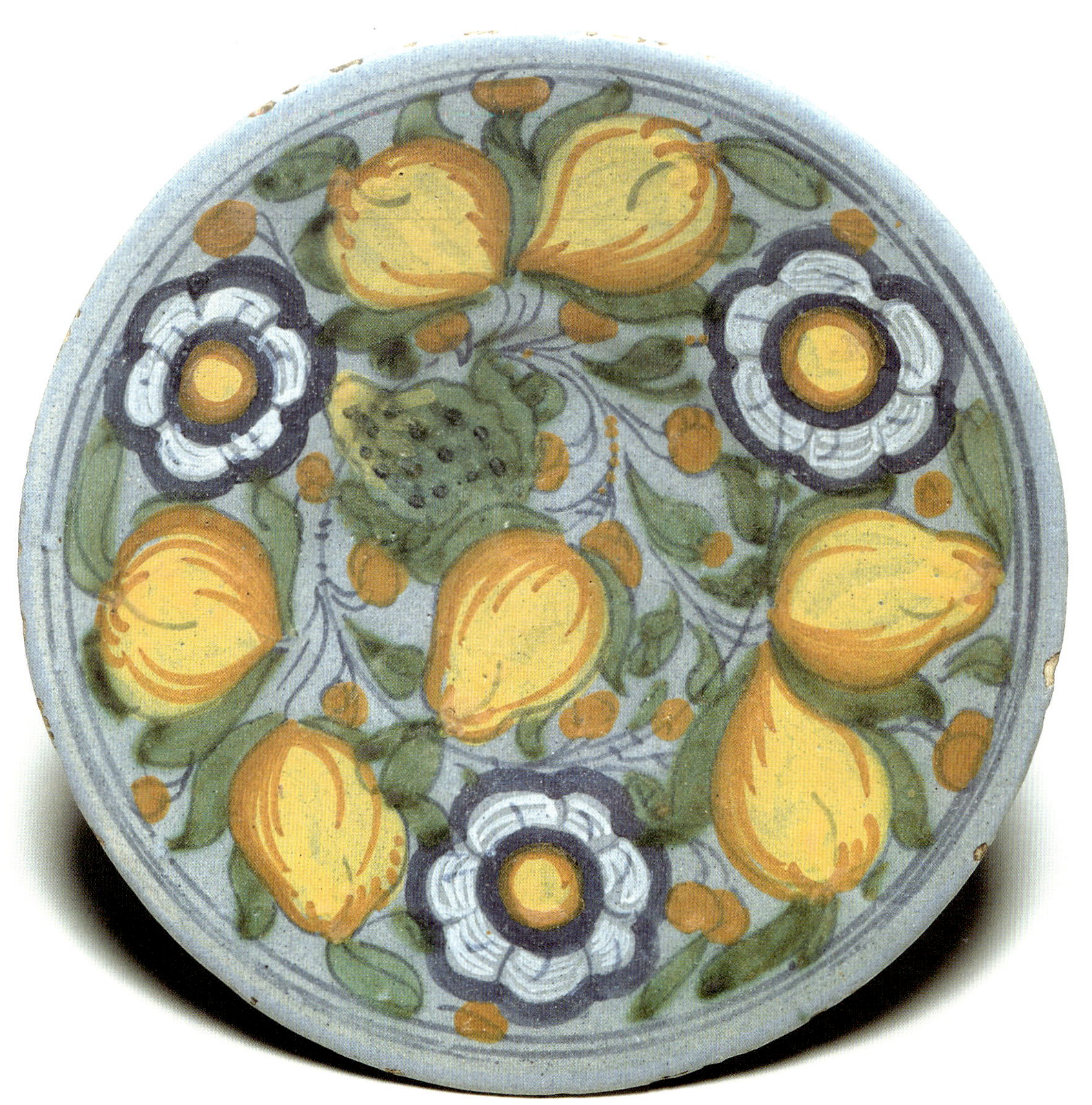

37

STORAGE JAR

VENICE, PROBABLY WORKSHOP OF DOMENEGO DA VENEZIA, *c.* 1560–70, OR LATER

Height 39.5 cm; width 28.9 cm.
C. B. Marlay Bequest. MAR.C.68B–1912.

This albarello represents a numerous class of large cylindrical and globular storage jars decorated with heads of men or women in scrolled panels, surrounded by stylized flowers, and foliage reserved in a dark blue ground incised with tendrils. When labelled they usually have the contents name '*Mostarda* F^{A}' (*Mostarda Fina*), which means either fine mustard or a fruit pickle or sauce, known as *mostarda*. Venetian recipes for this usually include a purée of quinces, or other fruit, such as pears and apples, cooked in white wine, to which are added chopped candied fruit, sugar, mustard and salt. This mixture is cooked until it becomes very thick before being put into containers.

These jars are usually attributed to the workshop of Maestro Domenego who was recorded in Venice between 1544, when he married Catarina, eldest daughter of the potter, Maestro Jacomo of Pesaro, and 1568. He signed and dated a globular pharmacy jar in 1562 and two dishes and an albarello in 1568. His date of death has not yet been found and it is possible that he lived for many years after this.

Some large albarelli have well-painted decoration comparable to the signed example by Maestro Domenego, but others are of a different shape and painted less carefully. This could indicate several things: a different painter, a later date, or even manufacture in another workshop. They are usually dated *c.* 1560–70, but it seems highly likely that some of them were made later. The young man on this example is wearing a *beretta a tozzo*, a soft high-crowned hat which was fashionable during the second half of the century, and particularly during its last twenty years or so.

Further reading Lessmann, 1979, p. 409, pp. 460–1, nos. 737–8. Angelica Alverà Bortolotto, *Maiolica a Venezia nel Rinascimento*, Bergamo, 1988. Angela Del Conte, *The Classic Food of Northern Italy*, p. 111, 'Mostarda di Venezia'.

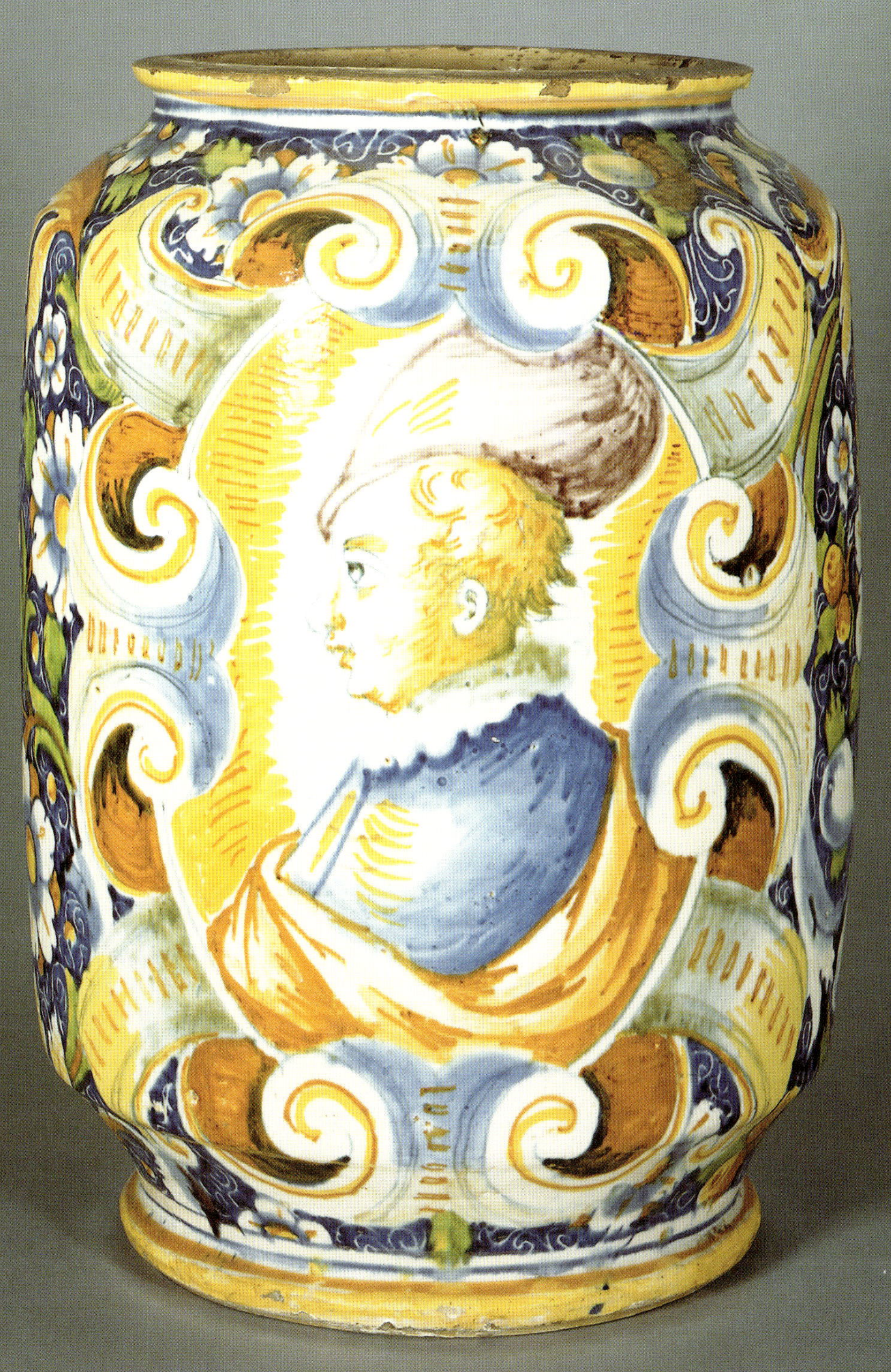

38

DRAGON-SPOUTED PHARMACY EWER

CASTELLI, POMPEI WORKSHOP, *c.* 1550–60

Height 25.9 cm; width 23.5 cm. F. Leverton Harris Bequest, 1926. C.64–1927.

This ewer contained '*Oymel composito*' (compound oxymel), a syrup made by evaporating clarified honey and vinegar with other ingredients. It is one of nearly 300 jars of several different forms decorated with busts and figures in a very distinctive style. Bernard Rackham named them 'the Orsini–Colonna pharmacy vases' after a two-handled bottle in the British Museum, decorated with a bear embracing a column and the words 'ET SARRIMO [*sic*] boNI AMICI', emblematic of a reconciliation between these rival Roman families. However, as the number of jars recorded increased, it became apparent from the repetition of drug names, and differences in decoration and lettering, that the jars formed more than one set. In maiolica literature published before about 1985 they were attributed by different authors to Siena, Deruta, Faenza, Cafaggiolo, or Castel Durante, and dated to *c.* 1515–30.

They are now securely assigned to Castelli on the basis of fragments found during an excavation between 1980 and 1982 of the waste tip on the hillside behind the house of Orazio Pompei (*c.* 1510–20 to after 1590), a member of a large and flourishing potting family in Castelli. The connection between Orazio and the jars is supported by the inscription 'OC/OPVS/ORATII' on a dragon-spouted ewer in the MICF. In addition there are strong similarities between female busts on some jars and figures on two panels attributed to him. One, of the *Virgin and Child*, dated 1551, was once situated at the entrance to his house. The other, of the *Annunciation*, dated 1557, now belongs to the *comune* of Chieti. The date on the latter suggests that some of the jars could have been made as late as *c.* 1555–60.

The reattribution and dating of this group demonstrates the crucial role being played by archaeology in maiolica studies, and is a forceful reminder that it is not always possible to make secure attributions of maiolica on stylistic grounds.

Further reading Rackham, 1940, I, pp. 78–80, nos. 250–7. Wilson, 1987, p. 143, no. 219. Giorgio Baldisseri, Rino Casadio, Raffaele Colapietra, Claudio de Pompeis, Vincenzo de Pompeis, Carmen Ravanelli Guidotti, *et al.*, *Le maioliche cinquecentesche di Castelli. Una grande stagione artistica ritrovata*, Pescara, 1989.

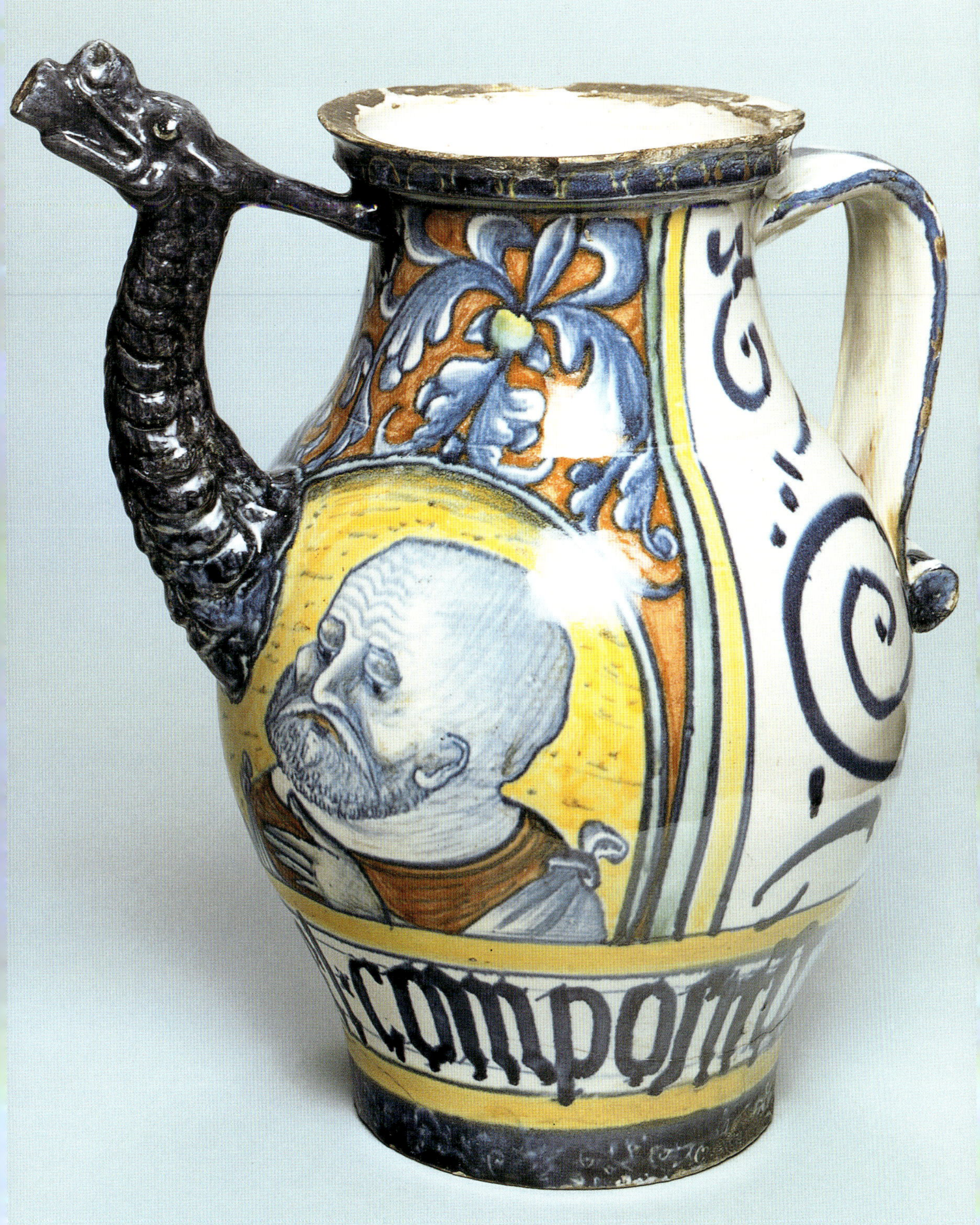

39

TWO-HANDLED VASE

PROBABLY FAENZA, *c.* 1557–68

Height 56.6 cm; width 39.5 cm. Given by the Friends of the Fitzwilliam aided by grants from the National Art Collections Fund and the Regional Fund administered by the Victoria and Albert Museum. C.10–1995.

Faenza white ware (*bianchi di Faenza*) was the most influential development in maiolica production in the mid sixteenth century. It was being made by the 1540s and became increasingly fashionable during the second half of the century. It was imitated in Italian towns such as Deruta, and its export to other parts of Europe resulted in tin-glazed earthenware becoming known as 'faïence'. Its popularity stemmed from its clean, milky-white appearance which resembled porcelain, and its cheapness in comparison with highly decorated *istoriato* wares.

Much white ware was undecorated, particularly vessels with moulded ornament imitating embossed silver, such as basins, flasks, and cisterns. Any decoration was usually rather sparse and in *compendiario* style (see nos. 40–2). This vase is decorated on both sides with the arms of Jean Parisot de la Valette (1494–1568), who was appointed Grand Master of the Knights of St John in 1557 and led their heroic defence of Malta against the Turks in 1565. He was known for his austere life, and this suggests that the vase was made after the siege, perhaps as a gift. The circumstances of its production are not known, but it seems likely that it was made in Faenza.

The vase is exceptionally large for maiolica, and its relief decoration suggests that it was designed by a painter or engraver rather than a potter. Its small foot embellished with shells and dolphins, and its triton handles illustrate the mannerist taste for sea creatures and have parallels in silver and sculpture. Designs for such vases survive by leading painters such as Polidoro da Caravaggio (1492–1553), and by lesser figures, like Marco da Faenza (d. 1588).

Further reading G. Morazzoni, 'Tre pezzi eccezionali di maiolica faentina', *La Ceramica*, 7 (August 1952), pp. 31–2. Giuseppe Liverani, 'Bianco di Faenza. The development of white maiolica', *Connoisseur*, 140 (November 1957), pp. 160–3.

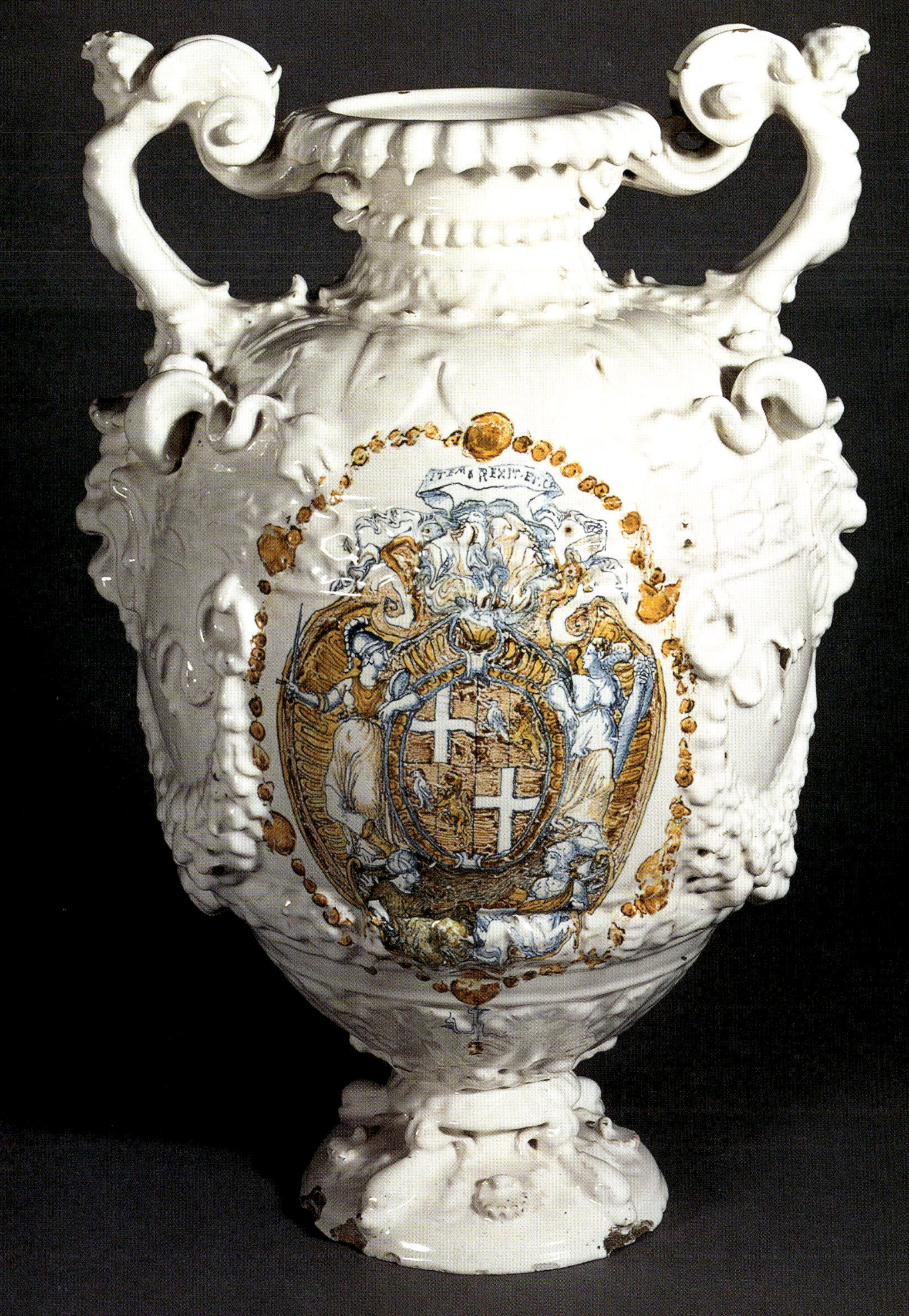

40

DEEP BOWL ON LOW FOOT

FAENZA, PROBABLY WORKSHOP OF LEONARDO DI ANTONIO BETTISI, ALIAS 'DON PINO', *c.* 1568–89

Height 12.2 cm; diameter 33.5 cm.
Dr J. W. L. Glaisher Bequest. C.2188–1928.

This deep fluted bowl illustrates two of the most characteristic types of decoration on Faenza white ware. Its central roundel is painted in *compendiario* (outline or summary) style and its sides with radiating panels *a ricamo* (resembling embroidery). Bowls of this form were made from at least the early 1560s. An example with different decoration, in the Hermitage at St Petersburg, is inscribed 'in Faienca/1563'. Bowls and basins (*bacini* or *catini*) are mentioned in sixteenth-century inventories of Faenza services, and it therefore seems likely that they were used for hand-washing or perhaps rinsing fruit at table. A water cistern for cooling bottles was usually described as a *rinfrescatoio*.

The Fitzwilliam's bowl is not marked, but was probably made by Leonardo di Antonio Bettisi, known as 'Don Pino'. Two analogous bowls from armorial services are signed with short forms of his nickname (see no. 41). One, in the Silesian Museum, Opava, bears the arms of a member of the Piccolomini family, and the other, in an Italian private collection, has the arms of Girolamo Michelozzi and Caterina di Braccio Alberti of Florence, who were married in 1571.

By then Bettisi was a well-established potter. In 1568 he had supplied a service of 307 pieces to the Grand Duke Francesco dei Medici of Florence and, in 1570, he leased the workshop of Virgiliotto Calamelli, from his widow, Isabetta. During the later part of his life he was assisted by his son, Antonio, who took over the workshop on Leonardo's death. This occurred in or before 1589 when Antonio alone was named as the supplier of tableware to the Grand Duke Ferdinando I.

Further reading Conte Luigi Zauli Naldi, 'Pezzi firmati di Don Pino', *Faenza*, 47:5 (1961), pp. 129–31. Eros Biavati, 'Leonardo Bettisi fu Antonio ed il figlio Antonio junior detti ambedue "Don Pino"', *Faenza*, 65:6 (1979), pp. 367–70. Carmen Ravanelli Guidotti, *Monte dei Paschi di Siena, Collezione Chigi Saracini, 5, Maioliche Italiane*, Siena, 1992, pp. 202–6, no. 41.

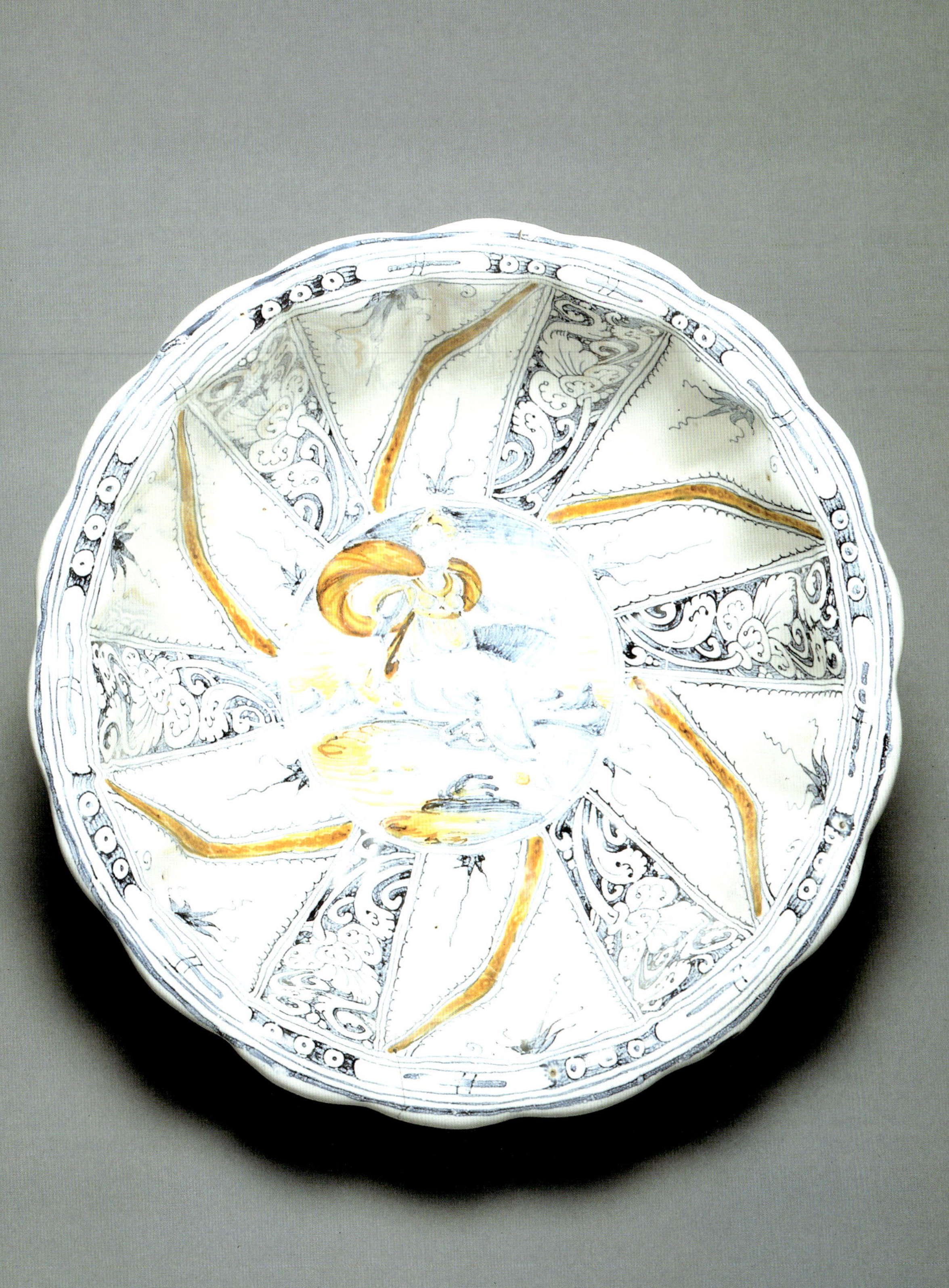

41

BROAD-RIMMED BOWL FROM THE ALBRECHT V SERVICE

FAENZA, WORKSHOP OF LEONARDO DI ANTONIO BETTISI, ALIAS 'DON PINO', 1576

Marked on the base '.D̄O. P̄î'. Height 4.1 cm; diameter 25.2 cm. H. S. Reitlinger Bequest, 1950. C.179–1991

During the sixteenth century substantial quantities of maiolica were exported to the German states from Venice, Urbino and Faenza. Much of this maiolica has been dispersed in Europe and America, but its original destination is known from the coats of arms of the wealthy merchants and rulers who owned it. This dish bears the arms of the Wittelsbach dukes of Bavaria, and once formed part of a service which belonged to Albrecht V (ruled 1550–79). The service was probably made in 1576, the date on one dish. Its original extent is unknown, but an inventory of 1751 mentioned 116 pieces. Of these, 84, including dishes of 4 different shapes, 2 salts, 4 flasks, and a candlestick, belong to the Residenzmuseum in Munich. Several more including a large circular cistern are displayed in the Bayerisches Nationalmuseum there, and a few dishes are in museums in Germany, France, and Italy. Many of the pieces are marked '*.D̄O. P̄î*' for Leonardo di Antonio Bettisi of Faenza, known as 'Don Pino' (see no. 40).

The dishes are decorated in *compendiario* style with scenes from the Bible, classical mythology, and Roman history derived mainly from Bernard Salomon's illustrations to Damiano Maraffi's *Figure del Vecchio Testamento con Versi Toscani*, Lyon, 1554, the *Trasformazioni* of Lodovico Dolce, Venice, 1553, and the cruder woodcuts in the *Deche di Tito Livio vulgare hystoriate*, Venice, 1493, or later editions in 1502 and 1511. The scene on this dish is titled '*cavaleria di popeo simoue / cotra cesare*' (Cavalry of Pompey advances against Caesar), and probably represents the battle between Caesar and Pompey at Pharsalus in 48 BC, described in Appian, *Civil Wars*, II, 11. It may have been inspired by one of the battle scenes in the illustrated Livy, but does not resemble any of them very closely.

Further reading Luisa Hager, 'Ein Majolika-Tafelgeschirr aus Faenza im Residenzmuseum München', *Pantheon*, 23 (1939), pp. 135–9. Rasmussen, 1984, pp. 254–5, no. 170. Ulrike Zischka, Hans Ottomeyer, and Susanne Bäumler, *Die Anständige Lust von Esskultur und Tafelsitten*, Munich, 1993, pp. 123–5. Rome, 1993, p. 138, no. 56.

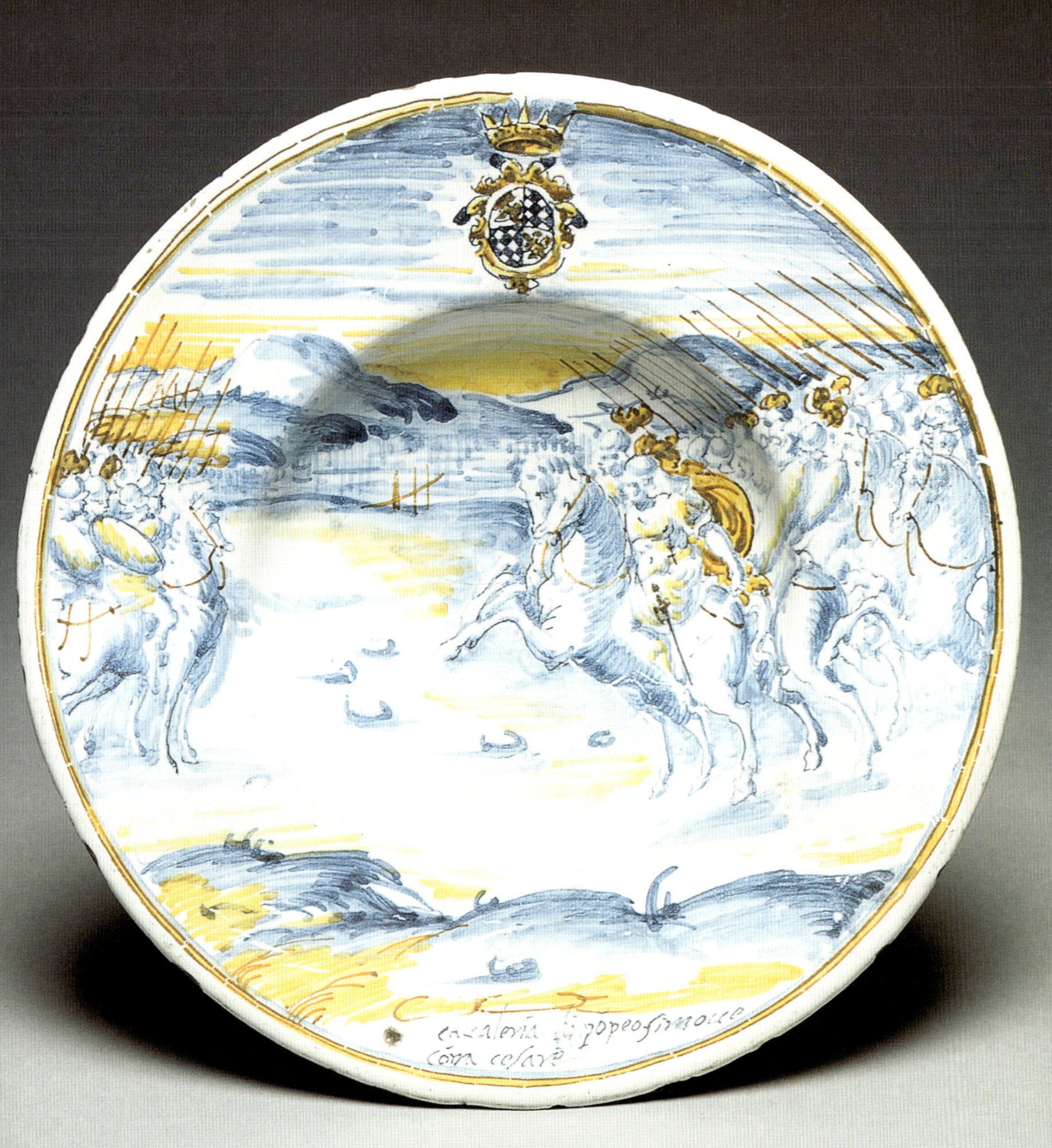
cavaleria di popeo si move
cõtra cesarē

42

DISH: DIANA AND ACTAEON

FAENZA, PROBABLY BY STEFANO ACCARISI, *c.* 1585

Height 5.7 cm; diameter 44.8 cm.
H. S. *Reitlinger Bequest,* 1950. C. 178–1991.

The myth of Diana and Actaeon from Ovid's *Metamorphoses*, III, 138–252 was one of those most frequently illustrated by maiolica painters in the sixteenth century. Actaeon was hunting when he came upon Diana and her maidens bathing in a pool. Fearing that he might reveal to others what he had seen, the affronted goddess transformed him into a stag. Terrified, and unable to speak, he was attacked and killed by his own hounds.

The scene on this dish was derived from an etching of *Diana and Actaeon* in a series of *Landscapes with Mythological Subjects* by Antonio Tempesta (1555–1630). Tempesta went to live in Rome in 1575 and probably learned to etch there in the 1580s. One of the prints in this series bears the name of Niccolò van Aelst (active 1582–1613), so it is unlikely that the dish was made much before 1582. It is an exceptionally fine example of narrative painting in *compendiario* style, and illustrates very well the difference between this and earlier *istoriato* decoration. The design is lightly sketched and shaded in a restricted palette leaving large areas of the white background visible, whereas earlier polychrome designs covered most of the surface, which was usually very pale beige rather than white.

Large dishes decorated in this style are not common, and have only recently received the appreciation they deserve. Most of them do not bear workshop or painter's marks, and are therefore impossible to attribute securely because there were several workshops operating in Faenza in the 1580s, including Don Pino's (see no. 40). Several dishes, including this one, appear to be by the same hand, whose vigorous drapery painting caused Francesco Liverani to name him the 'Master of the Draperies'. He was probably Stefano Accarisi (active 1576, died 1626), who signed a panel of the Virgin and Saints in 1610.

Further reading Francesco Liverani, 'Figure e stemmi in maioliche compendiarie faentine', *Faenza*, 50:1–3 (1964), pp. 52–4. Rome, 1993, pp. 119–21, nos. 45–7. Francesco Liverani, 'Per Stefano Accarisi', *Faenza*, 82:1–3 (1996), pp. 61–3.

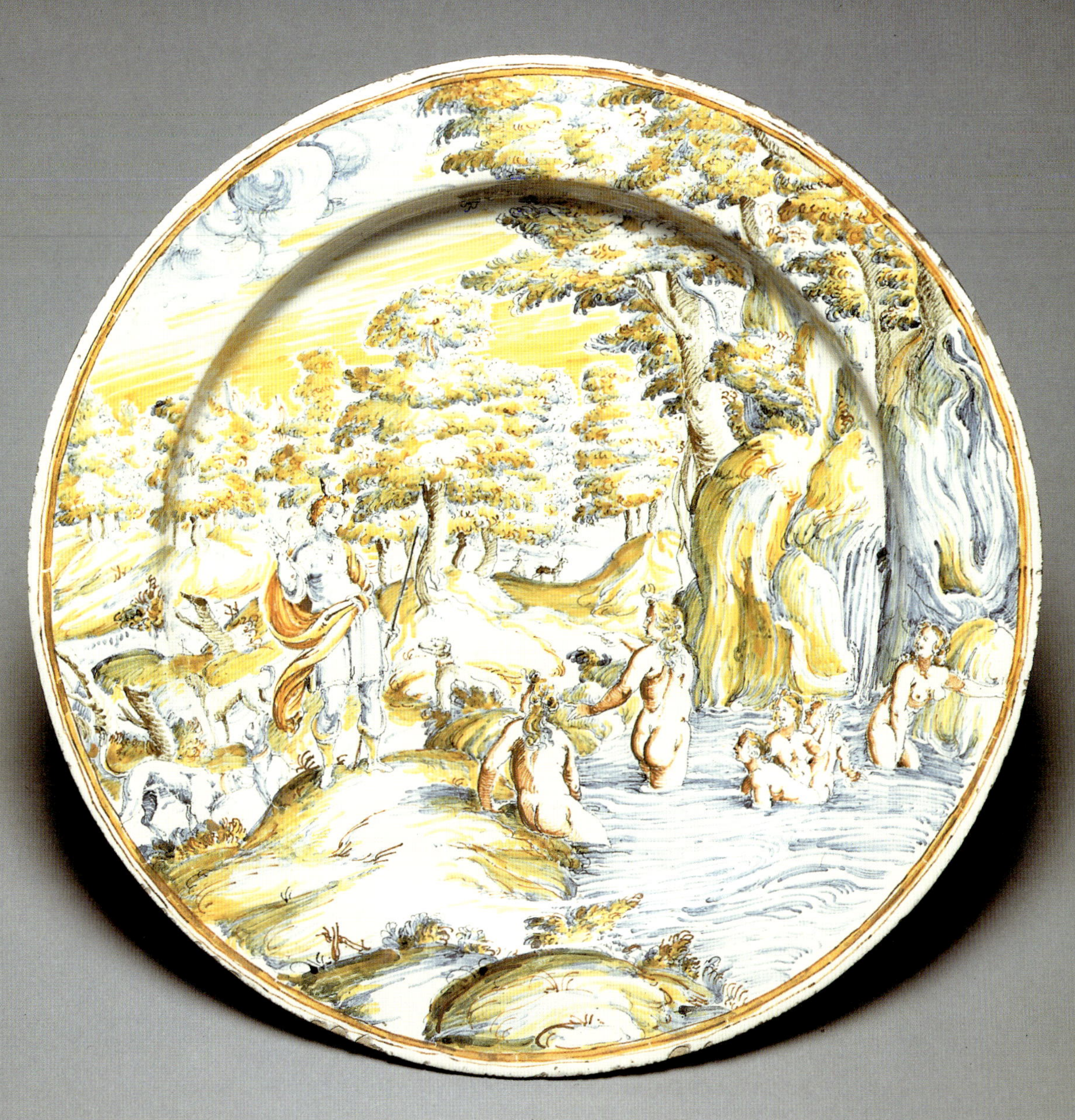

43

EWER

CASTELLI, POMPEI WORKSHOP, *c.* 1580–1600

Height 20.9 cm; width 21.3 cm.
Dr J. W. L. Glaisher Bequest. C.2338–1928.

The helmet-shaped ewer was one of several maiolica ewer forms common in the late sixteenth century, and became increasingly popular during the seventeenth. Many examples have a mask under the lip and a dolphin-shaped handle. Like other three-dimensional maiolica forms, such as candlesticks, flasks, salts, and cisterns, the helmet-shaped ewer was derived from metalwork. This example has dark blue glaze, known as *maiolica turchina*. It is usually sparsely decorated in white, or white and yellow, but a significant group of high-quality tableware is decorated in gold.

Dark blue maiolica was made in several towns in Italy, such as Faenza and Padua, but this ewer is securely attributed to Castelli because it resembles sherds found during an excavation between 1980 and 1982, of the waste heap on the hillside behind the house of the sixteenth-century potter, Orazio Pompei. Dark blue maiolica was probably made there from about 1570 as the earliest dated examples are a few plates of 1574 in the Museo di Capodimonte, and some pavement tiles of 1576 which were either made or commissioned by Annibale Pompei for the church of the Madonna della Spina near Isola del Gran Sasso.

The introduction of luxury tableware with dark blue glaze at this date is interesting, because it was then that predominantly white maiolica with *compendiario* or grotesque decoration was fast overtaking *istoriato* maiolica as the fashionable type. The high status of *maiolica turchina* is shown by its gilt ornament and by the presence of armorials on many pieces, not merely of local nobles, such as the Acquaviva of Atri, but of outstanding connoisseurs, such as Cardinal Alessandro Farnese (died 1589), whose possession of a service is documented in an inventory of his Roman *palazzo*.

Further reading Carmen Ravanelli Guidotti, 'La produzione turchina: la nascita e l'affermarsi del nuovo gusto tra manierismo e barocco', in Giorgio Baldisseri *et al.*, *Le maioliche cinquecentesche di Castelli. Una grande stagione artistica ritrovata*, Pescara, 1989, pp. 126–34.

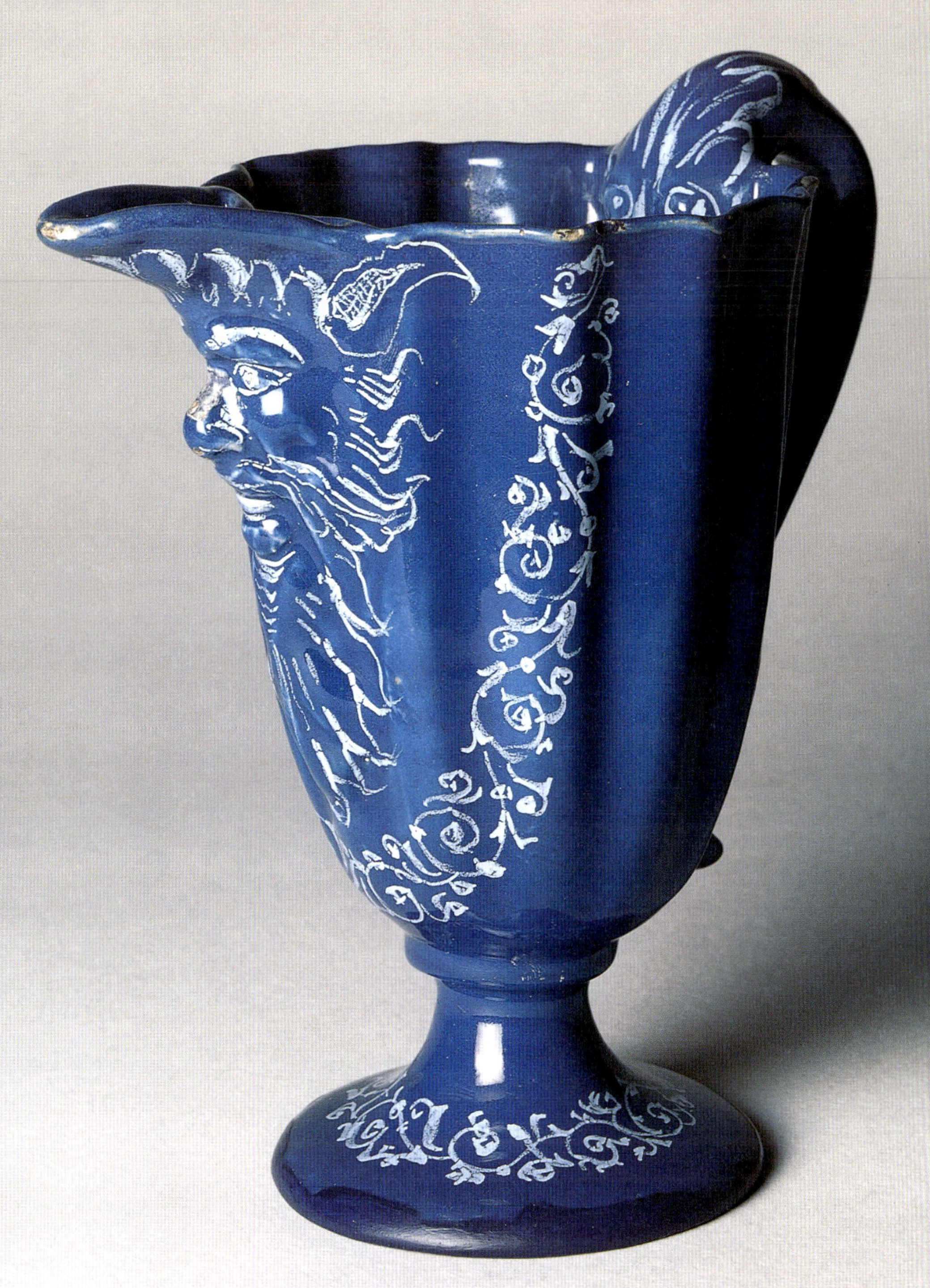

44

DISH WITH BROAD RIM: THE VIRGIN AND CHILD

URBINO, PROBABLY PATANAZZI WORKSHOP, c. 1600

Height 5.6 cm; diameter 33.4 cm.
L. C. G. Clarke Bequest, 1960. C.90–1961.

Grotesque decoration in a predominantly yellow palette on a white ground was introduced in Urbino about 1560 and continued in production until the mid seventeenth century. These ornamental designs were derived from Roman interior decoration (see no. 19), and from that in Renaissance buildings, notably the Vatican *Loggie*, designed by Raphael and executed mainly by Giovanni da Udine between 1516 and 1519. By the 1550s, this form of interior decoration was widespread and models were available to maiolica painters in the form of prints and drawings.

In the early 1560s, grotesques on a white ground appeared as borders for *istoriati*, but soon occupied much of the surface of tableware, vases, and ink-stands. Documents, including bills and inventories, and a few signed pieces indicate that the main producers in Urbino were members of the Fontana and Patanazzi families, and, in the early seventeenth century, the Grassi family.

Few pieces of maiolica of this type are dated, but some can be dated approximately because they bear armorials whose owners can be identified. The dish illustrated formed part of an armorial service of which at least five more dishes are extant; four decorated centrally with a saint and one with the coat of arms. It was probably made around 1600, because the grotesques are similar in style to those on a dish in the Louvre, bearing the arms of Cardinal Paolo Emilio Zacchia (1598–1605). The owner was a bishop who was probably a member of the Venetian Contarini family. Possible owners were Thomas Contarini, Bishop of Crete (1597–1605) and Hieronymous Contarini, Bishop of Capo d'Istria (1600–20).

Further reading Nicole Dacos, *La decouverte de la Domus Aurea et la formation des grotesques à la Renaissance*, London and Leiden, 1969. Wilson, 1987, pp. 152–6. Wilson, 1989, pp. 64–5, no. 28. Timothy Wilson, 'Maioliche del tardo Rinascimento dipinte a grottesche: nuove testimonianze della produzione di Pesaro', *Fimantiquari*, 7 (1995), pp. 33–9 (in English).

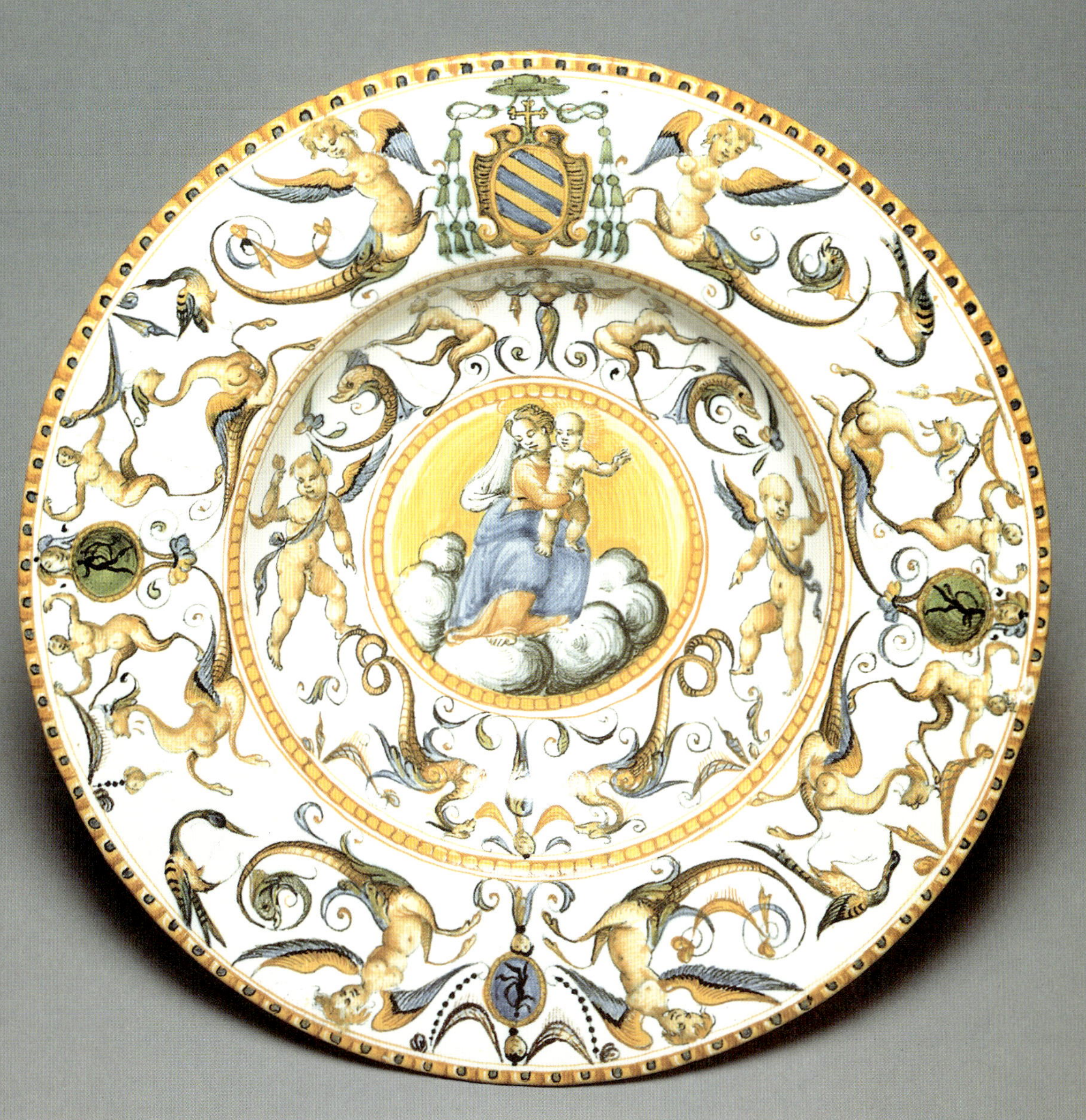

45

PLATE: A RIVER GOD

PROBABLY URBINO,

c. 1570–1600

Height 3.5 cm; diameter 26.1 cm.

H. S. Reitlinger Bequest, 1950. C.222–1991.

This unusual design was copied with minor omissions from a print by Cornelis Floris (1514–75) of Antwerp, in *Veelderly niewe inventien von antycksche sepultueren*, Book II, published by H. Cock in 1557. Its appearance on a maiolica plate is evidence for the flow of designs between northern centres of Mannerism, such as Antwerp, and Italy. The almost flat profile of the plate and its narrow footring suggest that it was not made until the last quarter of the century, when watery subjects and grotesques were fashionable as maiolica decoration. The back is simply decorated with yellow bands round the footring and outer edge.

Although Neptune is shown on the right side of the dish, the central figure can be identified as a river rather than a sea god. He holds an urn from which a river flows, and his head-dress is formed of bulrushes and perches for animals and birds. Water subjects, featuring marine deities, tritons, sea monsters, and river gods surrounded by prominent waves, were common on mannerist silver in northern Europe and Italy, and appear appropriately on maiolica water cisterns and ewer basins. The popularity of river gods in sixteenth-century art derived ultimately from their representations in Roman reliefs and from the five gigantic reclining statues in Rome.

Further reading F. W. H. Hollstein, *Dutch and Flemish Etchings, Engravings and Woodcuts 1450–1700*, VI, Amsterdam (1952), p. 250. John Shearman, *Mannerism*, London, 1967. Giacomotti, 1974, pp. 356–60, nos. 1077–80.

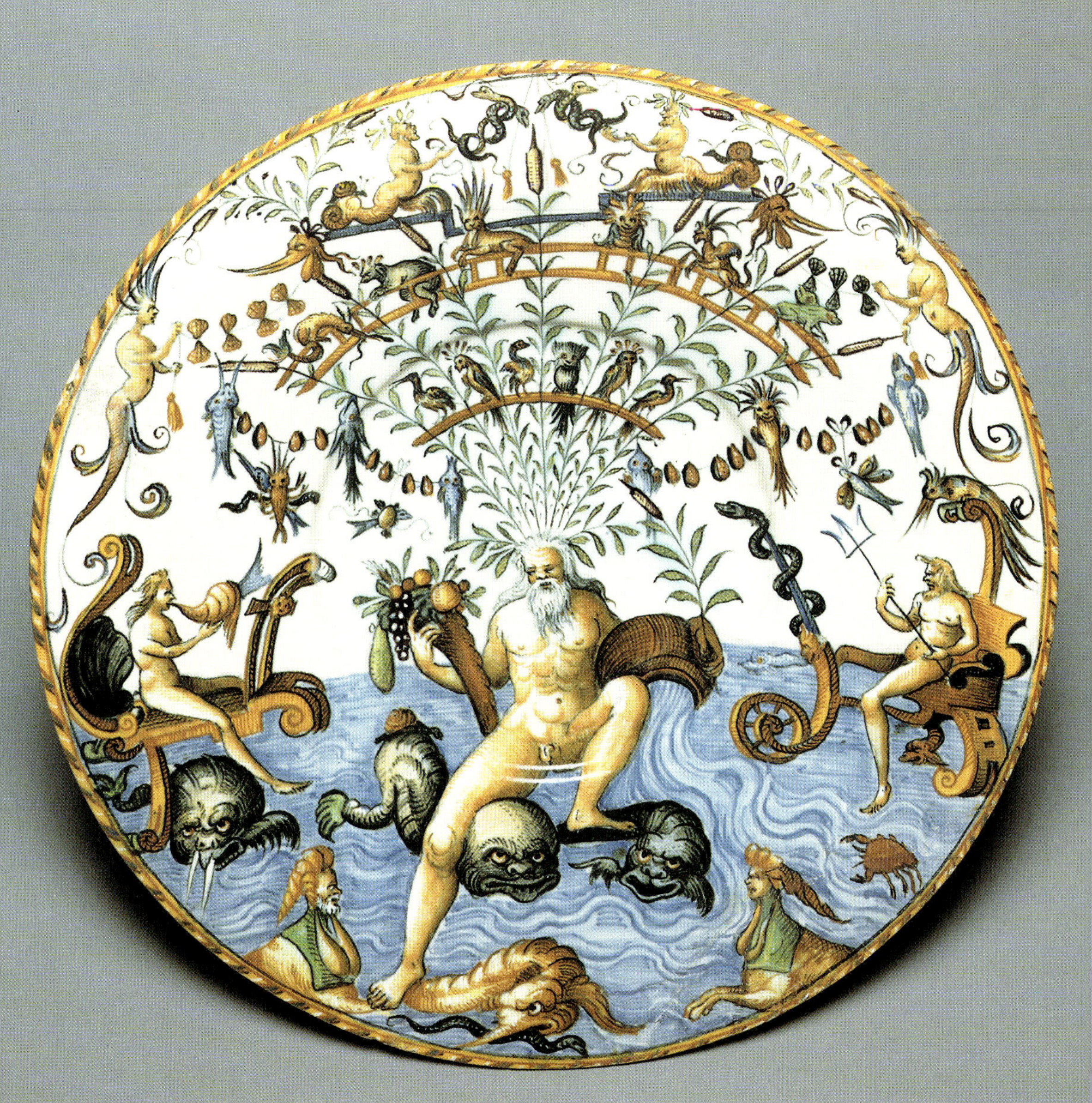

46

DISH

DERUTA, *c.* 1600–50

Height 5.6 cm; diameter 41.7 cm.
Given by Peter C. Wilson. C.4–1948.

Urbino-style grotesque decoration on a white ground was adopted in other maiolica centres in the late sixteenth and first half of the seventeenth century. These included Deruta, Montelupo, Pisa, Pesaro, Padua, and Rome. It seems to have spread partly by imitation of exported ware and partly through the movement of potters, such as Giovan Paolo Savino of Castel Durante, who signed two jars in Rome in 1600 and was back in his home town by 1609 when he signed a ewer basin (respectively in the Ashmolean Museum, Oxford and Waddesdon Manor, Buckinghamshire). As the seventeenth century progressed, the general trend was for the grotesques to become less and less like the classical and High Renaissance sources which inspired them.

It is not certain when Urbino-style grotesques were adopted in Deruta, but it seems likely to have been in the early seventeenth century. The only dated example is a ewer basin decorated with a central roundel of St Martin and dated 1644, which can be attributed to Deruta on account of its form and colouring. The identification of other Deruta grotesque decoration, which occurs *inter alia* on dishes, bowls, salts, holy water stoups, and jugs, depended on matching their forms, or the style of figure painting in medallions, with those of securely attributed pieces with different types of decoration. Among their chief characteristics is a tendency to be overcrowded, and for the individual motifs to terminate in comma-like scrolls which fill up the spaces. The dish illustrated was formerly attributed to Urbino, but the presence of these features suggests that it was made at Deruta.

Further reading Giacomotti, 1974, pp. 427–8, no. 1269; Fiocco and Gherardi,1988–9, I, pp. 144–5, 342–51, nos. 301–16.

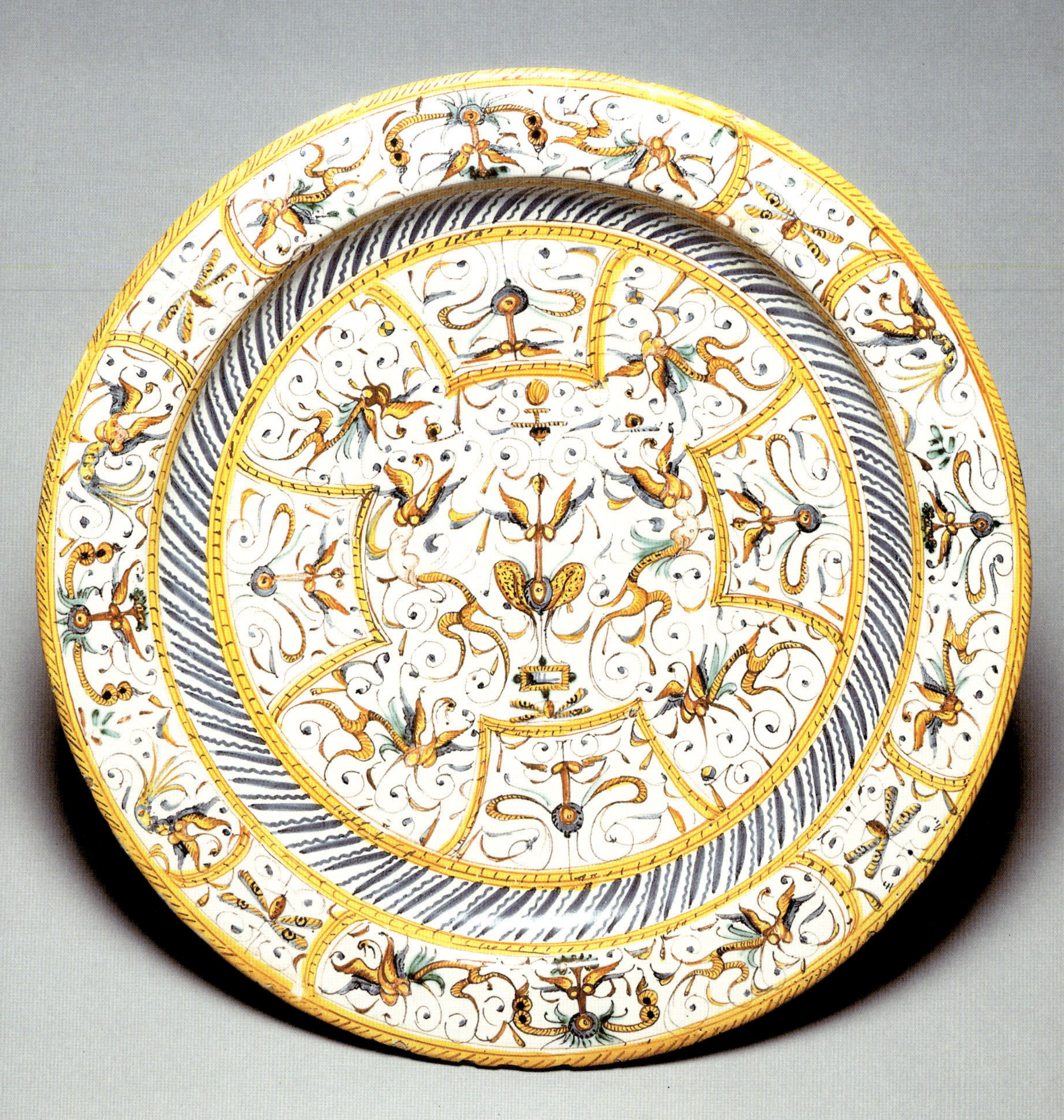

47

DISH

CASTELLI, c. 1600–20

Height 4.2 cm; diameter 39.9 cm.
H. S. Reitlinger Bequest, 1950. C.258–1991.

In the late sixteenth century the Faenza *compendiario* style and palette spread to other maiolica towns such as Deruta, Castelli, and Laterza. Castelli and Laterza also developed high-quality white glaze similar to that on *bianchi di Faenza*.

This dish was once thought to have been made in Laterza, but is now attributed to Castelli. One reason for considering that Castelli was its place of origin is that its decoration of foliage in compartments closely resembles that on a dish in the Victoria and Albert Museum, which has a central medallion containing the arms of a Visconti bishop, probably Giambatista Visconti, bishop of Teramo near Castelli (1609–38). A second reason is that the foliage resembles that on tiles decorating the ceiling of the church of San Donato at Castelli. Many of the tiles are decorated with busts of men or women, and, although none of the latter are identical to the woman in the centre of the Fitzwilliam's dish, they have comparable doll-like expressions. Some of the tiles are dated 1615 or 1616, and a date around then, or a little earlier, would be consistent with the exaggeratedly large and ornate ruff the woman is wearing. A third dish with analogous foliage and a central coat of arms is in an Italian private collection.

Further reading Rackham, 1940, I, Appendix, no. 1089B. Pasquale Calvario 'Segnalazione di un piatto datato' in *Castelli e la maiolica cinquecentesca italiana*, Atti del Convegno in Pescara, 22–25 April 1989, Pescara, 1990, pp. 240–1. Guido Donatone, Sergio Rosa, and Aleardo Rubini, *La Sistina della Maiolica*, Colledara (Teramo), 1993, pp. 45–59 (in English).

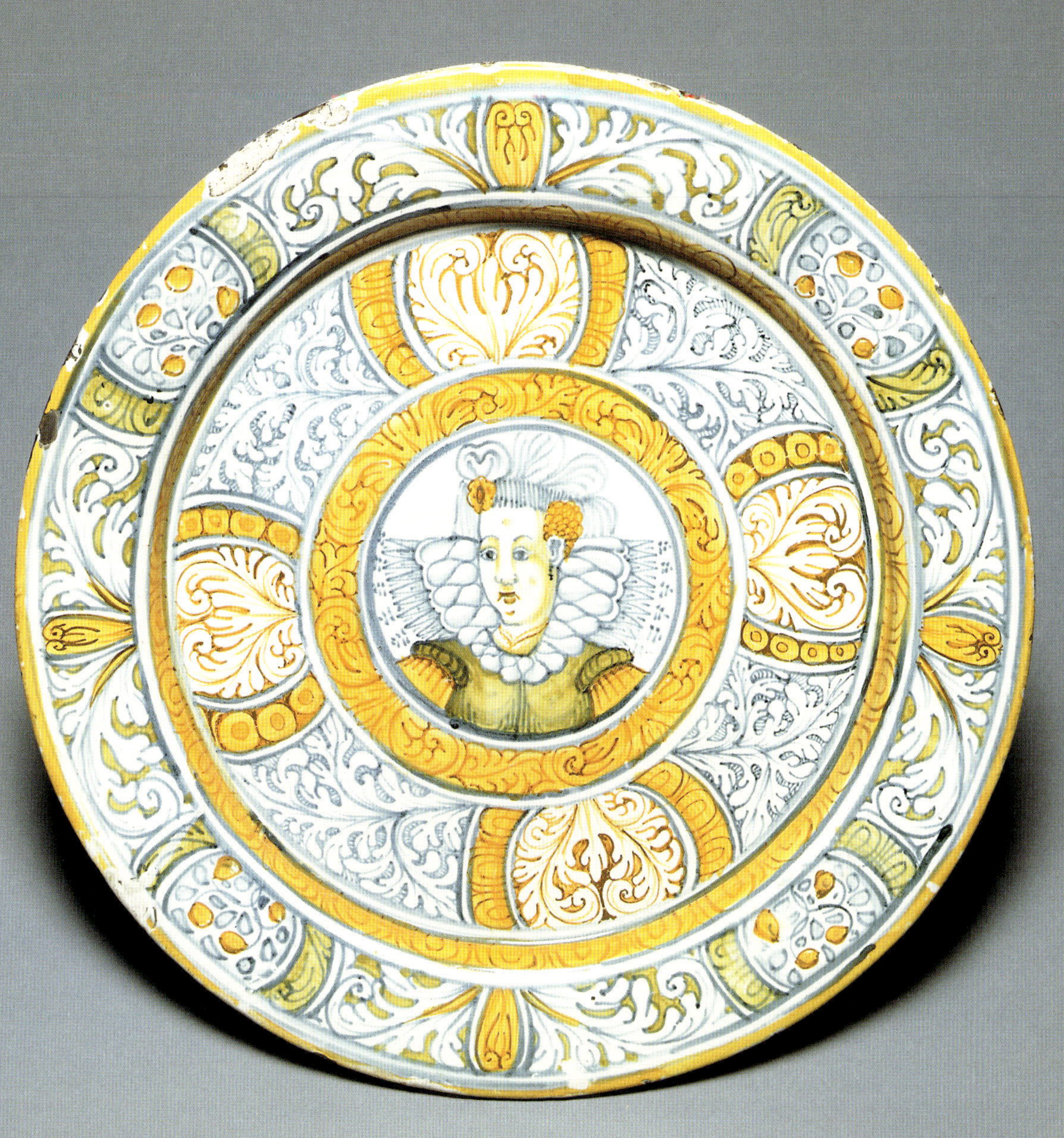

48

TWO-HANDLED JAR

LATERZA, *c.* 1630–1700

Height 30 cm; width 22.5 cm.
H. S. Reitlinger Bequest, 1950. C.259–1991.

Laterza, situated about half way between Matera and Taranto, was one of the leading maiolica centres in Apulia (Puglia). In the late sixteenth century a local historian, Geronimo Marciano, noted that it made pots 'similar to those of Faenza'. During the seventeenth and early eighteenth century its maiolica had high-quality white glaze, and much of it was painted in the *compendiario* palette, in manganese and blue, or in blue alone. Decoration included coats of arms, devotional subjects, and *istoriato* scenes, often surrounded by borders of baroque foliage, scrolls, and open fans. Many potters are recorded in Laterza, but only a few signed their work, including Lorenzo Gallo in 1652 and Angelo Antonio d'Alessandro (1642–1717), between 1678 and 1705. By the mid eighteenth century Laterza had over fifty potters, but a century later, in 1856, the number had declined to five, a sign of the impoverished economy of the area.

The political link between the Kingdom of Naples and Spain after 1503 was responsible for Spanish influence on the arts in southern Italy. The form of this jar (also made with plain handles), is comparable to examples made at Talavera and elsewhere in Spain in the seventeenth century. A smaller version intended for use as a drinking vessel can be seen in Zurburan's the *Miracle of Saint Hugh*, painted for the Charterhouse of Our Lady of the Caves at Triana, Seville, probably between 1641 and 1658.

This colour plate shows the floral pattern on the back of a Laterza jar. The lower part of the front is decorated with a medallion enclosing a woman holding a pot plant, who probably represents the Sense of Smell, and the neck with a panel containing a nereid holding up a drape.

Further reading Balbina Martinez Caviro, *Ceramica de Talavera*, 1969, pl. 19B. Guido Donatone, *La maiolica di Laterza*, Bari, 1980. Antonio and Carlo dell'Aquila, 'La maiolica dell '600 e '700 in Terra d'Otranto', *CeramicAntica*, 5:6 (June 1995), pp. 26–45.

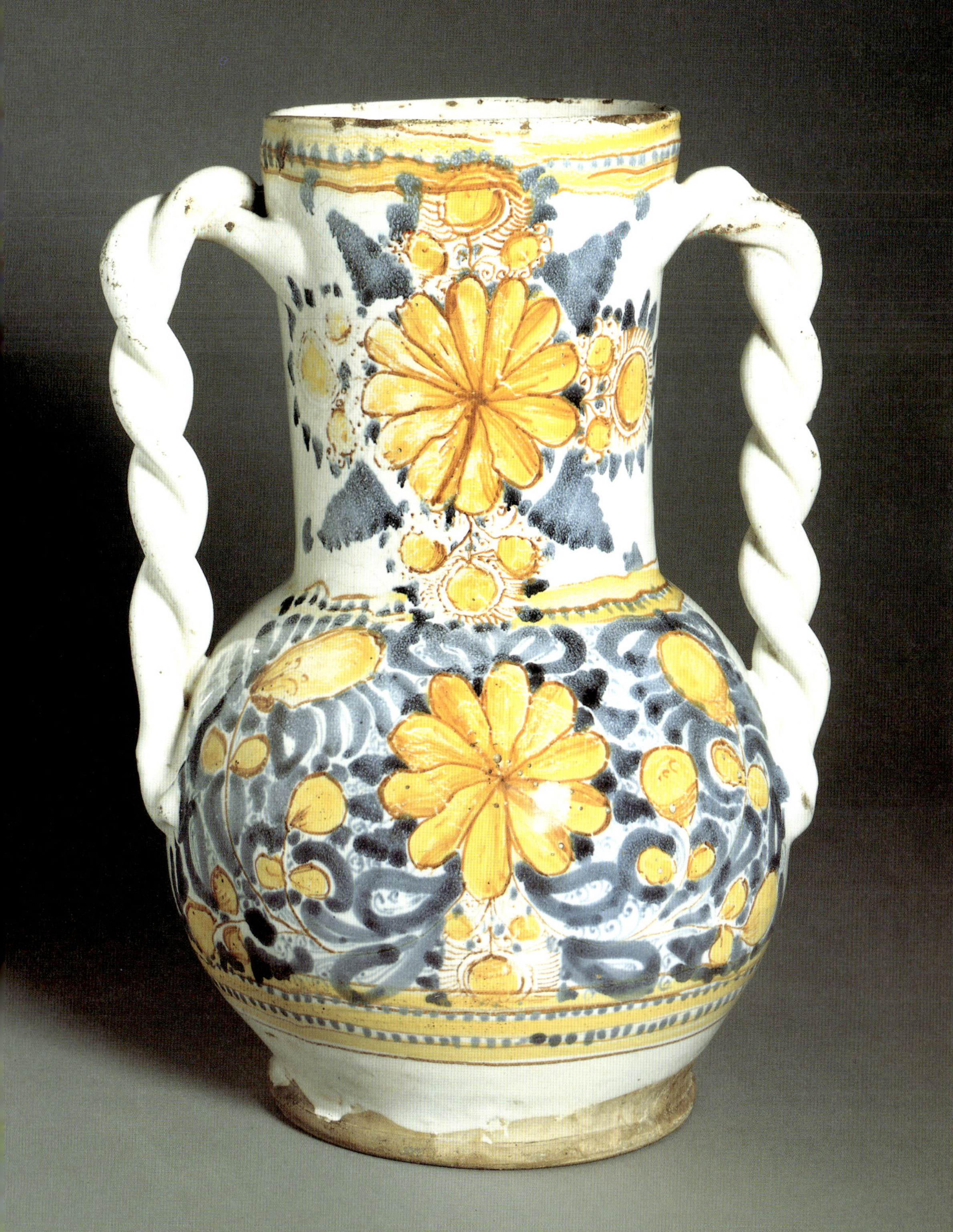

49

DISH

PROBABLY PADUA OR BASSANO,
MANARDI FACTORY, *c.* 1610–1705

Height 8.8 cm; diameter 48.8 cm.
Purchased with the Glaisher Fund. C.22–1932.

This unusually large dish is decorated in the style of Isnik pottery of about 1570–1600, which featured exuberant floral designs in blue, emerald green, black, and vivid 'sealing-wax red'. Exports of this splendid Ottoman ware to Italy must have been considerable, because it was there that many pieces were found by nineteenth-century collectors such as Charles Drury Fortnum.

Dated dishes show that maiolica influenced by this class of Isnik pottery was being made by the second decade of the seventeenth century, probably at Padua. However, the earliest dish with a large central 'saz' leaf in the design and blue squiggles on the back resembling those on the Fitzwilliam's dish, is dated 1633. This dish, now in the Musée National de Céramique at Sèvres, is inscribed 'S. Chandiana', for a nun, Suora (sister) Chandiana. The first nineteenth-century publications of that dish missed out the 'h' and consequently the whole class became known as 'Candiana ware' and was thought to come from Crete, known earlier as Candia. The latest recorded dish, in the Ca' Rezzonico, Venice, is dated 1705. Isnik decoration has also been recorded on ewers, bowls and vases.

The discovery of fragments of Isnik style maiolica including wasters, during an excavation in 1982 on the site of the Manardi factory at Bassano, indicate that it was also made there during the second half of the seventeenth century. This appears to be supported by a document of 1699 in which Giovanni Battista Salmazzo from Padua, who had worked at the Manardi factory for thirty years, and Bernardin Gollin who had worked there for twenty years, stated that they painted maiolica '*alla Turchesca*'.

Further reading Hausmann, 1972, pp. 337–8, no. 252. Nadir Stringa, *La famiglia Manardi e la ceramica a Bassano nel '600 e '700*, *Quaderni bassanesi*, 3, Bassano, 1987. Nurhan Atasoy and Julian Raby, *Iznik, the Pottery of Ottoman Turkey*, London, 1989.

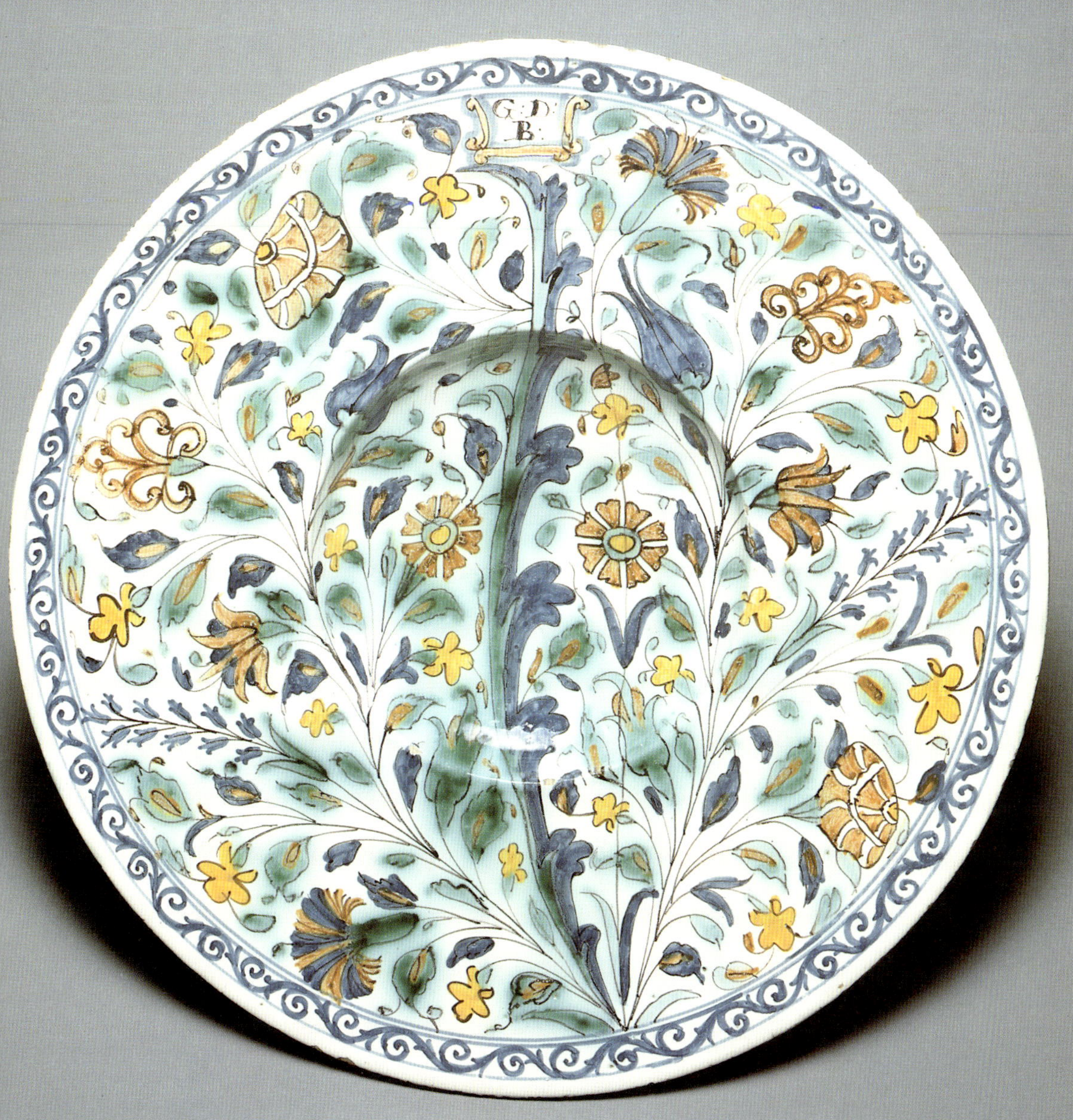
G:D:
B:

50

SQUARE BOTTLE

PROBABLY ALBISOLA *c.* 1630–1700

Marked on the base with a crown over a crossed shield.
Height 21.4 cm; width 8.8 cm.

Dr J. W. L. Glaisher Bequest. C.2229–1928.

The sides of this bottle are decorated with birds, deer, and rabbits among rocks and foliage in imitation of blue and white Chinese porcelain of the reign of Wanli (1573–1619). The first major shipments of this porcelain, captured from Portuguese vessels, had been sold in the Netherlands at Middleburg in 1602 and at Amsterdam in 1604. Two years later a consignment from Amsterdam reached Genoa. Blue and white maiolica was being made at Albisola and Savona, near Genoa, and at Turin by 1620, but the typical late-Ming style decoration known as *calligrafico naturalistico* was probably not common until the end of the decade. It was used on domestic and pharmaceutical wares throughout the rest of the seventeenth century and in the early eighteenth century, and was also adopted in Turin, Faenza, and Deruta.

Square bottles had been made in Medici porcelain and in maiolica in the late sixteenth century, but Ligurian bottles made in the seventeenth may have been influenced by Oriental examples. Square gin bottles were among the first European forms copied in porcelain by the Chinese, beginning in the reign of Tianqi (1620–7), or perhaps late in the reign of Wanli (1573–1619). In turn they were imitated in Persia, so it is difficult to determine whether maiolica bottles were influenced by Chinese or by Persian examples, exported when Chinese porcelain became scarce after the end of the Ming dynasty in 1644.

The crowned crossed shield mark, adopted from the arms of Genoa, occurs on maiolica attributed to Albisola in the second half of the seventeenth century. It is also thought to have been used at the pottery founded by the Ligurians, Giovanni Giacomo Bianchi, and Nicolò Corrado, at Reggio Parco, Turin, who operated it from 1646 to 1657, when Bianchi gave up the privilege and it was transferred to Enrico La Rivière.

Further reading Federico Marzinot, *Ceramica e ceramisti di Liguria*, Genoa. 1979. Arrigo Cameirana, *Ceramica in banca, 50 maioliche liguri della Cassa di Risparmio di Genova e Imperia*, exhibition catalogue, Albisola, 1989, pp. 21–4.

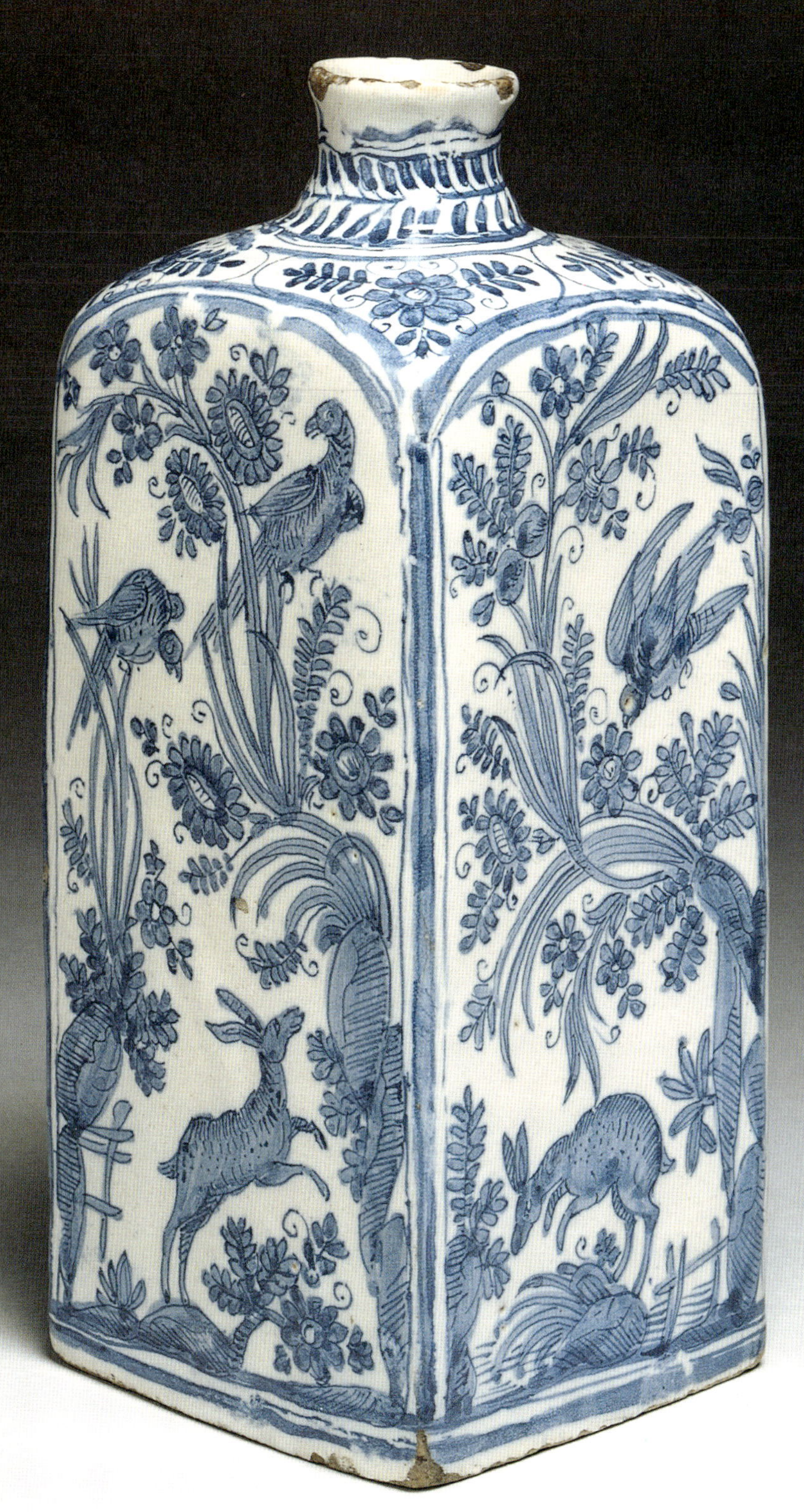

51

DEVOTIONAL PANEL: THE VIRGIN AND CHILD

DERUTA, SEVENTEENTH CENTURY

Height 46.5 cm; width 37 cm; depth 3 cm.
Dr J. W. L. Glaisher Bequest. C.2200–1928.

Maiolica associated with popular religious practices was made throughout Italy and painted panels and reliefs of religious subjects survive in large numbers. The most common are of the Virgin, the Virgin and Child, and well-loved saints, whose intervention was invoked to mitigate the hardships of daily life, or to intercede on a sinner's behalf. In the home, maiolica panels were an alternative to more expensive religious paintings and relief sculpture, and were hung up by suspension holes, or framed and secured to the wall. When displayed out of doors, they had a protective function and provided a focus for the prayers of passers-by. Many were built into walls over entrances and at street corners. Others were set over well heads and fountains or in small tabernacles alongside roads or in the fields.

Panels moulded in relief with this Virgin and Child were made mainly in Deruta. The image derived from a marble relief by Benedetto da Maiano (1442–97), formerly in the Orléans collection at Bologna and now in New York. Its location in the seventeenth century is not known, and it seems likely that the immediate prototype was a plaster cast. Some of the maiolica panels have a cherub's head under the Virgin's left elbow, a feature which appears in a painted plaster relief attributed to Benedetto da Maiano in the Sculpture Gallery at Berlin.

Variations in the moulding, colouring, and quality of the maiolica reliefs, suggest that they were made over a long period, as does their survival in large numbers in Italy and in museums elsewhere in Europe and North America. The only dated example known, in the Bowes Museum at Barnard Castle, is atypical in having a panel at the bottom bearing two coats of arms and the date 25 February 1633.

Further reading Maria Cecchetti, 'Il catalogo delle targhe devozionali al Museo di Faenza', *Faenza*, 68:5–6 (1982), pp. 328–32. Maria Cecchetti, *Targhe devozionali dell' Emilia Romagna*, MICF, Milan, 1984. Fiocco and Gherardi, 1988–9, I, pp. 328–9, nos. 278–9.

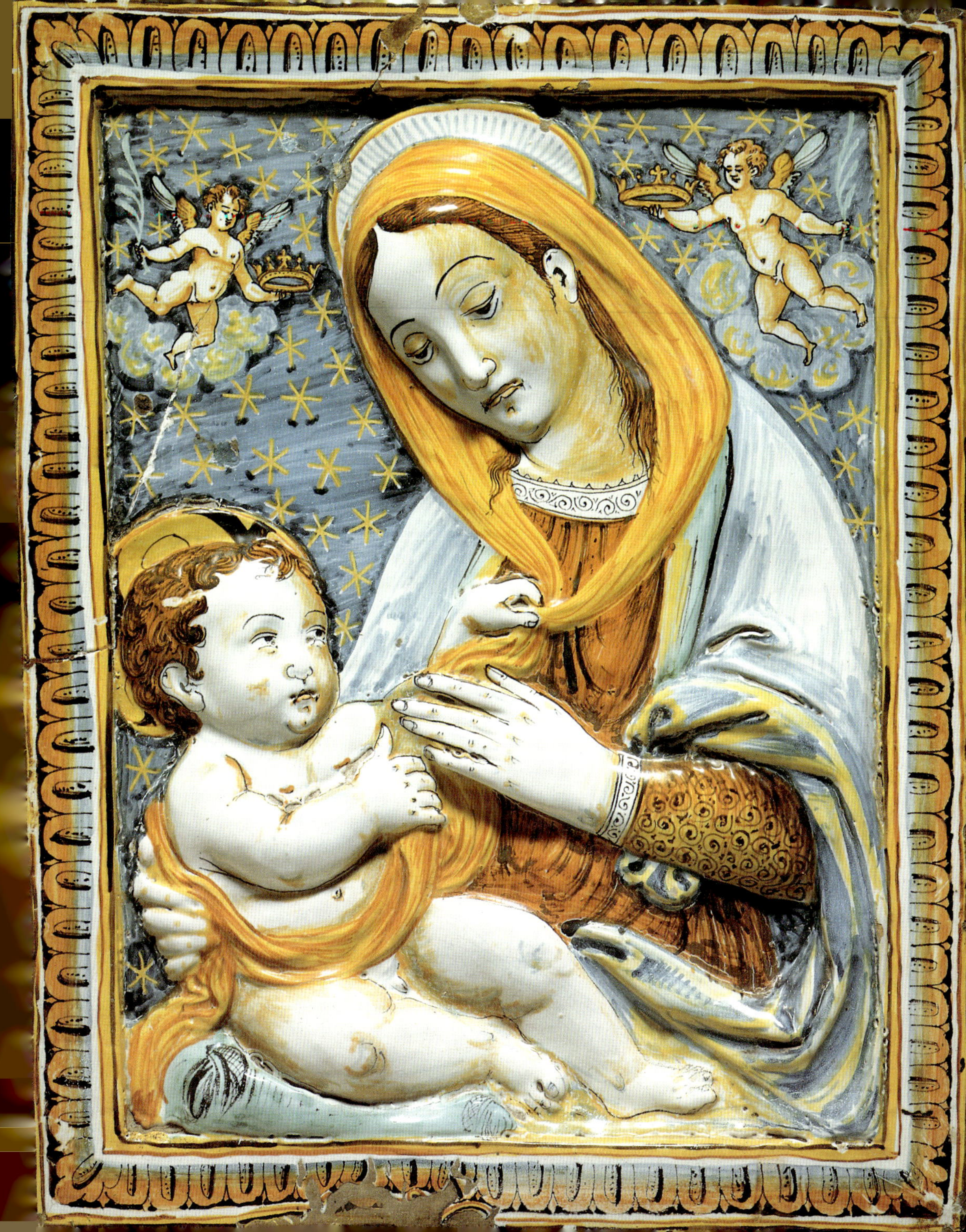

52

DEVOTIONAL PANEL: THE VIRGIN AND CHILD

PROBABLY CARPI, c. 1600–50

Height 38.3 cm; width 25.1 cm; depth 5.6 cm.
Dr J. W. L. Glaisher Bequest. C.1789–1928.

Incised slipware (*ceramica graffita*) was made in much of northern Italy by the beginning of the fourteenth century. Its production was at its peak in the second half of the fifteenth and sixteenth centuries and continued during the seventeenth and eighteenth centuries, but in gradually decreasing quantity and quality.

The technique involved coating the thrown or moulded clay object with white slip, through which the decoration was incised to reveal the reddish-brown body below. Alternatively the slip could be cut away from the background. After this the pots were fired for the first time and emerged from the kiln as 'biscuit'. The design was coloured in pigments derived from metallic oxides which produced green, brownish-yellow, brownish-purple, and, less commonly, greyish-blue. A translucent lead glaze was applied, and the pots were fired for the second time. During firing the colours often ran into the yellowish glaze, producing random variegated effects.

This moulded tabernacle enclosing the Virgin and Child is typical of devotional panels made in the region of Carpi and Modena. The letters 'IHS', at the top were a Latin transcription of the first three letters of the name 'Jesus' in Greek, but were also commonly misunderstood as standing for *Iesus Hominum Salvator* (Jesus Saviour of Mankind). A comparable panel is in the Museo Civico, Carpi. The image, also found on maiolica panels, probably derived from a late fifteenth-century Emilian or Lombard relief in terracotta or cartapesta, such as one made of the latter in the Victoria and Albert Museum.

Further reading Giovanni L. Reggi, *La ceramica graffita in Emilia-Romagna dal secolo xiv al secolo XIX*, Modena, 1971. Giovanni L. Reggi, *Ceramica a Carpi dal XV al XVIII secolo nelle civiche Collezioni*, Carpi, 1981, p. 85, no. 215. Maria Cecchetti, *Targhe Devozionali dell' Emilia Romagna*, Milan, 1984, pp. 148–9, no. 12.

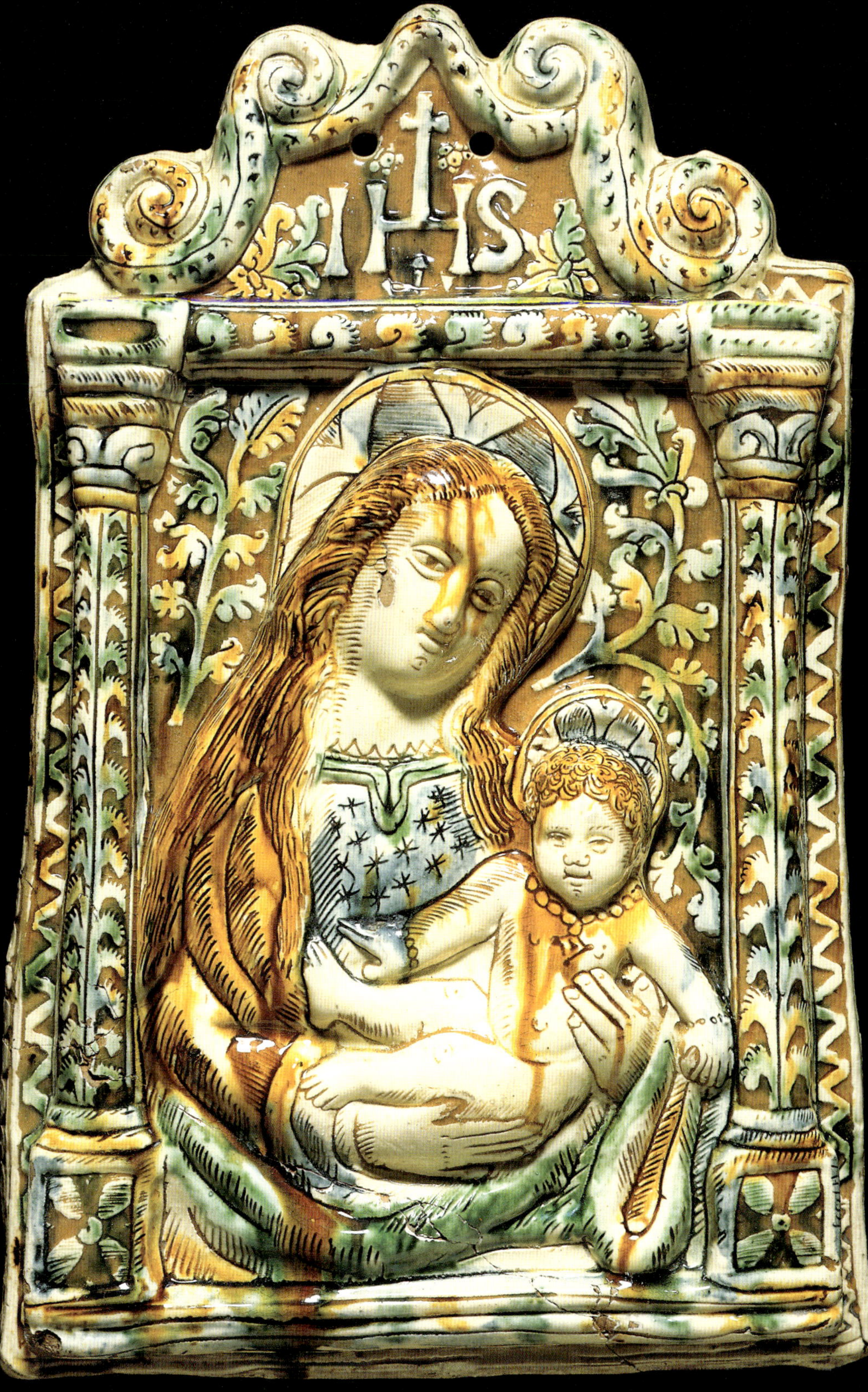
IHS

53

DISH: THE ENTOMBMENT OF CHRIST

URBANIA, PAINTED BY IPPOLITO ROMBALDONI (1619–79), *c.* 1670–9

Marked on the base in brown, HR in cursive monogram.
Height 6.2 cm; diameter 28.6 cm. H. S. Reitlinger Bequest, 1950. C.231–1991.

Castel Durante was renamed Urbania in honour of Urban VIII, whose birthplace it was, after he was elected to the papacy in 1635. The great period of *istoriato* maiolica painting was over by then, but during the 1660s and 1670s some fine decoration in baroque style was executed by Ippolito Rombaldoni (1619–79). Rombaldoni is known to have lived in Urbania from documents which mention his participation in local government and his activity as a painter, which was probably his main occupation, as he is not referred to as a potter. His residence there is also recorded on two pieces of maiolica: a large vase decorated with figures of Innocence and Discretion and signed 'Hipolito Rom(ba)ldotti d'Urbania pinse 1678', in the MICF, and a dish decorated with the *Triumph of Flora* signed 'Hipollito Rombaldotti / Pinse in Urbania', in the Louvre. Usually, however, he spelled the end of his name 'oni', for example, on a panel decorated with the *Virgin and Child in a landscape* signed 'HIPPOLITO ROMBALDONI PINSE 1670' in the British Museum, and a panel of the *Virgin of the Snow* after Federico Barocci (1535–1612), signed 'HIPOLLITVS/ ROMBALDONVS / PINCHSIT / 1670' in the Diocesan Museum, Urbania. On most of his other signed work, he used the monogram HR in script or Roman capitals.

This dish, like most of Rombaldoni's, stands on a low foot and is rather unevenly glazed on the reverse. The design was derived, probably by means of a drawing, from either an *Entombment* by Lodovico Carracci (1555–1619) now belonging to the Bavarian state collection, or from a painting after it by Lorenzo Garbieri (1580–1654) for the church of Sant'Antonio dei Teatini in Milan.

Further reading Bologna, *Maestri della pittura del Seicento Emiliano*, exhibition catalogue, Bologna, 1952, pp. 20–1, no. 2 and p. 104, no. 44. Ravanelli Guidotti, 1985, pp. 230–5, nos. 188–91. Don Corrado Leonardi, 'Un Maestro dell'istoriato secentesco: Ippolito Rombaldoni', *CeramicAntica*, 5:3 (March 1995), pp. 56–61.

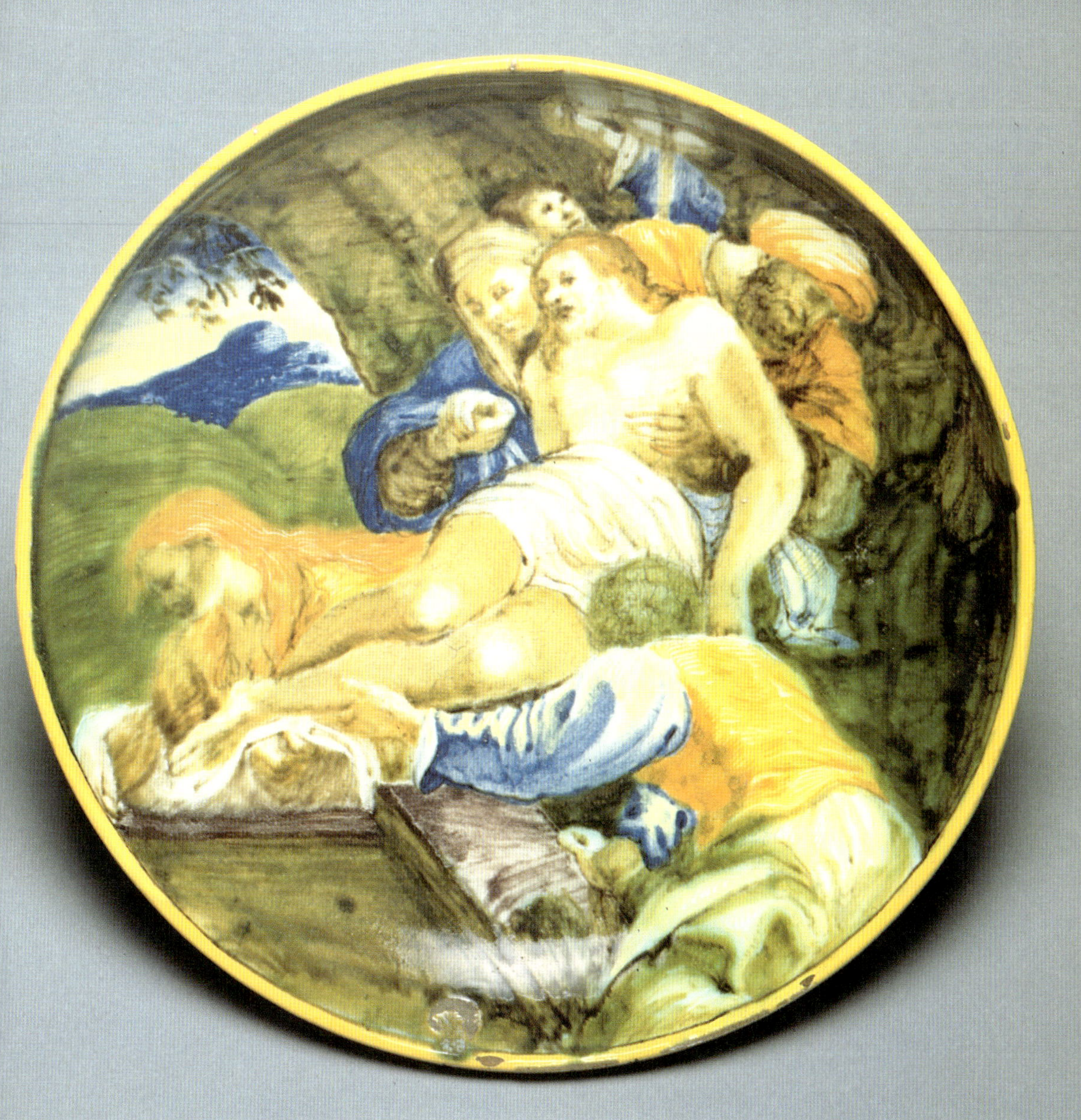

54

PLATE

NORTHERN ITALY, PROBABLY LOMBARDY, c. 1660–1720

On the back in manganese, five stylized plants and a mark, AF, attached to the shank of a grapnel. Height 2.1 cm; diameter 25.6 cm. H. S. Reitlinger Bequest, 1950. C.251–1991.

This plate belongs to a class of maiolica which includes tableware, vases, and ornamental panels, decorated with landscapes and figures dominated by the ruins of massive Roman architecture. Some pieces have large mythological figures in the foreground, and others have borders decorated in relief with scrolling foliage or flowers resembling those on seventeenth-century baroque silver. They can be linked to one centre and probably to one factory by the manganese marks on their backs. Many of them have either AF attached to the shank of a grapnel, or AF joined below two palms flanking a crown over a Maltese cross; others have monograms of JG or GR, CGR or GCR.

Most scholars are agreed that this group came from northern Italy, but so far neither documentary nor archaeological evidence has been found to identify the town or factory conclusively. Costantino Baroni considered that the mark stood for Fabbrica Angarano, and that the group were made at the Manardi factory, then thought to be at Angarano in the Veneto, but now known to have been situated in nearby Bassano. However, an excavation on the site and study of documents relating to the factory have not confirmed that attribution. A more recent suggestion is that they were made at Pavia in Lombardy in the factory of Carlo Giuseppe Rampini. *Rampino* means hook or grapnel, so, if correct, this attribution explains the mark.

Further reading Costantino Baroni, 'La disputa dei "latesini" nella storia della ceramica italiana', *Dedalo*, 13 (March 1933), pp. 147–74. Nadir Stringa, *La famiglia Manardi e la ceramica a Bassano nel '600 e '700*, *Quaderni bassanesi*, 3, Bassano, 1987. Elena Pelizzoni, 'Sono di fornaci lombarde le maioliche attribuite ad Angarano', *Rassegna di Studi e di Notizie* (Castello Sforzesco, Milan), 17 (1993), pp. 195–9. Luciano Rizzi, 'Sul problema attributivo di grande attualità, Angarano, Pavia o Bassano?', *CeramicAntica*, 4:8, (September 1994), pp. 36–43.

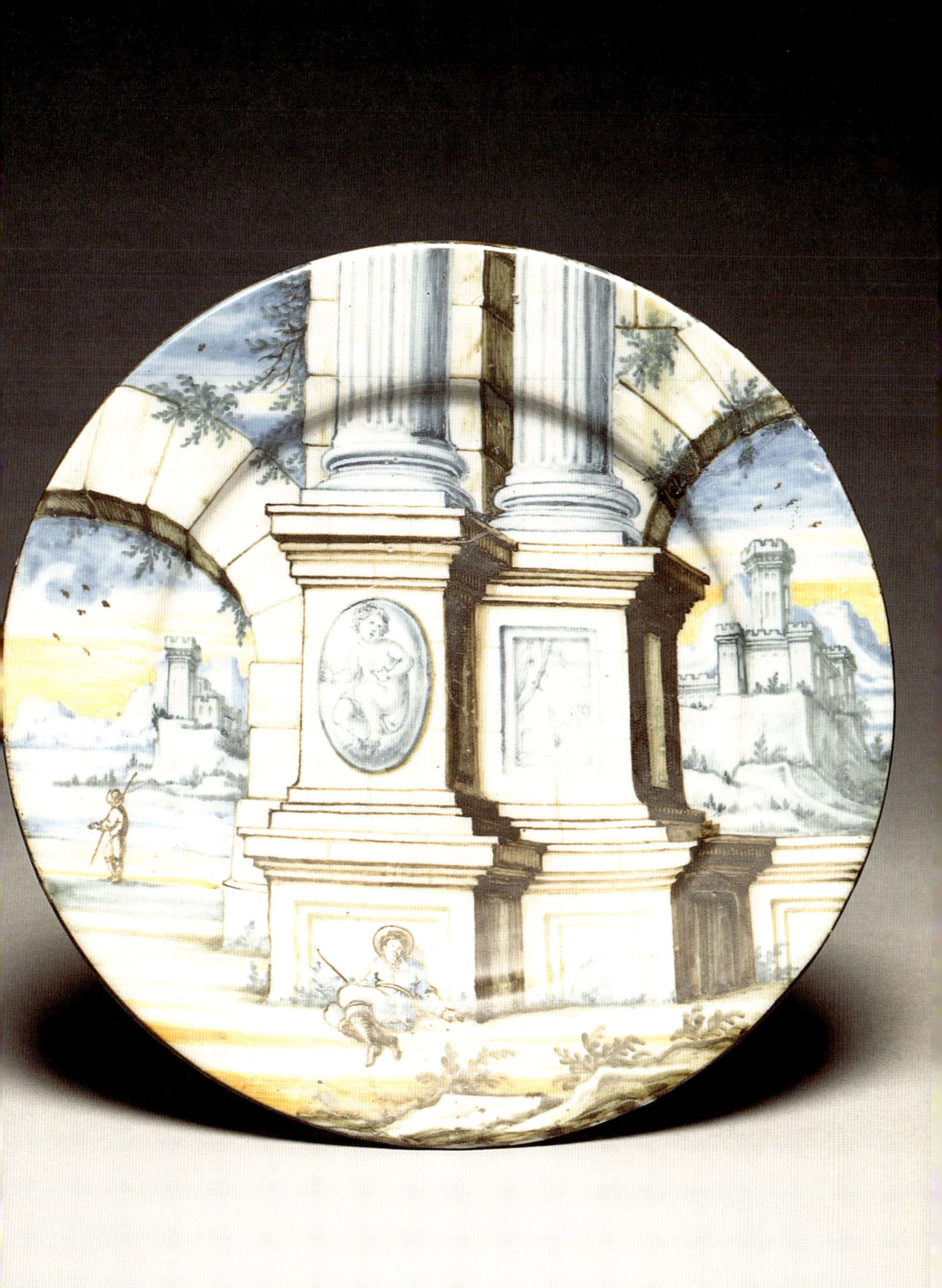

55

EWER

FAENZA, c. 1680–1720

Height 20.5 cm; width 22.5 cm.
Dr J. W. L. Glaisher Bequest. C.2216–1928.

Bianchi di Faenza continued to be made throughout the seventeenth and early eighteenth century. Much of it was moulded to resemble embossed metalwork and was sparsely decorated mainly in blue, with coats of arms, scattered motifs, and narrow borders. In the early eighteenth century, French faïence painted in the style of Jean Berain (1637–1711) was influential and resulted in more elaborate designs made up of strapwork, diapered panels, scrolls, masks, and vases.

This ewer is decorated with a common type of narrow running border, described as *a peducci* (pedestals). In reality the small repeated motifs do not always resemble pedestals, but are made up of small half scrolls, scallops, and pendants of small leaves or dots. The ewer is difficult to date precisely. The form was probably derived from a mid seventeenth-century silver ewer, and would have been old-fashioned in the early eighteenth century, but *a peducci* decoration continued well into that century. Vessels decorated in this manner are shown in the *Last Supper* by Michele Marchetti and Sebastiano Canavari, painted in 1751 for the monastery of Santa Chiara in Faenza.

Further reading Ravanelli Guidotti, 1985, pp. 264–6, nos. 229–30. Gian Carlo Bojani and Carmen Ravanelli Guidotti, *Ceramica di Faenza. Selezione di opere dal Medioevo al XX secolo*, 1992, pp. 55, 57, nos. 49, 51–2.

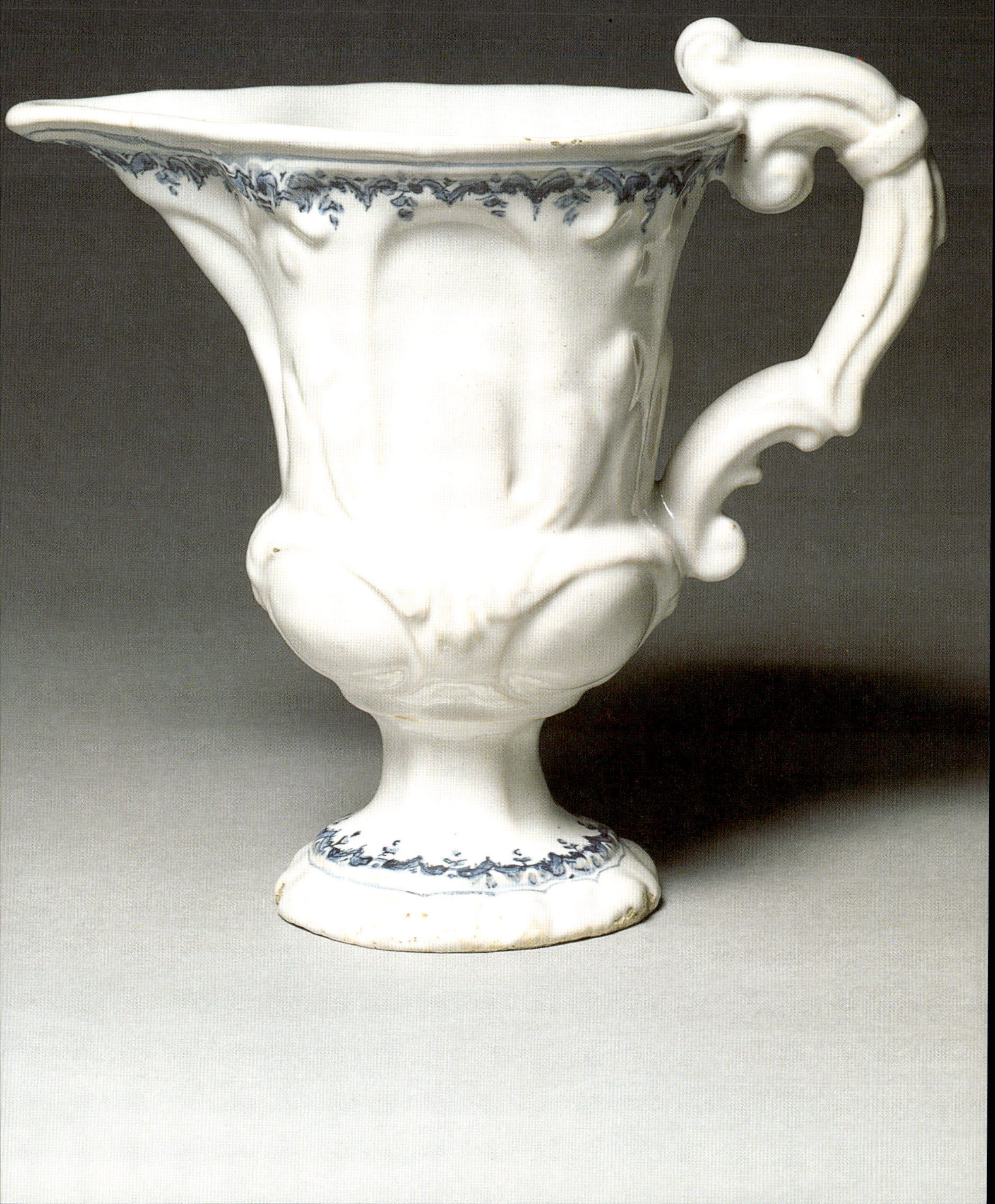

56

DISH

SIENA OR BASSANO DI SUTRI, C. 1730–45

Height 4.5 cm; diameter 31.4 cm.
H. S. *Reitlinger Bequest*, 1950. C.197–1991.

A revival of *istoriato* painting on maiolica took place in a small factory at San Quirico d'Orcia near Siena at the end of the second decade of the eighteenth century. The leading painter was Bartholomeo Terchi who was born at Trastevere in Rome in 1686 or 1691 and was employed in San Quirico from about 1717 to 1724. By 1725 he was established in Siena, where he remained until 1735 when he moved to Bassano di Sutri in Lazio. He returned to Rome in 1753 and died between 1767 and 1768. During the period that Terchi was at Siena he worked in close proximity to Ferdinando Maria Campani (1702–71), a talented portrait painter who had turned to maiolica decoration and signed work between 1733 and 1749.

The subject-matter and style of maiolica by these painters is very alike, and, although they both signed panels and dishes which can be used for comparison, it is difficult to differentiate their work. They both painted mythological and biblical scenes derived from engravings after artists such as Raphael and Agostino Carracci, and pastoral scenes after Bassano. This dish used to be attributed to Ferdinando Maria Campani, but is almost identical to one in an Italian private collection which was attributed to Terchi in the first work cited below.

Further reading Elena Pelizzoni and Giovanna Zanchi, *La maiolica dei Terchi*, Florence, 1982, see p. 69, no. 54. Carmen Ravanelli Guidotti, *Monte dei Paschi di Siena, Collezione Chigi Saracini 5, Maioliche italiane*, Florence, 1992, pp. 31–43, pp. 247–306, nos. 60–81. Curnow, 1992, pp. 85–7, nos. 101–3.

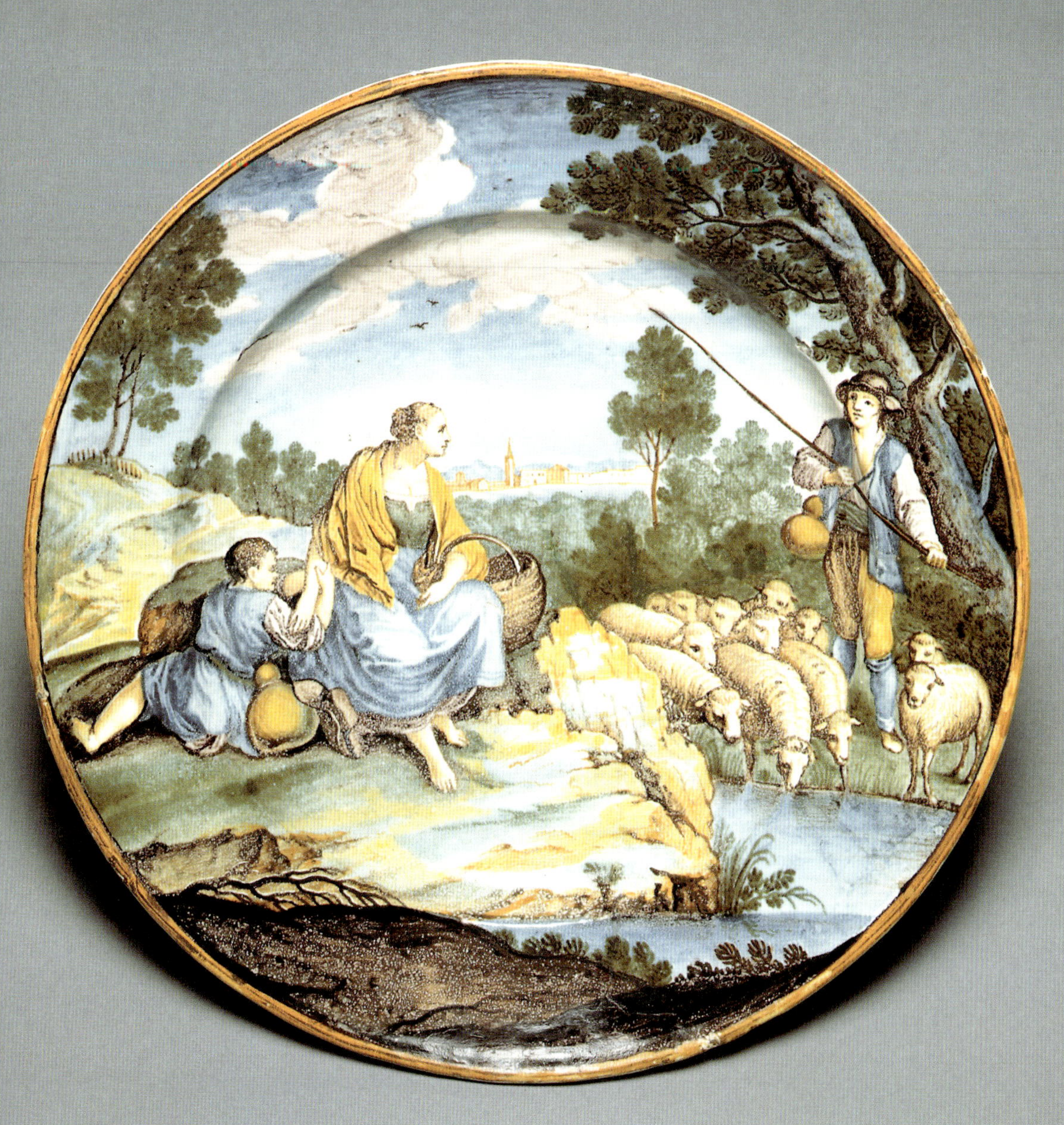

57

PILGRIM'S SOUVENIR BOWL

PROBABLY MADE IN THE MARCHES, PERHAPS IN THE LORETO AREA, EIGHTEENTH OR NINETEENTH CENTURY

Height 3.9 cm; diameter 10.9 cm.
Dr J. W. L. Glaisher Bequest. C.2244–1928.

According to the legend, related *c.* 1470 by Pietro Giorgio di Teramo, in 1291 the Virgin Mary's home at Nazareth was saved from the Infidels by angels who transported it to Yugoslavia. In 1294 they moved it again to a forest near Recanati in the Marches and, after yet another move, it finally came to rest inland at Loreto about 1295. Loreto developed into an important pilgrimage centre and a great church, completed in 1500, was built around the 'house' which was encased in a marble shrine in the early sixteenth century. In addition to the Holy House, pilgrims came to venerate a statue of the Virgin and the Holy Bowl said to have been used by her.

Souvenir bowls for pilgrims bear the words 'CON POL DI S CASA' (con polvere di Santa Casa), referring to the adding of dust from the sweeping of the Holy House to the clay from which they were made. Bowls like this one are fairly common. The scene inside was probably copied from a woodcut on one of the printed attestations, which pilgrims acquired as evidence of their visit to the shrine. The Virgin is shown wearing a stiff robe similar to that worn by the famous statue, and stands in front of the church of the Santa Casa. Another common design is painted in baroque style, mainly in blue and yellow. The origin of most of these bowls is uncertain. Some can be attributed to Castelli, and it seems likely that the others were made near Loreto, or elsewhere in the Marches.

Further reading Floriano Grimaldi, *Musei d'Italia, Meraviglie d'Italia, Loreto Palazzo Apostolico*, Bologna, 1977. Curnow, 1992, p. 92, nos. 113–14. Wilson, 1989, pp. 74–5, no. 33.

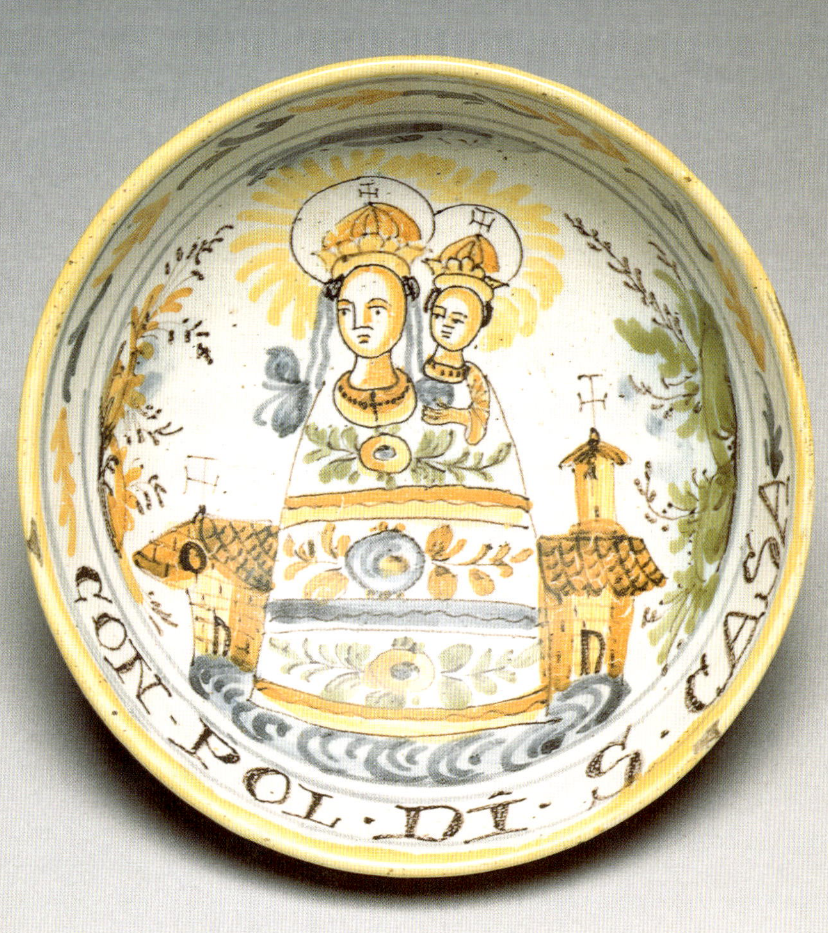
CON·POL·DI·S·CASA

58

TEA POT

PESARO, PROBABLY GIUSEPPE BARTOLUCCI'S FACTORY, *c.* 1757–62, OR CASALI AND CALIGARI, SHORTLY AFTER

Height 21.5 cm; width 22.8 cm.
Given by Lady St John Hope. C.3–1949.

Fluted silver tea and coffee pots were fashionable in the mid eighteenth century, and maiolica forms were derived from them, although maiolica is not a medium which stands up to hot liquids very well. The attribution of this teapot is not entirely certain, but its decoration suggests that it was made in the factory founded in Pesaro in October 1757 by Giuseppe Bartolucci (d. 1800) of Urbania, in partnership with a financier, Francesco Fattori. The earliest documentary piece from the factory is a dish on a foot (*alzata*) inscribed 'F.B/Pesaro/1758', in the MICF. The duration of the partnership had been set at nine years, but in 1762 Bartolucci returned to Urbania and the workshop at Pesaro was taken over a year later by Casali and Callegari.

The sketchy foliage and tiny landscapes with buildings on this pot are similar in style to those on an oval dish in the Victoria and Albert Museum, a plate in the MICF, and a cruet and vinegar bottle in a private collection, which are marked 'Pesaro 1760'. The fluted form, though more extreme, is comparable to a coffee pot in the Museo Civico, Pesaro. These designs, which sometimes include figures, appear to have been derived from etchings by Jacques Callot (1592–1635). Decoration of this type also occurs on maiolica attributed to Imola near Faenza, and to Albisola and Savona (see no. 59).

Further reading Grazia Biscontini Ugolini, 'Giuseppe Bartolucci e la rinascita della maiolica nel settecento a Pesaro', *Faenza*, 68:1–2, pp. 36–41 and pls. IXd–XII. Grazia Biscontini Ugolini, *Ceramiche pesaresi dal XVIII al XX secolo*, MICF, Bologna, 1986, pp. 30–2, figs. 2–3, pp. 50–1, no. 250.

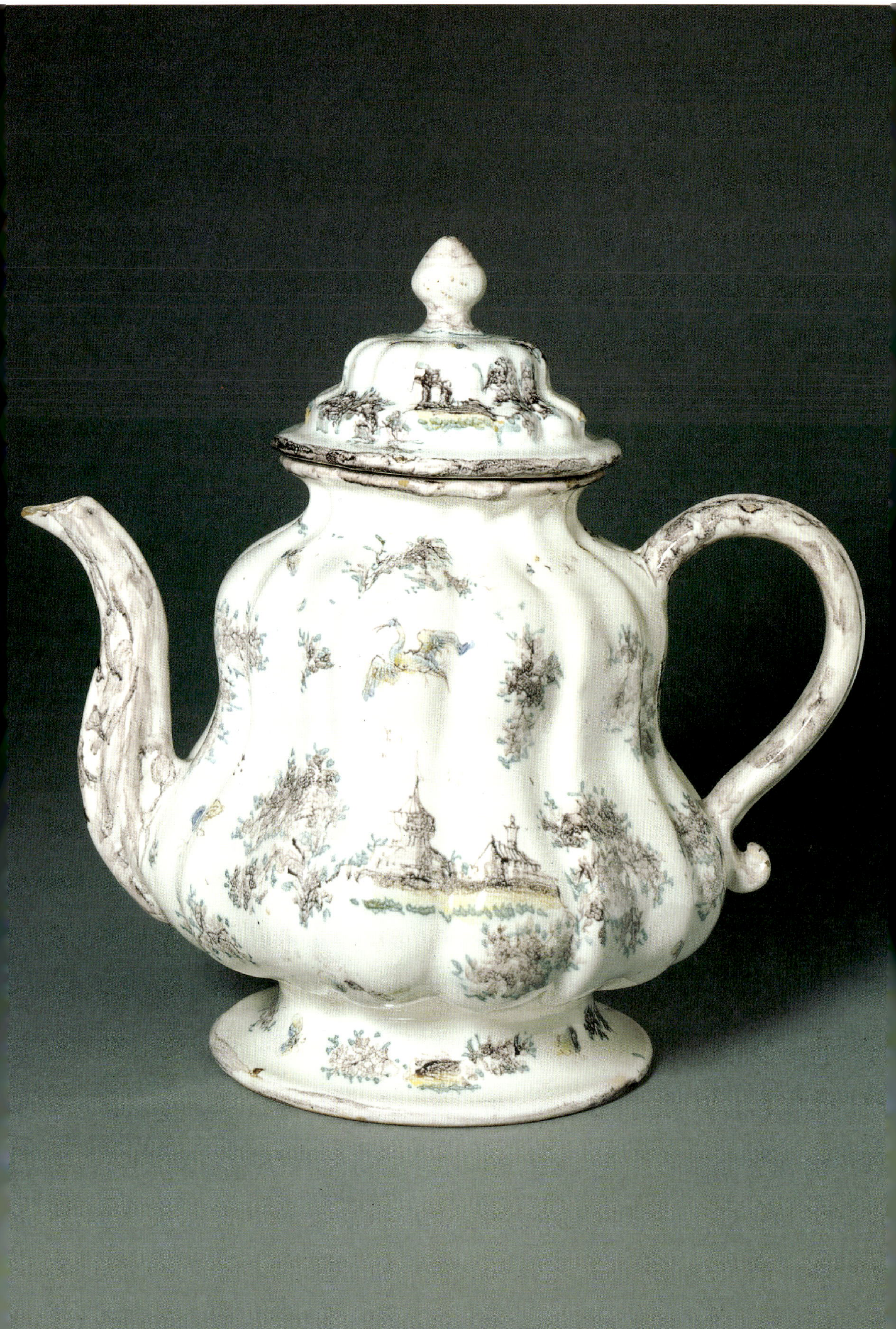

59

PUNCH BOWL

PROBABLY SAVONA, *c.* 1740–80

Height 27.7 cm; rim diameter 47.8 cm
Given by Mrs W. D. (Frances) Dickson. C.79–1950.

Italian maiolica punch bowls are very uncommon, and this is an exceptionally large example. The name 'O FARIELL', written across the centre of the inside, resembles the Irish name O' Farrell, and suggests that the owner was Irish, as was the donor. Possibly it was commissioned by someone on the Grand Tour, or a naval officer calling at the port of Genoa which was the nearest large city to Savona.

The exterior is decorated on one side with Pluto carrying off Proserpine to the Underworld in his chariot, and, on the other, Proserpine is shown seated with her hands tied behind her back, attended by two putti, one of whom holds a fruit, probably a pomegranate. Ceres, the mother of the goddess, pleaded with Jove for her release, and he eventually agreed that she could return to earth if she had not eaten anything in the Underworld. Unfortunately Proserpine had eaten seven pomegranate seeds, but, to please Ceres, Jove agreed that Proserpine should spend half the year with her and half with Pluto.

The landscape background with its low buildings and small figures was probably inspired by landscape etchings by Jacques Callot (1592–1635). The bowl is unmarked, but may have been made in either the Folco or the Levantino factories which are known from marked pieces to have produced maiolica decorated in this soft, predominantly manganese and green palette, whose green tends to run into the glaze.

Further reading Federico Marzinot, *Ceramica e ceramisti di Liguria*, Genoa, 1979. Nancy, Musée Historique Lorrain, *Jacques Callot 1592-1635*, exhibition catalogue, Paris, 1992, 'Les paysages italiens', pp. 229–304.

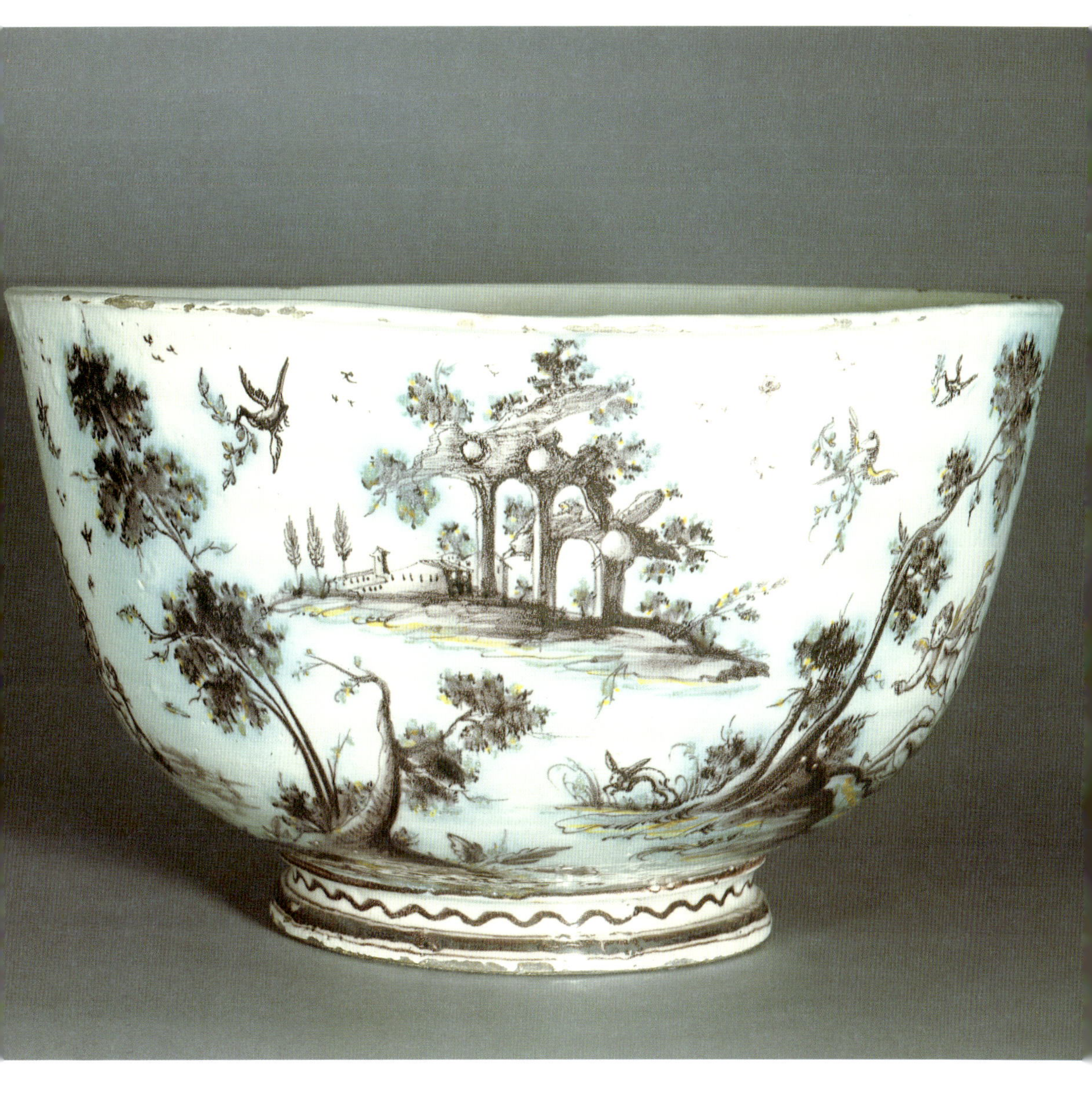

60

STAND FOR AN OVAL BASKET

FAENZA, FERNIANI FACTORY,
c. 1770–1800

Height 2.7 cm; length 26.8 cm; width 20.5 cm. Dr J. W. L. Glaisher Bequest. C.2190–1928.

In 1693 Conte Annibale I Ferniani purchased from Artemisia Cavina Grossi and Lodovico Tonducci the workshop in Faenza which in the sixteenth century had been occupied successively by Virgiliotto Calamelli and Leonardo Bettisi. Under Conte Annibale II (1736–84), who succeeded to the title in 1768, it entered an extremely productive and innovative phase of its existence, in which the forms and decoration of its maiolica were strongly influenced by Oriental and European porcelains and French faïence. This was not simply a matter of directorial taste, but an essential measure to enable the factory to compete with foreign imports.

Tableware with pierced basketwork borders was made by many European porcelain factories and was imitated in faïence and maiolica. This stand was originally accompanied by a matching oval basket. The central area is decorated with one of the most popular Ferniani patterns, introduced in 1767 and still available in Faenza. It is known as *garofano* (carnation) but was inspired by a late seventeenth-century Japanese Kakiemon porcelain pattern featuring a chrysanthemum. Production continued for many years and pieces of this pattern can therefore be dated only approximately.

Further reading Teresa Strocchi, 'Note storiche' in 'L'officina di maioliche dei Conti Ferniani 1693–1890', *Collana di Studi d'Arte Ceramica*, 2 (1929), pp. 65–87. Giuseppe Liverani, 'Note d'arte', *ibid.*, pp. 91–120. Carmen Ravanelli Guidotti, *Donazione Paolo Mereghi ceramiche europee ed orientali*, MICF, Faenza, 1987, pp. 268–9, nos. 145–7.

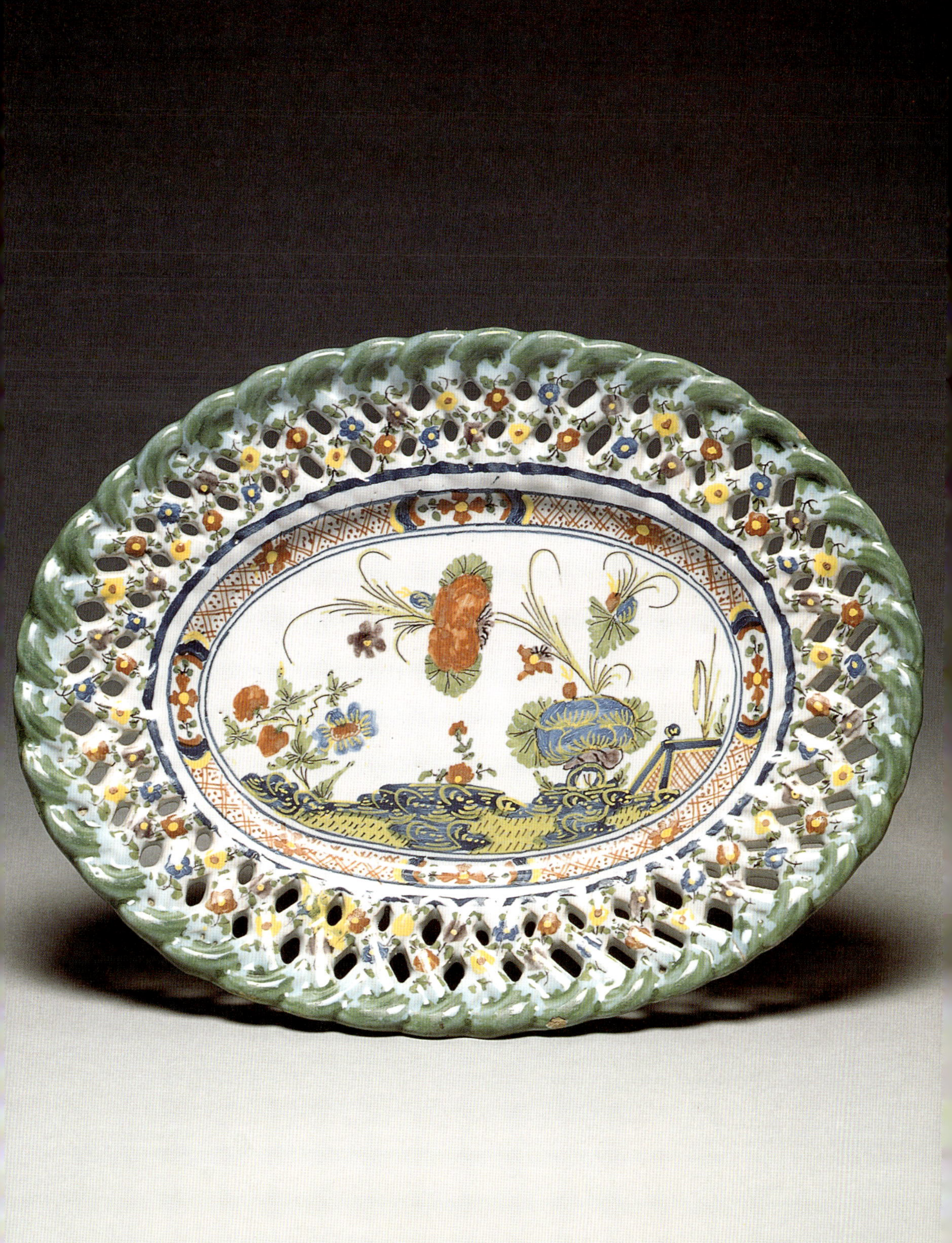

61

PLATE DECORATED WITH MUSICIANS

MILAN, PASQUALE RUBATI'S FACTORY, *c.* 1770

Marked on the back in red enamel,
'F./P.R./Mil^{no}'. *Height 3.4 cm; diameter 27.2 cm.*
Dr J. W. L. Glaisher Bequest. C.2247–1928.

This plate is decorated onglaze in enamels, a technique known in France as *au petit feu* and in Italy as *a piccolo fuoco*, because the decoration was fired at a lower temperature than the glaze – around 800 centigrade. It is also described as *a terzo fuoco* because the ware had already been fired twice before the enamels were applied and fired for a third time. Enamelled decoration on tin glaze had been employed at Delft in the Netherlands since about 1700, but was not adopted in Italy until the second half of the century. Its great advantage was that it gave painters a more varied palette including red (which was difficult to fire successfully at high temperatures), and shades of pink derived from gold.

Maiolica with enamelled decoration was made at three factories in Milan. The first, founded by Felice Clerici, was active between 1745 and 1788. The second founded by one of his employees, Pasquale Rubati, was founded in 1756 and, after his death in 1796, continued until about 1830. The third, run by the Confalonieri brothers between 1775 and 1782, was less important. The products of all three were strongly influenced by Oriental and European porcelains and by French faïence.

This plate is a charming example of European rococo decoration of around 1765–70. The subject would have appealed to upper-class interest in low life which was responsible for portrayals of beggars, craftsmen, and street entertainers in the fine and decorative arts. The initials on the back stand for Fabbrica Pasquale Rubati. A plate with the same design and mark is in the Museo Civico, Turin.

Further reading Costantino Baroni, *Maioliche di Milano*, Milan, 1940, compare p. 70, no. 80, and pl. 80. Museo Poldi Pezzoli, *Maioliche di Lodi, Milano e Pavia*, Milan, 1964. Saul Levy, *Le maioliche di Milano*, Milan, 1969.

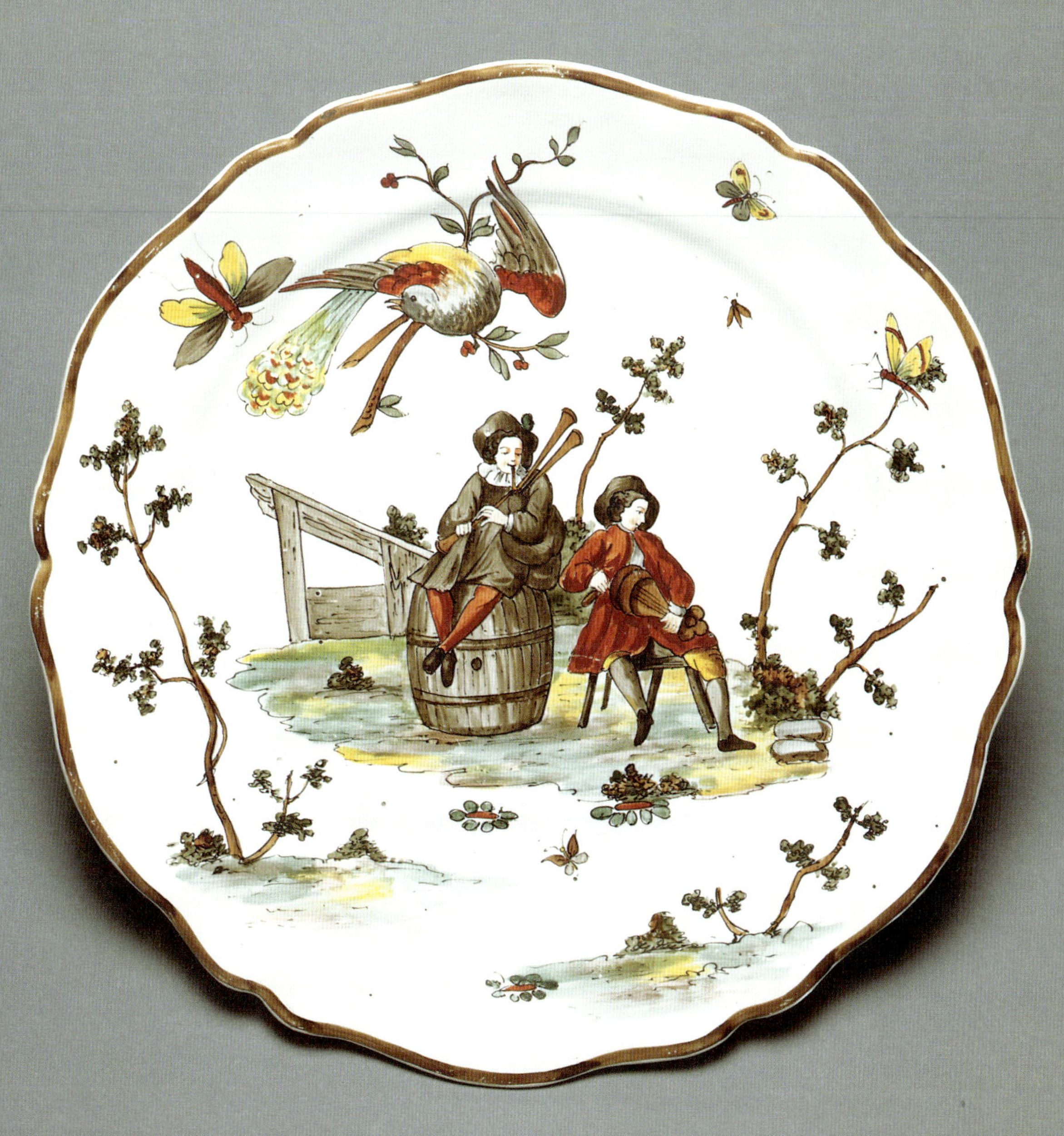

62

PUZZLE JUG

ARIANO IRPINO, *c.* 1790–1850

Height 23.5 cm; width 18 cm.
Dr J. W. L. Glaisher Bequest. C.2246–1928

Ariano Irpino is a small inland town about half-way between Avellino and Foggia in Campania. It seems likely that pottery was made there in the Middle Ages, but there is little evidence for its manufacture before the eighteenth century. Severe earthquakes in 1688, 1702 and 1732 probably disrupted the development of a pottery industry, but by 1753–4 11 workshops, 23 maiolica potters (described as *faenzari*), 1 maiolica painter, and 5 other potters were mentioned in the *catasto* (tax register). The industry flourished until the second half of the nineteenth century when there was a gradual decline.

Ariano potters were influenced to some extent by maiolica from Naples and Vietri, but, because of the town's remoteness from the leading centres of production, and its mainly rural or small-town markets, their products had an individual and 'popular' character. They included devotional panels and holy water stoups, zoomorphic and anthropomorphic flasks and lamps, salts and inkstands, large decorative dishes, and storage jars.

Puzzle vessels, including two-handled drinking cups, flasks, and jugs were a speciality, known in Italy as *vasi* and *fiaschi a segreto* or *beve se puoi* (drink if you can). This jug has a pierced neck which makes it impossible to pour or drink from it in the normal way. Instead it has to be tipped backwards so that the liquid passes through a tube inside the handle and round both sides of the rim to a sucking spout at the front. Its colouring and applied relief decoration are typical of Ariano pottery.

Further reading Carlo dell' Aquila, 'Note sulla maiolica popolare Campana, Ariano Irpino', *Faenza*, 63:4 (1977), pp. 87–94. Guido Donatone, *La maiolica di Ariano Irpino*, Naples, 1980. Ariano Irpino, Palazzo Anziani, *Antica maiolica popolare di Ariano Irpino*, exhibition catalogue by Guido Donatone, Rosa Carafa, and Irene Donatone, Naples, 1988.

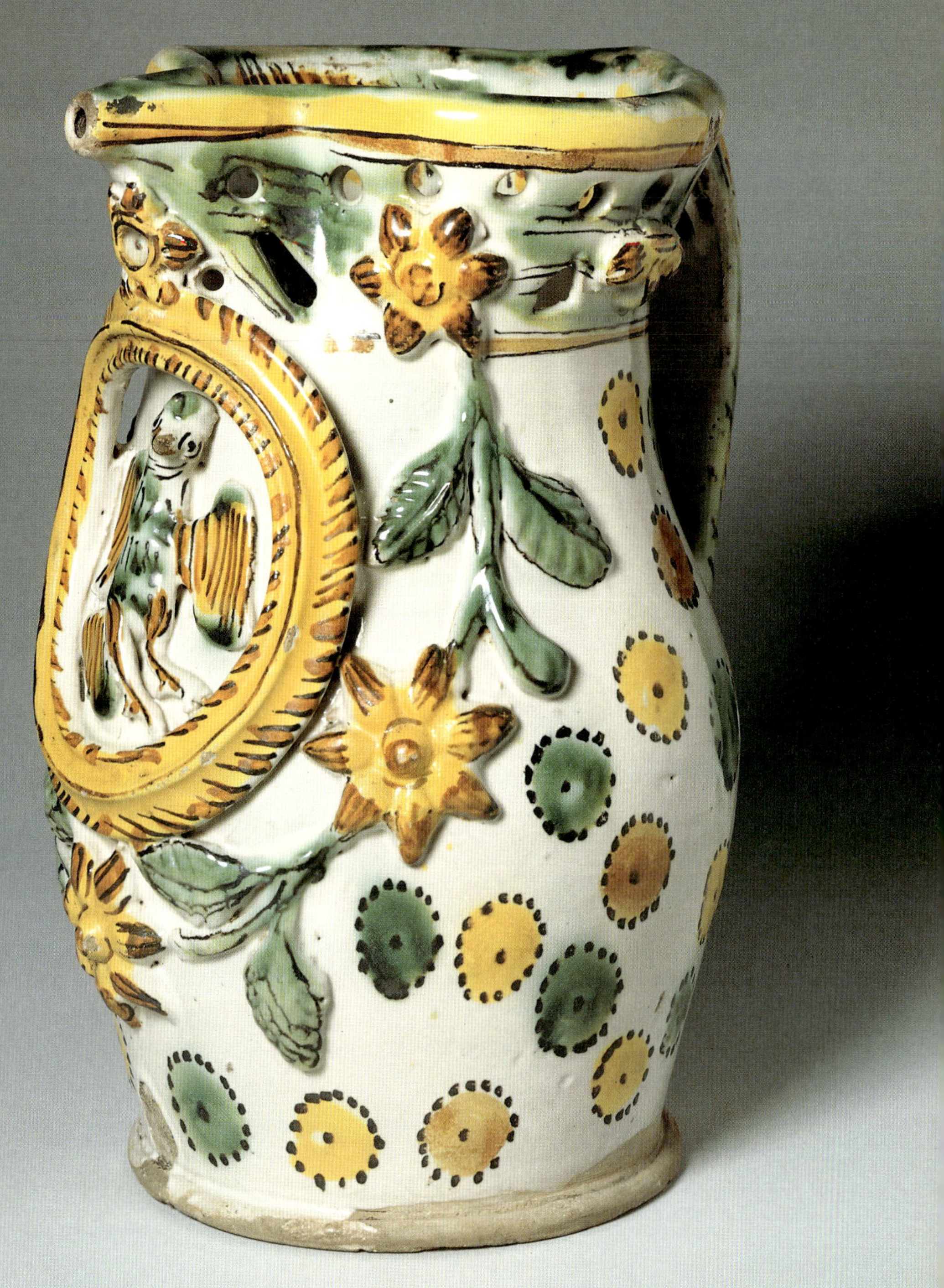

63

LAMP IN THE FORM OF A WOMAN

CALTAGIRONE, c. 1850–1900

Height 32.6 cm; diameter 16.5 cm.
Dr J. W. L. Glaisher Bequest. C.2260–1928.

Lamps fuelled by olive-oil were essential household equipment in Italy until the introduction of paraffin in the second half of the nineteenth century. After that their use gradually declined, although in country districts it continued well into the twentieth century. Most terracotta or maiolica lamps were utilitarian affairs, but in Sicily, from the sixteenth to the nineteenth century, there was a tradition of making decorative anthropomorphic lamps. Large numbers of them were made at Caltagirone, situated inland about 75 kilometres southwest of Catania. It was an important pottery centre from the thirteenth century onwards, and is sometimes referred to as 'the Faenza of Sicily'.

The earliest Caltagirone anthropomorphic lamps are in the form of finely dressed noblewomen whose bodies and skirts form the reservoir for the oil and whose headdresses have a hole for the wick. During the eighteenth century different characters were introduced and their construction changed. There was now only a small receptacle for oil in the figure's head or hat, and the base usually turned up at the edge so that it could save oil from dripping onto the furniture. By the nineteenth century, the heyday of these lamps, Caltagirone potters were making a wide range of male and female characters, such as monks, musicians, soldiers, and fashionable ladies.

This woman wears a flounced skirt and open-ended sleeves, which suggest a date of manufacture between the end of the 1840s and the mid 1860s. However, given the persistence of styles in places remote from fashionable cities and the popular character of the lamp, it may have been made some years later. Another lamp in the collection is in the form of a woman playing a mandoline (C.2258–1928).

Further reading Antonino Ragona, *La maiolica siciliana dalle origine all'ottocento*, 2nd edn, Palermo, 1986, p. 367, no. 199. Antonino Ragona, 'Graziose figurine in maiolica per rischiarare le notti siciliane', *CeramicAntica*, 1:2 (February 1991), pp. 45–50.

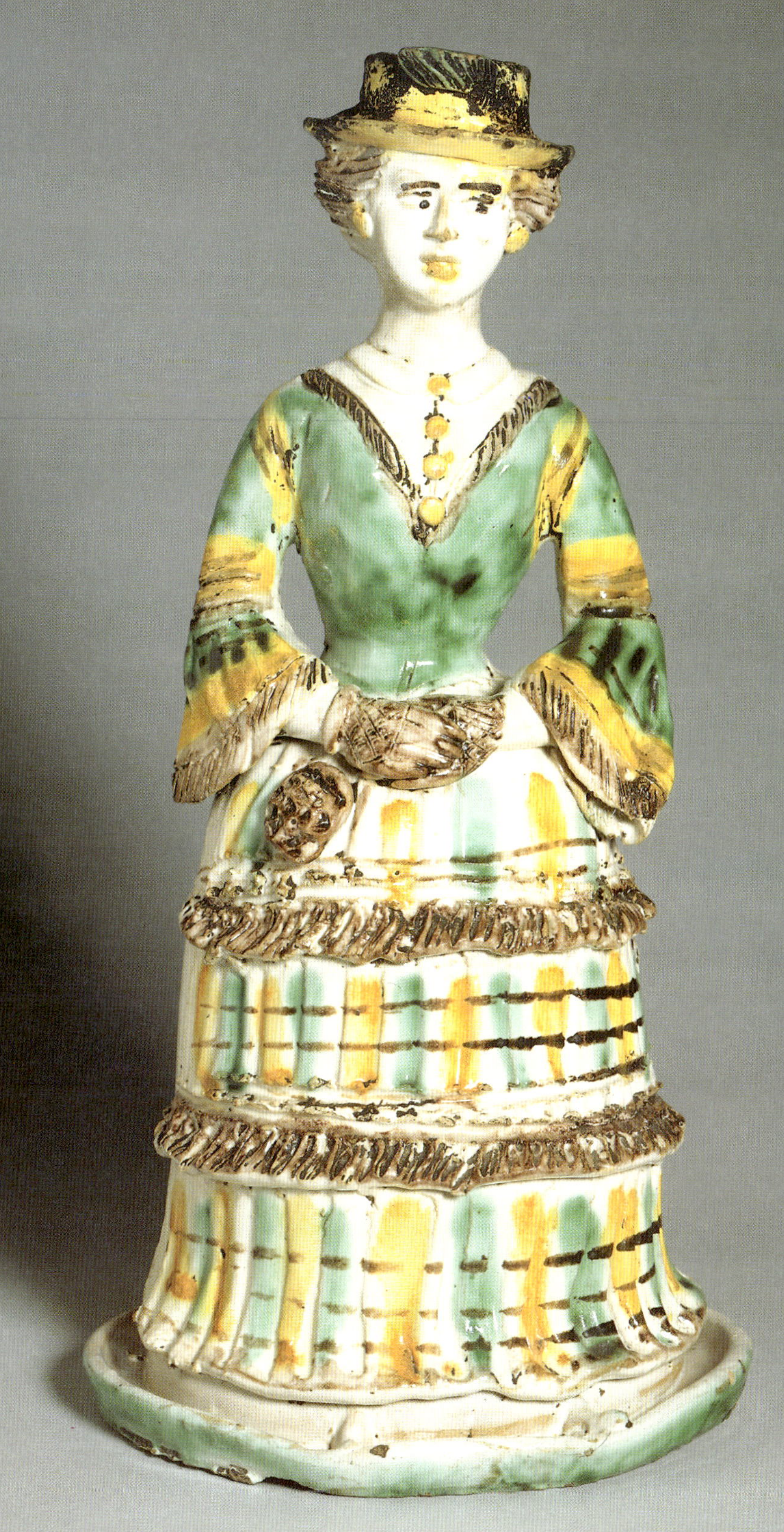

64

PANEL: THE REJECTION OF JOACHIM'S OFFERING

PESARO, PROBABLY BY FERRUCCIO MENGARONI (1875–1925), c.1900–25

Height 26 cm; width 17.7 cm; depth 1.1 cm.
L. C. G. Clarke Bequest, 1960. C.91–1961.

In art, the *Rejection of Joachim's Offering* was the first scene in the pictorial cycle of the legend of Joachim and Anna, the parents of the Virgin. The couple were childless, and when Joachim made his offering at the temple on a feast day, it was rejected because persons who had not fathered a child in Israel were not permitted to make sacrifices. Much saddened, Joachim went into the wilderness to fast and pray. During his absence his wife, Anna, was visited by an angel who told her that she would bear a child. Joachim also was told of their good fortune and returned home.

The scene on this panel was copied from either the woodcut in the *Life of the Virgin* by Albrecht Dürer (1471–1528), c. 1505–6 or an engraving after it by Marcantonio Raimondi. Prints by Dürer were copied frequently by maiolica painters in Faenza and elsewhere during the early sixteenth century. This panel has pale blue glaze which was a feature of much Faenza maiolica, and it is not surprising that it was attributed to Faenza when it was sold in London in 1934. After it was bequeathed to the Fitzwilliam, Bernard Rackham recognised it as a modern pastiche, and his opinion was confirmed by a thermoluminescence test in 1995. It was probably painted by Ferruccio Mengaroni (1875–1925) of Pesaro, an outstandingly talented potter and decorator, who produced a series of panels illustrating the *Life of the Virgin*. He began his career in the Molaroni workshop at Pesaro. Then, in 1914, he founded his own pottery, which continued after his premature death in an accident at Monza in 1925.

Further reading 'Maestro Ferrucio Mengaroni maiolicaro di Pesaro', *Collana di Studi d'Arte Ceramica*, 5 (1929), pp. 19–44. Grazia Biscontini Ugolini, *Ceramiche pesaresi dal XVIII al XX secolo*, MICF, Bologna, 1986, pp. 202–5.

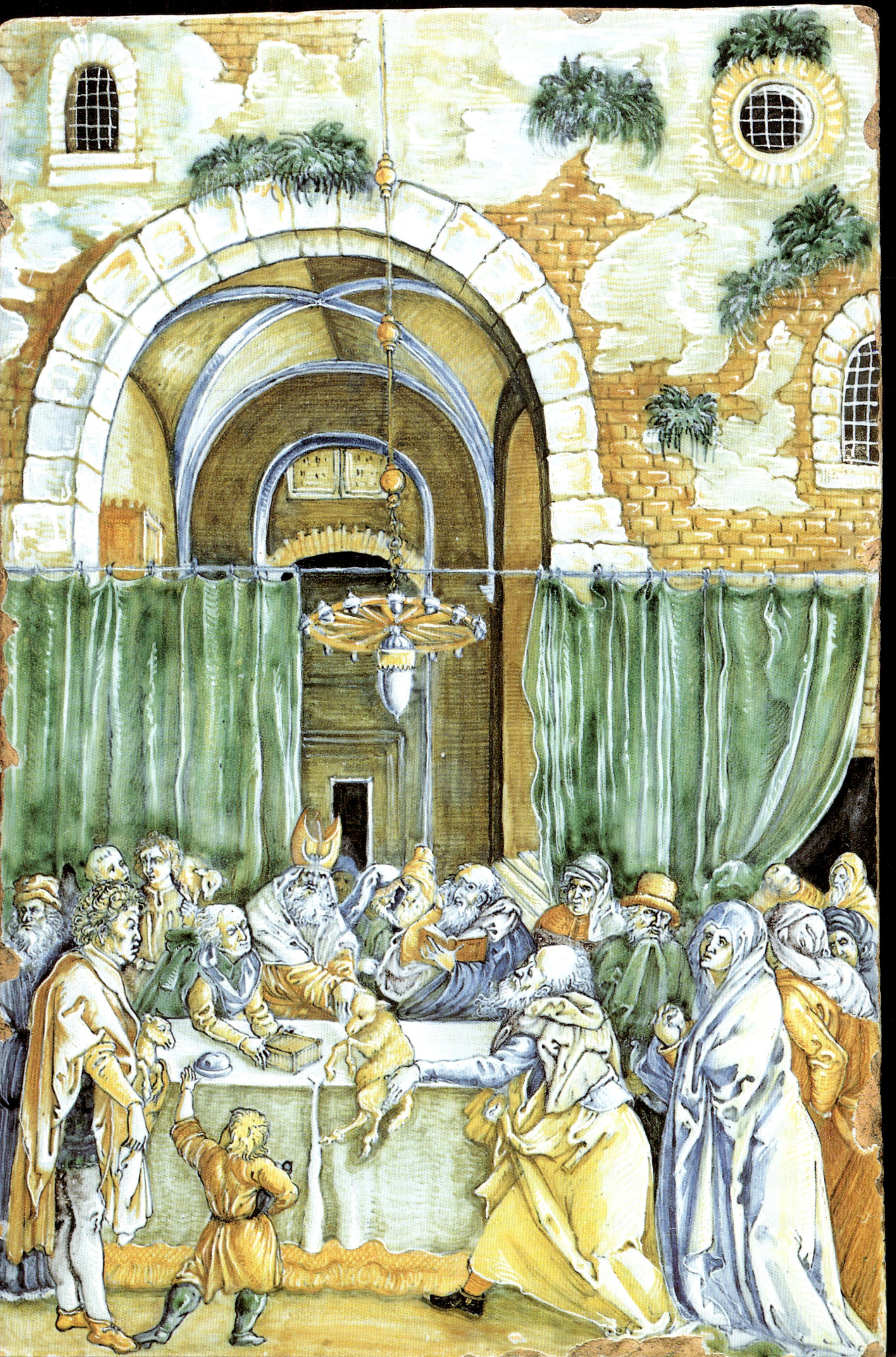

BIBLIOGRAPHY

All the maiolica in this Handbook except for nos. 33 and 39, was included in Julia E. Poole, *Catalogue of Italian Maiolica and Incised Slipware in the Fitzwilliam Museum Cambridge*, Cambridge, 1995. This is not cited under **Further reading** for each entry. Works mentioned once in this Handbook are cited in full under **Further reading**. The following are cited by the author–date system.

Albarelli, Giuseppe M., 1986, *Ceramisti Pesaresi nei documenti notarili dell'Archivio di Stato di Pesaro sec.* XV–XVII, ed. Paolo M. Erthler, Bologna.

Ballardini, Gaetano, 1933–8, *Corpus della maiolica italiana*, 2 vols., Rome, 1933 and 1938.

Cora, Galeazzo, 1973, *Storia della maiolica di Firenze e del contado secoli* XIV *e* XV, 2 vols., Florence.

Cora, Galeazzo and Fanfani, Angiolo, 1982, *La maiolica di Cafaggiolo*, Florence.

Curnow, Celia, 1992, *Italian maiolica in the National Museums of Scotland*, Edinburgh.

Fiocco, Carola and Gherardi, Gabriella, 1988–9, *Ceramiche Umbre dal Medioevo allo Storicismo, Parte Prima, Orvieto e Deruta*, MICF, Catalogo generale delle raccolte, 5, 2 vols. Faenza, 1988, 1989.

1995, *Museo Comunale di Gubbio, Ceramiche*, Perugia.

Giacomotti, Jeanne, 1974, *Catalogue des majoliques des musées nationaux*, Paris.

Hausmann, Tjark, 1972, *Kataloge des Kunstgewerbemuseums Berlin*, VI, *Majolika, spanische und italienische Keramik vom 14. bis zum 18. Jahrhundert*, Berlin.

Hess, Catherine, 1988, *Italian Maiolica, Catalogue of the Collections*, J. Paul Getty Museum, Malibu, California.

Lessmann, Johanna, 1979, *Italienische Majolika, Katalog der Sammlung*, Herzog Anton Ulrich-Museum, Braunschweig.

Norman, A. V. B., 1976, *Wallace Collection Catalogue of Ceramics 1, Pottery, Maiolica, Faience, Stoneware*, London.

Rackham, Bernard, 1940, *Victoria and Albert Museum, Catalogue of Italian Maiolica*, 2 vols., London; reprinted, with emendations and additional bibliography by J. V. G. Mallet, London, 1977.

Rasmussen, Jörg, 1984, *Museum für Kunst und Gewerbe Hamburg, Italienische Majolika*, Hamburg.

1989, *The Robert Lehman Collection X Italian Majolica*, Metropolitan Museum of Art, New York, in association with Princeton University Press.

Ravanelli Guidotti, Carmen, 1985, *Ceramiche occidentali del Museo Civico Medievale di Bologna*, Bologna.

1990, *La donazione Angiolo Fanfani, ceramiche dal Medioevo al XX secolo, Museo Internazionale delle Ceramiche*, Faenza.

Rome, 1993, Citta del Vaticano, Salone Sistino, *L'istoriato libri a stampa e maioliche italiane del cinquecento*, exhibition catalogue by Anna Rosa Gentilini, Carmen Ravanelli Guidotti, *et al.* with English translation, Faenza.

Watson, Wendy M., 1986, *Italian Renaissance Maiolica from the William A. Clark Collection*, exhibition catalogue, the Corcoran Gallery of Art, Washington, and the Mount Holyoke College Art Museum, London.

Wilson, Timothy, 1987, *Ceramic Art of the Italian Renaissance*, London.

1989, *Italian Maiolica in the Ashomolean Museum*, Oxford.

1993, 'Renaissance ceramics' in Rudolf Distelberger, Alison Luchs, Philippe Verdier, and Timothy Wilson, with contributions from Daphne S. Barbour, Shelley G. Sturman, and Pamela B. Vandiver, *Western Decorative Arts, Part I, Medieval, Renaissance, and Historicizing Styles including Metalwork, Enamels, and Ceramics*, National Gallery of Art, Washington. pp. 119–263.

Wilson, Timothy, ed. 1991, *Italian Renaissance Pottery, Papers written in association with a colloquium at the British Museum*, London.